MASTERFUL
COACHING

REVISED EDITION

Inspire an "Impossible Future"

While Producing Extraordinary

Leaders and Extraordinary Results

ROBERT HARGROVE

JOSSEY-BASS/PFEIFFER
A Wiley Imprint
www.pfeiffer.com

Published by Jossey-Bass/Pfeiffer
A Wiley Imprint
989 Market Street, San Francisco, CA 94103-1741   www.pfeiffer.com

Jossey-Bass/Pfeiffer books and products are available through most bookstores. To contact Jossey-Bass/Pfeiffer directly call our Customer Care Department within the U.S. at (800) 274-4434, outside the U.S. at (317) 572-3985 or fax (317) 572-4002.

Jossey-Bass/Pfeiffer also publishes its books in a variety of electronic formats. Some content that appears in print may not be available in electronic books.
Printed in the United States of America

ISBN: 0-7879-6084-5

Library of Congress Cataloging-in-Publication Data

Hargrove, Robert A.
  Masterful coaching / Robert Hargrove.— Rev. ed.
      p. cm.
Includes bibliographical references and index.
  ISBN 0-7879-6084-5 (alk. paper)
  1. Teams in the workplace. 2. Industrial efficiency. 3. Employee
motivation. 4. Employees—Training of. 5. Group relations training.
I. Title.
  HD66 .H37 2002
  658.3'124—dc21   2002008573

Acquiring Editor: Matthew Davies
Director of Development: Kathleen Dolan Davies
Editor: Rebecca Taff
Senior Production Editor: Dawn Kilgore
Manufacturing Supervisor: Becky Carreño
Interior Design: Yvo
Cover Design: Jennifer Hines
Illustrations: Lotus Art

Printed in the United States of America
Printing 10   9   8   7   6   5   4

CONTENTS

PART III: THE SECRETS OF MASTERFUL COACHES

LIST OF DIAGRAMS

Also by Robert Hargrove

Masterful Coaching Fieldbook

E-Leader: Reinventing Leadership in a Connected Economy

Mastering the Art of Creative Collaboration

*Masterful Coaching: Extraordinary Results by
Impacting People and the Way They Think and Work Together*

INTRODUCTION

COACHING IS HOT!

"Coaching is hot!" I wrote to start off the first edition of Masterful Coaching in 1995. It still is. Companies such as GE, Ford, Conoco, and others are exploring it. Decision makers in the United States, Europe, and Asia are creating powerful partnerships with executive coaches so as to become extraordinary leaders who create an extraordinary future for their organizations. Leaders at every level are recognizing that they can leverage their personal success in accomplishment by coaching others to be successful at accomplishment.

There is a Coaching University, flight schools and boot camps are popping up, and there are at least a dozen books on the subject. Yet for all this interest, there is no commonly held answer to the question, "What is coaching?" No coaching "method" is widely accepted and applied by leaders and managers. No real professional standards exist for practitioners. The website of a coaching collaborative I visited offered the same coaches for executives as they did for marriage counseling.

The intent of my company, Masterful Coaching Inc., is to provide what's missing that will make a difference in this exploding field. This book is written with the practitioner in mind (whereas the *Masterful Coaching Fieldbook* that I wrote a few years ago is written from the leader's and manager's point of view). Yet the guiding ideas, methods, and tools found here can apply to any individual who is committed to causing other people's success. I therefore encourage you, whatever your vantage point, to read the book in an extrapolative way, to look for the golden nugget and run with it.

One thing is certain, Masterful Coaching, as I will write about it here, is a powerful, profound, new domain, and it needs to be distinct. It is different from abstract training programs, which provide lots of information but have little impact on people's leadership ability. It is different from traditional "consulting," which provides reports and recommendations—most of which never are implemented. And it is distinct from the "coaching" and "counseling" done in companies on a remedial basis, which as often as not leave people feeling diminished.

WELCOME TO THE REVOLUTION!

This book is a call to arms. It is an invitation to the future. It is a cause. Join in, and welcome!

I would like to begin with a declaration: *Masterful Coaching is an idea whose time has come.* In the coming decades, decision makers will recognize that, if you are a leader, you are first and foremost a coach and teacher. Furthermore, coaching will displace traditional consulting and training.

In addition to this declaration, I would like to make four assertions.

1. I assert that Masterful Coaching is based on inspiring people to realize an Impossible Future they can passionately engage in; it is not a remedial activity.
2. I assert that Masterful Coaching involves personal and organizational reinvention. It is transformational as opposed to transactional.
3. I assert that Masterful Coaching—The Method™ that you will find in this book provides a powerful, repeatable technology for producing breakthroughs for people and breakthrough results.
4. Finally, a Masterful Coach is an extraordinary human being who combines wisdom, compassion, and a sense of humor with a proven track record of accomplishment.

MASTERFUL COACHING IS THE FUTURE OF COACHING

My purpose in writing *Masterful Coaching* and revising and expanding it now is to sound the tone—to say, "This is the future of coaching." The new paradigm of coaching that we will introduce here rests on the notion that coaching is about expanding people's capacity to create an extraordinary future, that it involves personal and organizational reinvention, and that it takes place in the domain of accomplishment, not psychology.

I say that this is the future of coaching because the new paradigm I intend to establish through Masterful Coaching is such a world apart from the prevailing paradigm of coaching today—based on performance appraisals, remedial counseling, and therapy, all of which occur behind a locked door—that it is almost unrecognizable.

A Masterful Coach is a "listening" for people's *greatness,* for bringing out the best in people, rather than being a listening for people's pettiness. A Masterful Coach is grounded in expanding people's capacity to achieve what they need to achieve, not therapy. A Masterful Coach's legacy is not only *breakthrough results,* but also *breakthroughs for people.*

Victor Hugo said that there is nothing as powerful as an idea whose time has come. When you sound the tone for an idea whose time has come, three things happen: Some people come to the tone and become proponents; others are indifferent to the tone and become bystanders; and others are detractors who are often eventually crushed by the tone. It is often my experience when I speak to people about coaching in organizations that, while they respond positively to the idea, they often try to reinterpret what I am saying by falling back into the prevailing paradigm.

I have found that there was an old conversation about coaching—or a "negative listening"—that made it difficult for people to hear the tone I was sounding. People would listen to my message intently, while a background conversation was going on in their heads consistent with the old conversation or paradigm. "Boy, maybe this is a cure for the CEO's or VP's attitude problem," or "The last time I got what my boss called coaching, I walked out of the room devastated," or " I don't have the time to coach."

These and other background conversations are based on a network of beliefs and assumptions I was to eventually label "The Four Myths of Coaching." I saw that these four myths were directly responsible for the fact that, in most organizations, there is little or no cultural clearing for coaching to show up at all. In fact, 85 percent of the five thousand managers I surveyed said they received "little" or "no" coaching, and when they did, it was "a negative experience."

EXPLODING THE MYTHS

It seemed that the first step in creating a cultural clearing that allowed for and pulled for coaching in organizations was to inaugurate a new conversation about coaching and break the grip of the old conversation. What was needed was a new conversation about coaching that would stimulate new ideas, fresh views, and perspectives. I undertook this work in writing the *Masterful Coaching Fieldbook.*

I was generously afforded the opportunity to carry the work of creating a new conversation about coaching forward with companies like Philips

Electronics, Motorola, and especially with Conoco, an innovative energy company in Houston, Texas. This work involved bringing the old background conversations to the foreground, so people could acknowledge them and move beyond them. Generating a new conversation about coaching involved teaching managers to begin to recognize and disperse the four myths described below.

MYTH 1. Coaching is a last gasp effort for washouts

I was giving a seminar on Masterful Coaching in which, after the first day, one of the vice presidents came up to me and said, "I have been sitting here all day wondering why I resist coaching so much." This was coaching both from his boss and from the Masterful Coaches who were working in his organization. He continued, "I now realize that I am not going for an Impossible Future, but rather a predictable future, and for that I don't need a coach." Then he continued, "Coaching has always been suggested to me as a kind of punishment or disciplinary action because I don't listen very well. I now want to create an inspiring Impossible Future, and for that I will need coaching."

REALITY: Coaching is for winners who seek an edge or advantage

After every Masterful Coaching seminar, I offer a free coaching session to every participant. Interestingly enough, I am usually only approached by the "winners," people with top positions (or top potential) and the highest personal and organizational aspirations. These are also people with very strong wills, who, at the same time, have a basic attitude of humility, curiosity, and learning. My observation is that these people seek an edge or advantage in reaching their goals and sense that coaching can give it to them.

MYTH 2. Coaching is about identifying and filling GAPS

Like dissecting a frog to find out the secret of life, most leadership and management development programs tend to dissect leaders to find out the secret of their art. First the corporate university comes up with a list of ten leadership characteristics (with five dimensions for each trait). Next comes the obligatory round of computerized 360-degree feedback, followed by a list of strengths and gaps. Finally comes the "push" approach to coaching and training, designed to fill these gaps. This psychological, mechanistic approach is based on a fundamental misconception of how leaders actually develop.

REALITY: Coaching is about creating futures, not just filling gaps

One of the most powerful realizations I have made with Masterful Coaching Inc. is that, when leaders declare an ambitious aspiration for themselves and their organization, it creates the pull for coaching. It does this all the more so when the ambitious aspiration is coupled to a desire for accomplishment and a basic attitude of curiosity, humility, and learning. Thus, all of our coaching starts with asking the question, "What is an inspiring Impossible Future you can passionately engage in?" Next we ask, "Who do you need to be in the matter?" In other words, "Where is the gap?" It is my experience that *winners* love living in the gaps, whereas *losers* love to pretend they don't exist.

MYTH 3. Coaching is about development for individuals

In most companies, performance and development are seen as entirely separate domains. It is usually the manager's job to deal with performance, HR's or the corporate university's job to deal with development. As a result, most managers tend to do a totally inadequate job of developing their direct reports. Worse, they also tend do a totally inadequate job of managing performance. This is because they tend to manage by objectives and to see coaching as interfering. The motto is: "Here's the goal; come back and see me at the end of the year when you have the results." Finally, when coaching does occur, it is seen as focused on the individual, not on the team.

REALITY: Coaching integrates performance and development with people in groups

Years ago, as CEO of an entrepreneurial organization, I had to develop leaders rapidly to head up far-flung new business centers. First, I tried the prevailing paradigm of "transactional learning"—enrolling leadership candidates in leadership training, 101 tips and techniques. This had little impact on people's actual leadership ability. I then tried "transformational learning." The leaders were given a stretch assignment in a new center—an extraordinary result they needed to produce in ninety days, along with a Masterful Coach. To obtain the results, people would have to shift their attitudes and behaviors fundamentally. Bam! It worked.

MYTH 4. Coaching is an isolated "event" that happens at the yearly performance appraisal

Richard Severance, a Conoco leader, told me that until he participated in the Masterful Coaching course, he always considered coaching as something with a "little c." In other words, coaching and feedback were isolated events that happened one to two times a year during the annual goal setting and performance appraisal. What he realized after taking the course was that coaching was actually a "big C" word. If you are a leader, you are a coach and teacher. I have discovered through research that the best leaders in the world spend 40 to 50 percent of their time coaching and teaching people in groups to produce personal and business breakthroughs.

REALITY: Coaching is a continuous, but not continual process

We have discovered in providing Masterful Coaching for executives that it takes a year or more to impact an individual or to bring about fundamental change in an organization. Coaching on this basis is not an obligatory appraisal, but a powerful partnership in which the coach empowers people to accomplish what they need to accomplish. This does not just involve an isolated conversation, but rather a network of conversations in which the coach and coachee are continually engaging in such questions as, "What happened? What's missing? What's next?"

MASTERFUL COACHING—THE METHOD™

After writing the first edition of *Masterful Coaching* in 1995, I began doing Masterful Coaching seminars in Global 1000 type corporations, a three-day program designed to shift the mindset about what coaching is and to build coaching skills and attitudes. I would introduce people to the "Four Myths of Coaching" as a way to create a new cultural clearing that would support coaching. This lead to many executive coaching assignments for Masterful Coaching Inc., which in turn significantly contributed to my stock of knowledge regarding the "what" and "how" of individual and team coaching. Some of this was captured in the *Masterful Coaching Fieldbook,* and it evolved into what I call Masterful Coaching—The Method™.

Following the publication of the *Fieldbook,* I began receiving many requests from both top executives/managers and coaching practitioners who were committed to becoming Masterful Coaches and wanted more specifics than the first two books offered in terms of guiding ideas, methods, and techniques for catalyzing breakthroughs for people and breakthroughs in results. The intent of this new edition of *Masterful Coaching* then is to take a quantum leap forward in terms of Masterful Coaching—The Method™.

Masterful coaches make sure the model is the servant, not the master.

Mental Models for Being a Coach

This book will make it clear that the starting point for Masterful Coaching is a powerful partnership with the person or group being coached, which is based on an emotional commitment to who people are and what they are up to in life. Commitment unlocks the wisdom, intuition, and natural knowing needed to coach people effectively in any situation. Without commitment, what one is left with is a bottomless quagmire of technique. At the same time, it is helpful to have a mental map or coaching model. As with any model, the model should be the servant, not the master.

The coaching model most frequently used is the "doctor/expert" model. This model is useful when people need a quick fix, for example, when they are upset or want a remedy for an attitude or behavior problem or need an answer to an immediate issue or problem. There are certain problems with this model. The doctor/expert model often does not do enough to involve the patient in the learning process necessary to eliminate the problem or create a remedy. For example, a "patient" might not accept the "doctor's" diagnoses. Also, the expert may bring solutions that the patient does not or cannot apply.

The "guru/catalyst model" is useful when people are seeking to create a powerful new future that requires personal and organizational reinvention. The coach as guru or catalyst must have a strong intention to get inside the person through inspiration, a teachable point of view, and provocation so as to initiate the desire to learn and change. We have discovered in our research a three-step process for promoting transformation.[1]

- *Step 1. Unfreeze. The "heat" of the guru or catalyst can help the "initiate" surface and call into question underlying thinking patterns or practices that get him or her into trouble.*

- *Step 2. Change. The coach (guru/catalyst) provides guiding ideas with the intent of helping people make a fundamental shift in their thinking and practices.*

- **Step 3. Refreeze.** *This involves making the new ways of thinking or practices smooth and automatic through practice and study.*

Teaching, coaching, and training all too often mean transferring knowledge from one person's head to another's. Fred Kofman of MIT suggests that a "learning enzyme" is a more appropriate metaphor, especially where reaching high-performance goals requires creating new knowledge or building new skills.[2] The coach and coachee co-mingle and generate a new learning system between them that allows both to learn in the context of doing the job.

The coach is asking, "How can I help?" The coachee is asking, "How do I get unstuck?" Instead of giving people the answers or directly instigating change, the learning enzyme usually provides ideas, tools, and methods of inquiry with the intent of helping people expand their own capacity to learn. The drawback of this approach is that it can lack the heat of the guru or be too coolly intellectual to cause people to make a shift.

Whether it is the doctor/expert, the guru/catalyst, or the learning enzyme, a Masterful Coach has the flexibility and insight to take on the model that will be most useful to the coachee and the situation at hand.

Masterful Coaching in Three Parts

The book has three parts:

> Part I. *Transforming Individuals;*
>
> Part II. *Transforming Groups; and*
>
> Part III. *The Secrets of Masterful Coaches*

The first part deals with declaring an Impossible Future and, stepping into the reinvention paradigm, starting with who you are as a leader.

Part II deals with reinventing the organization. It takes you beyond creating a plain vanilla vision statement and shows you how to coach people to create a powerful context that becomes the vision, climate, and spirit of the company.

Part III deals with key secrets of Masterful Coaches and gives you the inside scoop on what Masterful Coaches do to impact people and the way they think and work together.

In Coaching Individuals or Groups Within Organizations, You Eventually Reach a Crossroads

Masterful Coaching involves unleashing the human spirit into action, setting ambitious goals and aspirations, and then acting as your coachee's thinking partner to create new openings for possibility and action that were previously unknown to him or her. I want to emphasize that this work is about significant accomplishment, and *it is not remedial. It is transformational, not transactional,* in nature.

Once you step into this context, you enter the zone of Masterful Coaching. From then on, the journey to Masterful Coaching is a matter of practice and study. This involves taking the guiding ideas, tools, and methods you learn and applying them to coaching real people in real situations. It is also a matter of finding a Masterful Coach yourself—one who has the necessary wherewithal to accelerate your progress on the journey.

IN CLOSING. . .

I very much enjoy hearing from people who have read my books, and I promise to respond to you. I would not only appreciate your comments on the book but would like to learn about how you applied it on your own journey to Masterful Coaching. My email address is **Robert.Hargrove@Masterfulcoaching.com.**

PART I

TRANSFORMING INDIVIDUALS

The focus of Part I will be on mapping out the territory of Masterful Coaching for professionals, leaders, and managers. It will show you how to coach people to take a stand for the Impossible Future they passionately care about and to take action to make it a reality. Part I is based on the premise that realizing an Impossible Future will require personal and organization reinvention. The focus is on the individual: If you want to reinvent your organization, you need to reinvent yourself first. You will be introduced to Masterful Coaching—The Method™, which is based on Triple Loop Learning and which is transformational, as opposed to transactional, in nature.

Masterful Coaching is about inspiring, empowering, enabling people to live deeply in the future, while acting boldly in the present.

Chapter One, "The Journey," answers the question "What is Masterful Coaching?" I wanted a definition that was big enough to include all of who and what a powerful leader or coach/teacher is and does. I wanted a definition that broke the grip and excelled beyond the conventional humdrum notions of coaching for improved performance or coaching for improved development.

I assert then that a Masterful Coach, whether a leader of an organization or coaching practitioner, is someone who impacts people's vision and values in a way that is consistent with their highest human aspirations. Most people stand in the present too mired down with politics, circumstances, and events to think about the future. A Masterful Coach inspires, empowers, and enables people to live deeply in the future, while at the same time acting boldly in the present.

Most people in organizations are in the proverbial "pea soup." A Masterful Coach enables people to get out of the pea soup so that they are able to see things much more clearly and, as a result, act powerfully.

Chapter Two, "Becoming a Masterful Coach: A Coach Is Something That You 'Be,'" shows that all you have as a coach is "who you are being." You can choose to *be* inspiring or you can choose to *be* depressing. You can choose to *be* empowering or to *be* disempowering. You can choose to *be* enabling or to *be* crushing.

You have the power to choose who you are being at any given time by taking a stand—by making a commitment to come from a place that is inspiring, empowering, and enabling. You have the power to choose who you are being, because you have the power to determine how you speak and listen with people. This in turn determines how they will respond to you.

Chapter Three, "Coaching Happens in Conversations," emphasizes that a coaching conversation is one in which we speak and listen with the intent of making a difference. Veronica Pemberton, one of our Masterful Coaches, quite frequently begins every conversation with this statement: "It is my intention that this conversation make a difference for you."

You will also be introduced to some very specific coaching methodologies, including a Six-Cap Coaching Conversation System and a formula for having a successful coaching conversation. We have found that just being introduced to these two methodologies allows people to start having incredibly successful coaching conversations.

Masterful Coaching gives people access to a new kind of power, the power to make the impossible happen.

Chapter Four, "Masterful Coaching Is Transformational," explores this very powerful fundamental which is the foundation for personal and organization reinvention. Creating an Impossible Future does require transformational, not just transactional, learning. In this chapter we continue to put forth Masterful Coaching—The Method™. The Triple Loop Learning model is introduced as a way to develop extraordinary leaders in the process of producing extraordinary results. This will help you to bring about fundamental shifts in thinking and attitude. You will also learn how to turn "rut" stories (stories that get people stuck) into "river" stories (that move people forward), allowing people to be freed up to take powerful action.

Chapter Five, "Coaching Executives and Leaders at All Levels," will provide specific methods for coaching leaders and managers. The first part of the chapter, which is entirely new, will reveal how to create and design an extraordinary coaching relationship. The premise behind the chapter is that an extraordinary coaching relationship is generative by its very nature. It is focused on creating a powerful new future, rather than something that is remedial in nature. This starts with setting an Impossible Future (such as an inspired organization and a billion dollars in earnings) that people passionately care about so much that they would be willing to reinvent their entire selves in order to achieve it. The chapter will then provide a specific, step-by-step recipe for coaching leaders to accomplish their Impossible Future over a year-long period or more in their business with colleagues, amid change and complexity.

CHAPTER ONE

THE JOURNEY

What Is Masterful Coaching?

Masterful Coaching involves expanding people's capacity to make a difference with individuals, their organizations, and their world. It involves impacting people's visions and values and offering them a powerful assist in reinventing who they are being, their thinking, and behavior that is consistent with achieving what they need to achieve.

Masterful Coaching involves challenging and supporting people to be extraordinary leaders, as well as to achieve extraordinary levels of performance. It starts with becoming clear on the goals and aspirations people passionately care about and offering them a powerful assist in calling forth who they need to be in the matter. It requires building new skills and capabilities so as to bring out the best in those around them. It means fostering not just individual excellence, but also creative collaboration.

Masterful Coaching is based on being completely committed to the person(s) you are coaching and engaging with them in conversations (or, actually, a network of conversations) that leave them inspired, empowered, and enabled with respect to their concerns. The acid test is that when you leave the presence of a Masterful Coach, you have "freedom to be" and you have new openings for possibility and action in areas where you were stuck and ineffective.

A JOURNEY, NOT A DESTINATION

Masterful Coaching is a journey, not just a destination. Whether or not you will embark on the journey depends not on whether you are a leader, project manager, or individual contributor; it depends on whether you dare to see and meet the calling to make a difference, whether in the life of one person, a group, or an institution. We admire others who make a difference, who have an impact, who are effective.

Perhaps our inspiration to take the journey to Masterful Coaching comes from these people. Each of us can remember a handful, but only a handful, of coaches, teachers, and mentors who touched our lives with new possibilities we didn't see before, who enabled us to achieve results that we never dreamed of or dared to imagine. They were people who held up an honest mirror, one that led to a revelation of our own foolishness. They had conversations with us about the lessons we needed to learn about life, laced with a sense of humor.

The journey is driven by passion, commitment, and zeal. It calls for a hungry spirit, a person who not only has the desire to be a *success* but also to be a *contribution*. It calls for those who know that the true joy in life is to bring people together to create and invent the future, rather than just trying to predict it. It entices those who have achieved something splendid at some point only because they dared to believe that there was something inside them that was superior to circumstance and now they want to pass that on.

It calls for leaders who recognize that the highest leverage in the adventure of business (and living) is elevating their concerns to making an Impossible Future. This can only happen if people let go of being the hero and being in the center of the action and focus on developing the next generation of leaders in the process of getting the job done.

It involves recognizing that Masterful Coaching is a journey, not a destination. To be sure, the ideas, tools, and methods offered in this book will provide you with a roadmap and the necessary wherewithal to get you on your way. Yet, as with mastering anything, it can take a lifetime to develop the skills and capabilities. It involves dedicated study and practice, a continuous cycle of making progress, plateauing, striving, and reaching the next level—from individual to group, from group to organization.

While it takes a powerful commitment to become a Masterful Coach, there are different stages along the way and each must be valued:

1. Beginner (sometimes a nuisance);

2. Advanced Beginner (does okay with supervision);

3. Competent (capable);

4. Virtuoso (brilliant); and

5. Mastery (invents new rules, becomes a legend).

The Setting Is Today's Workplace

The setting for the journey we are making to Masterful Coaching begins not in sports or the performing arts, but in the workplace—government, business, schools, hospitals. The performance bar has been raised for all. There is a growing clamor to reinvent organizations for the 21st Century. In order for this to happen, executives and leaders at all levels must first reinvent themselves. Coaching makes it possible to dramatically accelerate this process, without stepping on landmines. The time to take the journey is now.

- *Every Global 1000 corporation needs coaches who can help people to set unreasonable expectations and stretch their definition of themselves and their business to reach them.*

- *Every legislative body needs skilled facilitators to assist them in moving beyond government gridlock to building common ground.*

- *Every school is facing a crisis in how to educate students that demands teachers be less enforcers of curriculum-directed learning and more enablers of learner-directed learning.*

- *The world as a complex social and biological system is presenting us with ever more pressing dilemmas, and to solve them, we need coaches who can help us think and work better together and accelerate the process by which we produce results.*

This is the domain of Masterful Coaching. I invite you to hear the sounding of the tone . . . to come to the tone . . . and to join in sympathetic resonance with it.

THE FIVE COMPASS POINTS OF MASTERFUL COACHING: MAPPING THE TERRITORY

To me, the lifelong journey toward Masterful Coaching is one of the highest expressions of what it is to be a human being, even though it is fraught with challenges. For at its very core, it means bringing people into alignment with their highest human goals and aspirations, while at the same time linking them to the needs of their organization. It involves taking a stand that it is possible to make a difference, even when the mountain is high, the winds strong, the climate cold, and the road lonely. It is a journey filled with joy and pain, comedy and tragedy—all the ironies of life.

A Masterful Coach is a leader who by nature is a vision builder and value shaper, not just a technician who manages people to reach their goals and plans through tips and techniques. To be able to do this requires that the coach discover his or her own humanness and humanity, while being a clearing for others to do the same. At the same time, Masterful Coaches know when to shift weight to the opposite foot and focus on expanding people's capacity to accomplish what they need to accomplish. Such coaches know that being extraordinary is the key to producing extraordinary results, and they consistently bring out the best in those around them.

Masterful Coaches are not only great human beings, but also "monsters of effectiveness." They have the ability to inspire people to declare an Impossible Future they passionately care about to be possible and then to make it a reality. It is by standing with people inside a nonnegotiable commitment to an Impossible Future that the coach sets the stage for breakthrough results and breakthroughs for people. People see that the limiting factor is their level of intention and imagination, not their level of staffing and resources.

A Masterful Coach enters into the learning system of the individual or group with the intent of producing breakthroughs for people and breakthroughs in results.

Masterful Coaches show people how to take mere possibilities and translate them into live opportunities by formulating concrete projects that have a beginning, middle, and end. Their presence on a team is felt as having objectives agreed on, doing inventive and effective planning, ironing out conflicts, and creating a rallying momentum. They look for new openings for possibility and action in places where people are stuck or ineffective, honestly acknowledging all breakdowns and providing what's missing that will make a difference.

Masterful Coaches possess within themselves a potent combination of toughness and compassion, which shows up as a "listening for people's greatness" and at the same time "speaking to penetrate illusions that get people in trouble." They encourage people to stretch their minds and skills in pursuing results that are beyond and out of the ordinary. They return people to themselves and their promises in the face of disappointment or upsets brought on by unintended results.

At the same time, while Masterful Coaches are effective, they are not just results machines. They have the generosity of spirit to step back from their own preoccupations on the front lines and give someone the gift of their presence. "Got a problem? Let's talk about it." Such a person always has a touch of what the Buddhists call "crazy wisdom" (being colorful, dramatic, shocking, and wise).

I am often asked, because all of this sounds like a tall order, "Just how does one become a Masterful Coach?" The following Compass Points map the territory to be crossed in this journey. They are the navigational aids for the voyage, the street signs that let us know whether or not we are in the right neighborhood. If you have at least some of the right makeup that we have been describing, by following these navigation points you will eventually get there.

The Compass Points that you will find here were discovered from the direct experience and hard-won lessons gained in coaching leaders; they are not just an intellectual exercise. For the most part, they take the form of rich stories that are full of many lessons, like hidden jewels for those who care to look for them. Some of the stories are based on extraordinary successes and others on failures and honest mistakes. That's the purpose of creating a map. By using it, you can greatly increase your changes of succeeding and avoid dangerous rocks.

The intent here is to guide the reader into a different world. At the same time, while there are no magic bullets, you will be provided with guiding ideas, methods, and tools that will help you develop as a coach and that can be put to practical and immediate use. The starting point is with the people you most want to work with and in those areas where you have the most control.

COMPASS POINT I. Coaching Is a Powerful Partnership

Augusta, Georgia—There were thousands upon thousands of golf fans at the Augusta National in May 2001 who would have killed for a moment of Tiger Woods' time. Butch Harmon, Tiger Woods' coach, had Tiger's undivided attention for well more than an hour on the putting green. Then Harmon jogged over to the caddie shack, pulled on the requisite white coveralls and, at Woods' request, carried his clubs in the Masters' rain shortened par-3 tournament. One reporter said, "I actually had a guy in the gallery ask me—I swear this happened—if that fellow over there by Butch Harmon was Tiger Woods."

Butch and his prize pupil have been practically joined at the hip since 1997 when Woods dominated the field and won his first professional Gold Major at the Masters at the age of twenty. Tiger was sitting in his house studying the videotapes from his performance, blasting 300-yard drives, hitting crisp iron shots right at the pins, draining putts from everywhere. Yet something he was seeing wasn't sitting right with him. He called Harmon, a respected coach, and said, "My swing really sucks."[1]

He knew he wasn't in the right position at various points in his golf swing and had won because "my timing was great." At the same time, he knew that his swing wouldn't hold up under pressure for the long haul, so he told Butch Harmon, who was the former golf coach to the King of Morocco, that he wanted to make serious changes in the way he struck the ball. Harmon concurred with this assessment, and told him that it would take months to groove a new swing, and that his game would get worse before it got better. This might lead some to say that Tiger's success at the Masters was a flash in the pan.

Like Tiger Woods, the real leaders in sports, the performing arts, and business aren't content to merely be good. They want to be great.

Tiger told Harmon that it didn't matter. He relayed something that his pal Michael Jordan had told him: "No matter how good they say you are, set incredibly high goals and keep working on your game." He told Harmon his goal was to eventually surpass his cherished idol Jack Nicklaus (eighteen golf majors), and that he was sure he couldn't get there on his own. He wanted to build a powerful partnership with Harmon, who had worked with him on and off since Tiger was seventeen. Harmon accepted.

Harmon began working with Woods day in and day out. He told Tiger he would have to pump more iron to get his forearms stronger. Tiger then went to work on a Kaizen sequence (Japanese for improvement) that could be described as "disciplined intensity": (1) pounding hundreds of practice balls a day; (2) reviewing tapes of the swing for hours so as to get meaningful feedback; (3) bringing Harmon with him to all his tournaments; and (4) repeating all of the above.

It's rare in golf when a top pro teacher like Harmon accompanies a player like Woods to a tournament and walks every fairway with him (as Harmon did in 1998), even carrying his bag during the practice round to get a bird's eye view of his swing under pressure, all the while giving some appropriately wise counsel. The fact is that most top professional golf teachers have egos about as big as the players do, and would consider such a thing to be beneath their station in life.

A powerful partnership is created when there is chemistry, lots at stake in shared goals, regular interaction, and disciplined intensity.

The reason Harmon did this was that he took the partnership with Woods seriously and became a celebrity in his own right as a result. Woods took it equally seriously, spending hundreds of hours practicing, with Harmon relentlessly giving him the same corrections. In golf, old habits die hard. In some practice rounds, Harmon would tell Woods the same correction fifty to one hundred times. "Here's the grip you need to have." Then holding the mirror up, "Tiger, you went back to your old grip position on that last swing." Or "Here is the position you want to be in at the top, Tiger." "No, you went over the top," and so on.

Harmon was wise enough to recognize the impatience of the twenty-year-old Woods. To make sure Woods mastered each piece of the swing, grip, stance, and swing plane, he only told him one piece at a time. Harmon didn't show him the next piece until he had completely integrated the previous one.

Eventually, it all paid off. One day in 1999, preparing for the Byron Nelson Classic, Woods noticed some real improvement. Then suddenly, on one swing he sensed for the first time in a year that he had accomplished exactly what he wanted to accomplish. The motion felt natural and relaxed, and the contact solid. The ball flew high and straight.

Excited, he rolled another ball into place, but didn't make the same swing. Another ball. Didn't get it. Another ball. Didn't get it. Then he hit another pure shot. A couple of misses. Another pure one. And another. Soon the good swing started flowing like popcorn popping in a microwave.

Masterful Coaches will tell you that it takes at least one year to accomplish something big, to break the grip and excel beyond old patterns.

Woods called Harmon and told him, "I'm back!" The same year he won six pro tour events in a row. Nicklaus never won more than three in a row in one year. With his victory at the British Open in 1999, Woods completed a career Grand Slam of golf's four major tournaments, a feat accomplished by only four other golfers in history.

It is interesting to compare the powerful partnership between Tiger Woods and his coach Butch Harmon to the average professional golfer (or 15 handicapper player) who takes three lessons with a pro at the driving range when the wheels come off his swing and doesn't come back again for years, playing with the same crippled swing forever. In point of fact, most professional and amateur athletes have anything but bold goals and tend to get by on the minimal amount of coaching, which is why they never get better.

The same can be said of most businesspeople. In my experience, coaching in most organizations is the exception rather than the rule.

Getting to the Next Level

The Tiger Woods/Butch Harmon story is intended not to inspire people in business to take up golf, but rather to see the power of coaching. In Masterful Coaching Inc., we strive to create with executives and leaders the same kind of powerful relationship that Harmon and Woods created.

The model I have found most useful to use with leaders is one of a powerful partnership, where you are joined at the hip over the course of a year or more. This is definitely not the three sessions at the driving range variety of coaching. The leaders we work with, like Woods in his field, are already successful, but on some level know that they can get to the next level—from good to great. Further, they know that coaching will give them an edge or advantage.

This involves not only setting ambitious goals and aspirations that represent taking their game to the next level and creating a concrete plan to realize them, but also actually making something happen with colleagues in their business—with colleagues amidst change, complexity, and competition. There is a world of difference between having a Masterful Coach in your corner, someone who is there to empower your specific situation, and a "B" school executive education or an abstract training program that offers too much, too soon, or too little, too late. The same applies to Masterful Coaching that is done by leaders and managers within organizations.

The Qualities of a Great Partnership

It is my experience that, whenever human beings excel to great heights, accomplishing something extraordinary, it is being achieved with a Masterful Coach either in the foreground or background. It is also my experience that Masterful Coaching is based on an extraordinary partnership, which has some extraordinary and rare qualities.

First, for a coaching relationship to be established, there must be a personal chemistry in the mix that draws two human beings to each other in the pursuit of goals and aspirations that each finds meaningful. There is a powerful human bond that develops as a result of the coach's sincere desire and relentless effort to cause the person's success, along with the coachee's listening for the coach. (As Butch Harmon told Tiger, "You need to lift weights ninety minutes a day.") While this human bond is important, the coach has to make clear at the start of the relationship that it needs to be okay to disagree, as well as to tell the truth. This means providing potentially embarrassing feedback needed for growth and learning.

A Masterful Coach stands for the future and space of possibility, while shaping concrete goals and prompting concrete action.

At the heart of the matter, Masterful Coaching dwells in what I call a "listening for greatness." The coach provides an environment for that person to find him- or herself, and find his or her greatness and capacity to be extraordinary. It is based on a complete commitment to the other person and to what that person is committed to and capable of, even beyond what he or she sees right now. The coach stands for the future and the space or spirit of possibility, while shaping concrete goals and prompting concrete action. The coach must be prepared to "go above and beyond" to cause the person's success, as Harmon did by carrying Tiger's golf bag in the Masters par-3 match so he could better observe and teach him.

It is this listening for people's greatness that allows the coach to see what is really possible for people and to open people's eyes so they can see and believe in it themselves. Once people are enrolled in that possibility, the coach is then in a position to support them to set more powerful goals for themselves or to make powerful "unreasonable" requests that no one else in their lives would dare make. For example, I once told an up-and-coming executive that he needed to go sing in the subway at the top of his lungs to break through barriers he had to full self-expression. He did it.

Another extraordinary and rare quality in this kind of partnership is that the coach stands committed to the coachee in the face of breakdowns. In going for powerful breakthrough goals, the person being coached will inevitably produce breakdowns that in any other relationship would be highly annoying. This can take the form of becoming heavy-handed with direct reports, making the same mistakes despite repeated correction, or not following through on key actions that have been promised.

A Masterful Coach is a listening for people's greatness.

As Masterful Coach Veronica Pemberton says, "I am listening for people's greatness and who they are when they forget their greatness and descend into pettiness. The person I am coaching can do no wrong in my eyes (assuming it is ethical). If who they are being at a meeting is counterproductive with others, if they make repeated mistakes or don't deliver on promises, I never make them wrong. That just makes people defensive. Instead, I return them to their commitments, address the breakdown in a very matter-of-fact way, and identify what's missing that, if provided, can make a difference."[2]

It is important to point out that the coach needs to come to each and every conversation with the person without any other agenda except the agenda of that person. As a Masterful Coach, one of the things that keeps my agenda from getting in the way is that I only take on coaching engagements for a minimum of a year, and secondly "coachees" need to pay me a big chunk of money in advance. There are, as a result, never any hidden agendas about "continued work" or "money." If I have an agenda I want to talk about, then I can be frank about that.

If the Masterful Coach is in a leadership role within an organization, it is important to first align around goals and expectations that meet the needs of the person and meet the needs of the organization. This allows you to focus the conversation on being a listening for the coachees' concerns, offering them a powerful assist in accomplishing what it is they need to accomplish.

"The only way to discover the limits of the possible is to go beyond them into the impossible and discover possibilities you didn't see before due to veil of your own beliefs."

—Arthur C. Clark

COMPASS POINT II. Stand in the Future People Want to Create

Richard W. Severance is a vice president of Conoco Downstream North America (a refining and marketing group), the fourth largest oil company in the world. "Severance," as he calls himself, is a charismatic, good-humored, sharp-as-a-tack Texan who looks just a mite like Tommy Lee Jones, and sounds just a mite like him too.[3] As someone told me, "When Severance struts into the Marlin Room," a sancta sanctorum named after the company's founder, "you have no doubt who the leader of this business is." He fills the entire space with his presence, which is true grit.

I met Severance as a result of putting on a number of Masterful Coaching seminars for Conoco. I should explain that in an oil company, you have two powerful organizations: an upstream company whose business is exploration and production, and a downstream organization, which has to do with refining and marketing. The downstream business, which generally produces a lower return on capital employed than the upstream, received the message that, in effect, their purpose was not to grow, but rather to be cost-efficient and produce excess cash for upstream. The reason: New refineries cost a lot of money and building new gas stations, at $3 million each, on pennies for gross margin, ain't that profitable.

This purpose had been put in place by a real fireball of a leader, Jim Nokes, Severance's boss. The reason: Dupont, the company's previous owner, had threatened to sell the downstream organization if its results did not significantly improve. Nokes' message to the troops was, "Wake up and take charge of your own destiny. The Indians are coming and there's no cavalry." His refining and marketing approach, "Run full and run cheap," saved the day, and then the law of unintended consequences took over: a climate of resignation where people did not feel they had the opportunity to be creative, innovative, and take risks.[4]

A Masterful Coach stands in the Impossible Future people are committed to and encourages them to act boldly in the present.

When Severance got wind of the power in creating an Impossible Future in the Masterful Coaching course, he decided to take a stand to transform the climate of resignation that existed in the company into a climate of opportunity. He asked me to be his executive coach and I told him, "While I appreciate the request and like you, it's got to be a big enough game. I'm not interested in doing remedial leadership BS." I carefully select every coaching client I work with on the basis of who they are and what they are up to.

I saw Severance as a bag full of possibilities, the kind of person who not only has vision, but who can also rally larger numbers of people and actually make something happen. Severance is generous and warmhearted, but his view of a shared vision and an aligned organization could be likened to sitting around the campfire and pondering what trail to follow the next day with a group of trusted hands, and then the next morning proclaiming, "Well, we're burning daylight, let's go." Sure, Severance had some warts as a leader, like being dismissive of those who are "all hat and no cattle" or people who "talk big, but don't do big," and was bull-headed at times, but these seemed small compared to the possibilities.

We agreed on a focus for our Masterful Coaching partnership of creating a powerful new future for Downstream (DS) Conoco, which involved producing extraordinary results and creating a climate of possibility and opportunity. I told him that we would only focus on calling forth who he needed to be as a leader to get the job done. I wanted to make it clear here that this was to be a true partnership. Over the coming year, the role of "master" and "student" changed many times. I was to learn as much from him as he from me. For in setting the bar very high for himself, he also set the bar high for me as a coach to take my craft to the next level. An email he sent me said, "Hargrove, I intend to set the bar around here so high you have to go back to school."

Defining an Impossible Future

The next step was to define the Impossible Future that he wanted to create in the company, going beyond the predictable future, based on the company's winning strategies and history. One day at a meeting in the stateroom of Severance's 46 Grand Banks Trawler, I suggested that he discuss the idea of designing an Impossible Future at the next monthly meeting of his executive staff. He replied, "Man, we have a packed agenda." "What do you and your staff create at those meetings?" I asked him. Suddenly a light went on in his eyes: "We don't create anything, we run the business."

> **The first step in creating an Impossible Future is to create some Big Hairy Audacious Goals that force people to challenge orthodoxies.**

Severance saw that, to transform the company, he had to shift his viewpoint and start thinking in terms of *Creating the Business (CTB),* rather than merely *Running the Business (RTB).* At his next executive team meeting, he told people he had a vision he wanted to share with them. He then declared his commitment to creating an Impossible Future that would result in an inspired, energized organization, one that would take him and the rest of the organization beyond running the business to creating the business.

The first step in creating an Impossible Future was to create a vision of an inspired, energized, engaged organization. I often tell leaders that to realize their vision they need to create a Teachable Point of View (TPOV) that will shift the prevailing mindset or point of view in the organization.[5] For example, Coca-Cola's Roberto Goizueta had a teachable point of view used to grow the business. It was "share of stomach," as opposed to the prevailing point of view of "share of market." Andy Grove's teachable point of view is: "Only the paranoid survive."

I asked Severance what his teachable point of view was, and he told me a story from when he was in high school on the baseball team. It was 110 degrees and, between innings, he told the coach that he was too exhausted to move. The coach's response was, "Take another salt tablet and get back in the game." "That's my teachable point of view," said Severance, chuckling out loud. "Hey, a lot of leaders in business today have lost their drive, determination, and edge." Severance has another TPOV: "Extraordinary leaders, the kind who can create an inspired organization, develop in the process of producing extraordinary results."

The next step in creating the Impossible Future was to create what Severance called BHAGS—Big Hairy Audacious Goals—in the area of leadership, profitable growth, and real process improvement (reduced costs), the kind that comes from creating a sustainable competitive advantage. The idea behind the BHAGS was to both raise the bar— "We're gonna be a high performance organization"—and also to create a new managerial frame to get people to think outside of the same old boxes.

Structure for Fulfillment

The next step is to design a structure for fulfillment. Creating an Impossible Future starts with declaring an exciting new possibility. Yet a structure of fulfillment is required to realize the possibility and make it a reality. I told Severance that you create a structure for fulfillment by design. Together we acted as thinking partners in looking at the question of what is missing to realize the vision and achieve the BHAGS. Diagram 1.1 illustrates the structure for fulfillment that we came up with.

The structure for fulfillment included creating a cadre of generative leaders, giving them each Masterful Coaches, as well as creating forums for strategic conversations to take place with new voices free to fundamentally question the strategy of "buying, boiling, and selling oil." The structure of fulfillment also included a "business concept incubator" and the implementation of a high-voltage Six Sigma process improvement program. "If we control costs through Six Sigma," said Severance, "that will create space to do some highly innovative things."

DIAGRAM 1.1 *The journey to creating the Impossible Future*

I saw it as my role as Severance's coach/partner to stand in this Impossible Future he was committed to creating, as well as to encourage him to focus his agenda on including "calendar time" for making that Impossible Future a reality. The fact is that most leaders don't have the power to create an Impossible Future, because they tend to become too easily sucked into squandering their time and attention on petty people issues, circumstances, and events. "Someone wants me to go to a meeting on refinery security. What the hell do I know about refinery security?" Severance said, as he began to question how he spent his time.

Obviously, the kind of Impossible Future we are talking about doesn't just happen; it takes leadership. A large part of my coaching was spent on working with Severance to be the kind of generative leader it takes to "source" the Impossible Future, as opposed to a reactive RTB manager. I provided Severance a teachable point of view about who he needed to be in the matter. He provided the charisma, leadership, and drive to get the "sourcing" of the Impossible Future formulation over the line (vision, TPOV, structure of fulfillment). He began rolling the Impossible Future out to hundreds of employees with the intention of enrolling people's voluntary participation in the process.

My role not only included supporting Severance in keeping the different dimensions of the Impossible Future at the top of his agenda and in taking bold and powerful action, but I also acted as cheerleader. "Man, that IF presentation was great!" I provided further coaching and feedback to address breakdowns and provide what was missing. One potential breakdown we observed was that, to source the Impossible Future, we needed to have generative leaders at every level, people who could re-create the sourcing (in other words, the vision and TPOV). We needed leaders who were coaches and teachers.

Take Bold and Unreasonable Action

Severance saw this and declared a personal commitment to become a Masterful Coach in his own right. He started by holding coaching sessions with his direct reports. He set the expectation with them that each become an inspiring leader, recreating the sourcing of the Impossible Future, and creating "line of sight" to it for the people in their respective organizations. He also asked each leader to set up some goals that were based on producing some extraordinary results for the coming year. This would take each of them showing up as a dramatically different kind of manager.

As coaching and teaching represented new territory for Severance, he sometimes came on a bit strong here, putting on not a coach's hat but a judge's, and asking, "What was wrong?" rather than "What's missing that, if provided, would make a difference?" (At issue here is that "what's missing" is not always obvious.) This sometimes caused people to react defensively and shut down. I emphasized to Severance that, while all coaches make judgments, not all judges are coaches. I began looking for someone or something that could serve as a role model or metaphor.

I found one totally outside the world of business. It was Ben Zander, conductor of the Boston Philharmonic orchestra, who invited me to attend his master class. Zander's job was to transform talented music students from being good technicians to being great musicians. They needed to learn to play with passion, but were afraid of making mistakes and not receiving an "A" grade. Zander was frustrated by this breakdown, but soon discovered what was missing.

As I shared with Severance, Zander said, "I am going to give each of you an 'A' in this class." The only thing they needed to do was to write a paper entitled, "Dear Mr. Zander, I got my 'A' because. . ." "It has to be a story of transformation," Zander told me, "from this to that." Then he asked people to stand in the Impossible Future of transforming into an "A" player (as opposed to a "C" or "D" player) and to act from that possibility. Further, he never diminished his listening for the students' greatness when they didn't transform overnight. There was a not-so-subtle suggestion here that Severance do this with his direct reports.

I told Severance that, while Zander extended people an "A," he also provided something else that was missing. He was totally relentless in coaching them to actually show up that way. I heard him interrupt a cello player, Carl, who was playing Bach in front of the class and say, "Carl, I am now going to make a comment to you in the context of your 'A.' You could get a job today with a symphony orchestra making $50,000 a year, and have a nice little wife, and a nice little house, and 2.7 kids. The only thing is that Bach didn't write this music for someone who wanted to make $50,000 a year and have a nice little wife, and a nice little house, and 2.7 kids. He wrote it for the glory of God. Play with more passion, Carl!" Moments later Carl broke through.

Masterful Coaches extend people an "A" and then relentlessly coach them to show up that way.

Severance and I had many debates about how this applied to a Fortune 500 company, which led to the creation of an enlightened A,B,C,D performance management system based on extending people an "A" where possible and then coaching them to show up that way. Soon Severance began showing up more like a Masterful Coach, making some powerful commitments to develop people in his group.

These leaders and others soon began to show up as inspiring leaders, recreating the "sourcing" of the Impossible Future in their respective organizations and in getting the job done. It wasn't long before the prevailing climate of resignation began to be transformed into a climate of possibility and opportunity. The different elements of the Impossible Future were all in motion, and a rallying momentum was being created. The extraordinary and tangible business results that came spoke for themselves.

One last story about Richard W. Severance: One of his favorite movies is the classic Western *The Magnificent Seven*. There is a scene that reminds me of him. Some of the top guns in the West happen to converge on a south-of-the-border town that is being shot up and ransacked by bandits. The Seven try to ignore this at first, but eventually it starts to stick in their craws. One of the guys takes the lead and straps on his gun. The others, although not really a group, follow suit almost without a word. "Let's get this done," as Severance says.

COMPASS POINT III. Leaders Must Reinvent Themselves First

Jann Jarvi, the newly anointed chairman and CEO of the European-based giant high-tech firm Global Electronics (pseudonym), ushered me down the grand marble steps of his corporate headquarters in Stockholm. At six feet, five inches, towering over me like a skyscraper, Jarvi gently slapped my back, graciously opened the door of his BMW 750, and asked his personal driver to take me to the luxurious Grand Hotel. His parting words as he stepped away from the car were, "I don't just think I want to move forward with the Masterful Coaching." He continued, "I *definitely* want to move forward, and boldly. The only way we are going to reach our vision of creating a high growth technology company is to reinvent this company, and I need your help."

"So far, so good," I thought.

To provide some background, Global Electronics had stumbled badly in the late 1980s due to a lack of competitive advantage and escalating costs. The company was brought back to financial credibility by early 1990 by a new CEO, and then began to enjoy an era of profitable growth, based on a matrix structure that allowed the different product divisions to operate as independent businesses without a lot of bureaucracy. This winning strategy reached its limitation, however, leading to a total lack of cooperation that made it difficult to respond quickly to new market opportunities such as the mobile phone and the PDA (Palm Pilot).

Soon after becoming CEO and chairman, Jarvi announced at a company meeting of the top one hundred leaders that he was standing for a new possibility, that of "bringing Silicon Valley inside" and of becoming a company that would foster "profitable growth" and "shape the future of our industry." This would require reinventing their corporate culture so that it was much more innovative and collaborative. It would require a Six Sigma approach, and it would require talented people at all levels with a radically different leadership style. To make this happen, every person in the room was going to use an executive coach.

What Jann Jarvi didn't realize is that he had vastly underestimated the extraordinary leadership that it would take on his part to make this reinvention happen and so he stepped into what's called the "Great Programmatic

Fallacy." One of Jarvi's behaviors was that he often tended to speak in terms of transforming other people as leaders and to deflect conversations about transforming himself. A company can do a lot of "programs," but unless the leaders see that, in order to transform the organization, they must first transform themselves, the programs are generally doomed to failure.

What happened next reminds me of something Jacques Barzun talked about in *From Dawn to Decadence,* a cultural history of five hundred years of Western Civilization. He said essentially that, without extraordinary leadership, the most inspiring vision tends to be diminished by the reactionary defenders of the status quo. Even those hungry spirits possessed with the calling to make the vision a reality tend to eventually give up and adapt their behavior to the absurd norms created by reactionaries. In Global Electronics' case, this is exactly what happened.

While the CEO, a lifetime employee whose father had worked in the company as a maintenance engineer, had made bold pronouncements at the meeting of the top one hundred managers, he soon became very tentative in implementing them. One staffer told me candidly that Jarvi once confided to him that he wasn't sure why they picked him for CEO. There were others he thought more deserving. "He isn't sure of himself or the solidity of his position and is highly conflict averse," this person told me.

While the powerful chieftains of the different product divisions liked the idea of becoming a high-growth technology company, they balked at the idea of losing any shred of independence in favor of the new flavor-of-the-month collaboration. They were also resistant to a corporate-wide Six Sigma effort and would back it only if they were allowed to implement it in their own separate ways.

When I coached Jarvi to take a stand with his product division managers and use the coaching network we were creating to foster alignment, the HR manager, fearing that the coaches would become too powerful, stepped in and deliberately sabotaged both the entire reinvention strategy and the coaching effort.

Reinvent yourself, rather than reduce your vision, when you hit the inevitable roadblocks.

Jarvi, seeking to avoid conflict, reduced the vision, "We will be a high growth technology company that serves the best interests of the product divisions." He also agreed to make the way Six Sigma was implemented discretionary. Finally, he delegated the coaching effort to the HR manager, who sentenced it to a kind of solitary confinement.

Under the HR manager, there would be no collaboration between coaches or comprehensive effort, as he claimed this would be too hard to control. Coaches were to coach only on leadership issues, not on business issues. (Let me note that we have found that the collaborative approach where the coaching is based on a marriage of leadership development and business performance allows the coaches to not only support the leaders they are coaching as individuals, but to also ensure that the coaching is aligned to the larger vision, mandate, and objectives of the organization.)

Jarvi chose to make the HR person's behavior undiscussable, covering it up with reasons and excuses. At this point, I had no choice but to withdraw our coaches from the assignment.

Yet before I did, I had one last meeting with Jarvi. I told him that what shapes the cultural clearing of any organization is who leaders are being, which shapes how people occur. "The way you and others think and act has been a key force in providing the cultural clearing of the organization that exists today," I continued. "I know that you started out with a grand vision for the company, one that you truly believed needed to happen for the company to get to the next level. Yet, when you met disagreement and dissention, you lowered the vision. I don't believe you know how much you are influencing the culture of the company and what is possible here. You may not like what I have to say, but to me, you are not showing up as the leader and, consequently, leadership is showing up as missing in the company. You are not showing up as a collaborative and, therefore, collaboration is missing. You are colluding with the organization's defensive behavior and so is everyone else." I concluded, "If you do not reinvent yourself before you begin this reinvention effort, then it will surely fail."

I have seen over and over again the most sincere, well-intended efforts to reinvent organizations fail, because without leadership reinvention, leaders do not have the kind of personal power they need to succeed. Powerful organizational reinvention requires leaders from the executive suite to the shipping dock to reinvent themselves. The excuse that is often given for organizations that fail to reinvent themselves is resistance to change: "People did not embody the new attitudes and behaviors and get on board with the change program."

As Tracy Goss points out, "If you are a breathing human being, you are resistant to change. Like all your fellow human beings, you are designed to be incapable of starting with a blank sheet of paper"[6]. That is why it is necessary to reinvent yourself first. If you are in a key leadership role and you want to reinvent the organization, reinventing yourself first is the only way you can create the kind of cultural clearing in which resistance to change can be resolved.

It is not that people on the leadership teams are resisting, it is that they come with a "master program" and don't have the ability to start from a "blank sheet of paper." Before you or anyone else can draw on your blank page, it is already filled up right to the edges. It is encrypted with your history, the company's history, the winning strategies you think are right for yourself and the business, thrown ways of being, thinking, and attitudes. Usually the things that have made us successful in the past eventually become a source of constraint and limitation.

Masterful Coaches support people to invent a new future that is not an extension of the past by unearthing what people passionately care about and then encouraging them to declare the impossible possible.

It is not until the leader(s) reinvent themselves that they are personally freed of the constraints of the past (of which past successes are a part) and begin to have the power to create a new future. This not only is a matter of declaring new possibilities for yourself as a leader and for the organization as a business or culture, but it is a matter of giving up old ways of thinking and operating that you have come to rely on. Diagram 1.2 illustrates this.

DIAGRAM 1.2 *Creating a possible future versus a predictable future*

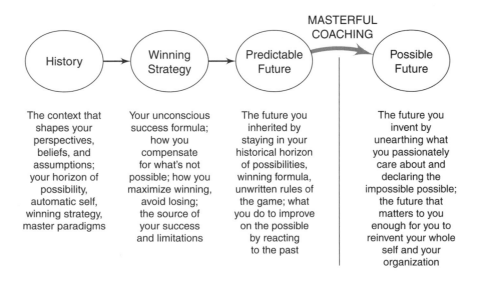

History	Winning Strategy	Predictable Future	Possible Future
The context that shapes your perspectives, beliefs, and assumptions; your horizon of possibility, automatic self, winning strategy, master paradigms	Your unconscious success formula; how you compensate for what's not possible; how you maximize winning, avoid losing; the source of your success and limitations	The future you inherited by staying in your historical horizon of possibilities, winning formula, unwritten rules of the game; what you do to improve on the possible by reacting to the past	The future you invent by unearthing what you passionately care about and declaring the impossible possible; the future that matters to you enough for you to reinvent your whole self and your organization

You can attempt to reinvent yourself on your own, but it happens much faster with a Masterful Coach around, for just as soon as people start preaching the new way, they revert to form without even being aware of it. Other people see this and model their behavior according to who you are being and what you are doing, not just what you are saying. Chris Argyris calls this shifting from your "espoused theory" (what you preach) to your "theory in use" or regular practice. This most often happens under conditions of pressure and stress.

In effect, what we are talking about here with respect to the CEO and leaders at all levels reinventing themselves is something transformational, not incremental. We are talking about transforming who we are being, which in turn shapes our thinking and actions. We are not simply talking about grafting on some new attitudes or changing a few behaviors. We are talking about an alteration of substance, not merely a change in form.

Leaders almost always show up in the world as a function of some way of being that they are presently unaware of. (Are you showing up as a leader or follower? As dominating or collaborative? And so forth.) This often results in them creating a cultural clearing that is inconsistent with their goal or intentions of reinventing the organization. The role of the Masterful Coach is to "rip the blinders off," to make people aware of what they are unaware of. It is also to empower people to declare their commitment to new ways of being and to call those forth into the organization. This is a key to the leader being able to create a new clearing.

The kind of personal transformation we have been discussing is intimately tied to organizational transformation. It goes hand in hand with declaring an Impossible Future for your business—and than acting boldly to make it a reality. In fact, it starts with people committing themselves to a future they care so passionately about that they are willing to reinvent their entire selves. Only then do human beings develop the individual and collective will to jettison the past and start over. (We will explore the ideas, methods, and techniques more deeply in Chapter Four, which is on transformational learning.)

COMPASS POINT IV. A Coach Is a Thinking Partner

"It is like trying to deal with an enigma, wrapped inside a conundrum, surrounded by a dilemma," Sheryl Steel said to Bill Brock, chairman of Shearing Inc. She was talking about her leadership role in Antigen, a subsidiary and a fast-track biotech company.

Brock laughed, recognizing the quote, which originally came from a comment Bertrand Russell made about dealing with the former Soviet Union. "There are a number of puzzles here that I am looking for a thinking partner on," said Steel. "Have you got about a week?" she joked.

First some background. In 2000, one of Antigen's project groups, previously lead by Carl Conti, succeeded after a decade of research in bringing to market a potential breakthrough bio-tech drug called "Arterio," a drug that is highly effective in treatment of congenital heart disease. However, the drug development process took five years longer than expected and ate up huge amounts of the company's research capital.

Steel, who had been lead marketing manager for the Schearing group, was appointed to head Antigen, with a special leadership role to play. "Keep the aspirations of the organization high. We can hit a home run here," Brock told her. "And bring some short-term discipline and rigor to the business at the same time." Brock affirmed, "It is a *both/and,* not an *either/or* situation."

Steel's appointment was made to the deep chagrin and anger of Carl Conti, who expected an upward promotion as a result of the Arterio success. Instead, Conti was moved sideways to a role of lead project manager for "CATS," which held the promise of being a breakthrough cancer treatment. After the move, he stopped showing up as the hard-driving leader he was previously, which confused the people in his organization. He also became highly defensive in his behavior.

First of all, Conti resisted even the most gracious attempts by the highly capable and affable Steel to build a relationship with him—resenting it when Steel asked him questions about the business. "Are you questioning my judgment?" he demanded to know. Another one of Conti's defensive routines was always to speak through rose-colored glasses about the new CATS project, touting it as a potential breakthrough, but refusing to look at any breakdowns that were occurring.

The issue was that "CATS" was a drug that could potentially treat many different forms of the disease. Conti and his team were out marketing various applications of the new biotech drug to the Big Ten pharmaceutical firms. A major issue for Antigen was that the pre-trial drug was still not out of the labs, and each different drug application required heavy capital investment to develop. When Steel asked questions about the wisdom of this approach, Conti said, "We don't know which of these drug applications will ultimately be successful, and we need to hedge our bets."

There was a distinct lack of purpose, focus, and discipline in Conti's organization. There were seven different development projects going on, which made it difficult to marshal enough resources to spearhead a breakthrough in any one of them. The word on the street was that the competition was moving fast in a highly focused way on related drugs in a key application area. Steel was not only puzzled about how to deal with Conti's defensive routines, but also her own as well. She told Brock, "I feel caught between trying to build a relationship with him and trying to bring some purpose, focus, and discipline to the business."

The whole festering situation boiled to a head when Bill Brock called Steel to his office that day to tell her that the board had noticed that the CATS project was a million dollars over its projected budget, and there was a need to make some very significant cutbacks. It was at this point that one of our coaches from Masterful Coaching, someone who had both a marketing and R&D background, was brought in to help sort out the situation.

The Coach, Thomas Halpert, framed it for Steel this way: "There are four dilemmas that you are faced with:

1. What strategic direction do we take the business in: Spearhead a breakthrough by focusing on one application, or spread our bets?

2. How do you deal with the defensive routines★ of Carl Conti: Build a collegial relationship to engender trust and safety, suppress dilemmas and defer to his reasoning, or confront dilemmas and ask him to make not just his views, but his reasoning public so it can be tested?

3. How do you deal with your own defensive reactions: Trying to be nice and avoiding conflict in order to be liked and accepted (Steel's own behavior) or unilaterally advocate your position?

4. If Carl Conti does not shift his attitude or decide to leave on his own, who will replace him? How do we not lose momentum?

Why a Thinking Partner?

First of all, shifting from the term "coach" to the term "thinking partner" can move people's thinking from "This is the boss telling me what to do" to "This

★A defensive routine is anything you do to avoid embarrassment or threat that does not remove the source of embarrassment or threat. Common defensive routines are withdrawing and distancing, suppressing dilemmas, making face-saving moves, easing into difficult conversations, and making hot issues undiscussable.

is a colleague who wants to offer me an assist." Second, a thinking partner is one of the most powerful ways to leverage the intellectual capital of any organization. When two people with different views and backgrounds come together with a basic attitude of curiosity and learning to solve a puzzle, the chances are that they will brainstorm ideas, question what they take for granted, and come up with insights that are not attainable on an individual basis.

Third, as to why a thinking partner, I am reminded of a quote from Wittgenstein: "A man's thinking goes on within his consciousness in seclusion, in contrast to physical action, which is an exhibition open to public view and thereby subject to scrutiny." Left alone to think in seclusion, there are any number of subjective factors that can distort the outcome. One benefit of using a thinking partner is that another person is able to bring some objectivity to the process.

Being a thinking partner often starts with simplifying people's thought processes, without overlooking complexity. I often start a conversation with people when there are overlapping dilemmas by saying, "This is not a trivial conversation, so let's be prepared to be in the confusion room for a while." It is okay to be in the confusion room on the way to clarity. At the same time, I say, "Let's see if there is anything we can simplify without overdoing it." To this I often cite a quotation from Oliver Wendell Holmes: "I don't give a damn about simplicity, from this side of complexity, but I would give everything for simplicity from the other side of complexity."

Roles of a Masterful Coach: thinking partner, sounding board, inquirer.

In the case of Sheryl Steel, Thomas Halpert first pointed out that she was stuck in a kind of pea soup, trying to think through the "people issues" and "business issues" at the same time. He suggested that the way to get out of it was to separate the business issues from the issues of organization defensive routines, and then to deal with each, one at a time. "Let's start with the issue of business strategy and then look at how we can begin to recognize and disperse (personal) organizational defensive routines."

Another key role of a thinking partner is to act as a "sounding board." The coach can do this by asking a question that gets to the heart of the matter and then by listening with an inexperienced ear. This empowers the person to make tacit knowledge (what they know but can't say) explicit. The coach creates the space for the coachee to do her own thinking and discover her own answers, keeping in mind that the coachee is nested in the situation and an information-rich context the coach doesn't have. The coach needs to draw out threads of insight and "half-baked ideas," with an ear to helping the person come up with inventive and effective solutions.

Halpert asked Steel a provocative question: "If you were a consultant who was being paid $5,000,000 if you could come up with the right solution, what would you do: Spearhead a breakthrough or spread your bets?" This led to a spirited dialogue in which they came up with a way of narrowing down their focus to three major initiatives, not putting their eggs all in one basket, but at the same time not spreading their resources too thin.

Then Steel and Halpert addressed the people issues and the defensive behavior. He asked about the relationship with Conti, "If you could wave a magic wand and have the relationship be a certain way, how would that be?" If you listen loudly enough, as well as "build and jump" on ideas, connecting disparate streams of thought, the person will often move beyond answers and come to the moment of true insight.

The answer that Steel came up with was that instead of she and Conti either withdrawing from each other, suppressing disagreement, or trying to advance their views on the drug development strategy through force of argument or pressure, they needed a radically different approach. "We need to engage in a learning process and stop being so defensive," Steel declared. The coach built on this idea by suggesting that they should (1) both make their reasoning process public by walking down the ladder of inference[7] (see Diagram 1.3); (2) jointly find ways to test disagreements; and (3) openly discuss with each other their defensive reactions and action.

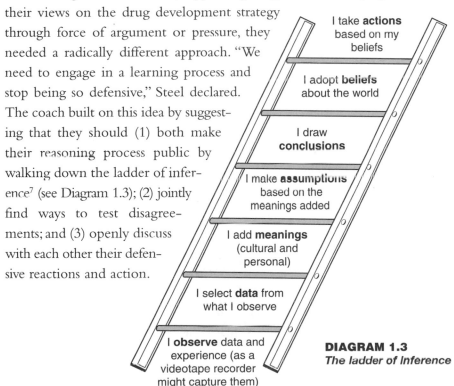

I take **actions** based on my beliefs

I adopt **beliefs** about the world

I draw **conclusions**

I make **assumptions** based on the meanings added

I add **meanings** (cultural and personal)

I select **data** from what I observe

I **observe** data and experience (as a videotape recorder might capture them)

DIAGRAM 1.3
The ladder of Inference

"Everything you say reveals you."

—Ralph Waldo Emerson

Acting as a "sounding board" and "drawing out" accomplishes two things. It allows people the opportunity to express what they know on a vague intuitive level but are not able to articulate. It also allows the coach to understand the underlying patterns of thinking that govern the person's thinking process that might cause distortion when he or she begins to draw conclusions.

One of the obvious traps is having frames of reference in our thinking that go unnoticed. For example, there are

- *Role Frames:* "I am the boss, I have more experience and therefore I am right."

- *Thought Frames or Pet Theories:* Seeing this situation as the one you were previously in and thereby thinking or doing the same thing.

- *Industry Frames:* Old orthodoxies that inhibit inventive and effective thinking.

- *Personal Mental Models:* Rigid patterns of thinking or thinking based on unexamined assumptions or assumptions that may no longer be accurate.

- *Gaps in Reasoning:* Conclusions ungrounded in data or jumping to conclusions.

- *Crooked Attitudes:* Ways of looking at what happened based on blame, shame, or guilt; they get in the way of making accurate interpretations of reality.

- *Emotional or Defensive Reactions:* Reacting to what happened based on past hurts in a way that is intended to defend and protect yourself; may cloud your ability to see clearly.

It is generally an excellent practice for the coach to question everything that the coachee takes for granted. This starts with graciously, but provocatively, challenging all assumptions and inferences. Here are some good stock questions to ask: "What lead you to that conclusion?" "Could you walk me down your ladder of inference?" "What is your reasoning process?" "Do you have any data to substantiate that opinion?"

COMPASS POINT V. Expanding People's Ability to Take Successful Action

Many coaches focus on speaking and listening in a manner that enables people to go beyond answers and come to a moment of true insight. It's my observation that people value a coaching relationship or session that creates a clearing for them to not only have powerful insights, but to also take effective action. The acid test for the effectiveness of any coaching session is: Did the person go back to work and take some powerful actions? It's very important then to end every coaching session with at least three action items.

Coaching people to take successful action not only involves setting goals, but also observing people on a daily basis, honestly acknowledging breakdowns, identifying what's missing that, if provided, can make a difference, and moving people into action with respect to it. My approach is to translate what's missing into a small project or doable action that can be accomplished in the next forty-eight hours (or at most two weeks).

There are different pathways to coaching people to take successful action. The first involves a fine-tuning (doing the same thing better). The second involves helping people learn to do something that is fundamentally different. This involves single-, double-, and triple-loop learning, which will be thoroughly discussed in Chapter Four.

A Masterful Coach is always asking penetrating questions: "What unintended results are you getting?" "How are you contributing to them?" "How are you looking at things now?" "How do you need to look at things differently?" "How could you look at the problem or solution in a different way?" "Where are you stuck in an old pattern?" "How do you need to shift your way of being, thinking, or behaving?"

It is very important for the Masterful Coach to hold people accountable to their word through some kind of follow-up. As Veronica Pemberton says, "I always presence people's commitment and I never let anything fall through the cracks." At the same time, there is a difference between presencing people's commitment at a monthly (or bimonthly) meeting and hovering over them on a day-in, day-out basis. It is very important to not only hold people accountable, but to act as a cheerleader for their accomplishments.

CHAPTER TWO

BECOMING A MASTERFUL COACH

A Coach Is Something That You "Be"

"I learned wisdom from all my teachers and teaching from all my students." —Ben Ezra, 2nd Century AD

Great coaches, teachers, or mentors seem to stand in a different place from the rest of us. They also come from a different place. This shows up in the way they are and in the way they think and interact with others. First of all, they stand in a commitment to make a difference in the life of the person and demonstrate this in every interaction. They listen from a place where they see that the coachee or student is committed to being great, not just merely good or mediocre and, as a result, they call that commitment forth. They speak from a place where the student is okay with them, even if the student has made a mistake, "Let's try that again this way."

Great coaches or teachers often display simple virtues like generosity of spirit, giving others the gift of their presence. They also seem to have the kind of clarity of mind that gets to the heart of the matter, the honesty and integrity to say what they know to be true, together with the compassion to do no harm. They have a basic human wisdom in dealing with countless situations. When we meet people who possess such virtues, they automatically become coaches for us, whether they are teachers, bosses, or janitors. When we leave them, we feel inspired, empowered, and enabled to take effective action.

PART ONE: IT'S WHO YOU ARE BEING, NOT JUST TECHNIQUE

The Japanese have a word, "kokoro," that has to do with perfecting one's inner nature. To be a great swordsman or tea master or Kojiki dancer, one must not only master the technique but also perfect the way of being that is consistent with the discipline—having a calm and centered inner spirit. A student learns as much from the master's quality of being as from the master's knowledge and technical skills. To be able to teach people in "the way," one must perfect his or her own inner nature.

In the West, we tend to underestimate the importance of a person's way of being. We focus instead on his or her knowledge, skills, or techniques. Yet, whenever people stand out in a particular domain, they are recognized as "being" a leader, "being" excellent, "being" creative, "being" effective, or "being" understanding.

In most cases in our society, people don't ask the question: "How do I *be*?" when it comes to learning. They think in terms of "What do I *do*?" and "How do I do it?" This makes sense in teaching simple skills or practices, but it becomes limited when we try to apply the same principle to learning certain roles, such as leadership or coaching. Although we may be able to describe or explain what great leaders, coaches, or teachers do, the source of their actions often lies beyond such descriptions and explanations.

It's no accident that in many spiritual traditions, such as Tibetan Buddhism or the martial arts, the master teaches the student both the spirit and the standard practices of the domain. Those who are able to embody the teacher's way of being, along with the skills and techniques, become part of the lineage. They become the next generation of masters, teachers, or coaches. It is their responsibility to pass on both the technical and mystical sides of the equation.

There is a story about a swordsman who went to study with a master in the mountains when he was just a young boy, and the master set him up in the kitchen washing pots and pans. The student begged the master to teach him how to use the sword, but the master didn't allow him to pick up a sword for over five years. Every time the master would enter the kitchen where the young boy worked, the master would pick up a stick, sneak up beside the boy, and whack him on the head.

One day the master silently walked into the kitchen and raised the stick to strike the student from behind, but the student picked up the top of a pot and blocked the stick. Soon it was almost impossible for the master to hit the student. The master had taught the student not only humility, but also how to defend himself from attack. The student went on to become one of the greatest swordsmen of Japan. He later said that it was the humility that his master taught him by making him work in the kitchen that developed his soul as a samurai. It taught him the spirit of true service . . . and to be ready at all times.

For over ten thousand years, this is the way that most things have been taught in human culture; but in Western society we have separated the process of developing a way of being from the process of learning. In most management books, articles, and courses, there is little or no importance placed on how you have to "be" in order to excel at something; the emphasis, rather, is on skills and practices. The typical management seminar is more likely to lead to colorful plastic binders full of information and a list of "how to's" than to an alteration of a person's way of being.

Becoming a Masterful Coach

As Jacob Bronowski said in The Ascent of Man, "Man may be lower than the angels, yet he has a set of gifts which make him unique. He distinguishes himself from the other animals by his imaginative gifts. He makes plans, inventions, and new discoveries by putting his talents together in more subtle and penetrating ways." Bronowski goes on to say that man's greatest inventions are not just the wheel, the telephone, and the printing press, but his "ability to reinvent himself."[1] This ability to reinvent ourselves is what makes it possible to learn new ways of being.

As the Japanese swordsman learned, becoming masterful in a particular domain starts with making a commitment. To become a Masterful Coach, the first question to ask, then, is not "What do I do?" but "How do I 'be'?" You may say to yourself, "I don't have those ways of being." Keep in mind that the essence of being a human being is to be able to create something.

All You Have Is Who You "Be"

All we have is who we "are," and this in turn shapes what we do. Being is sometimes thought of as something intangible, abstract, or even ineffable, but it is actually quite real. *Inspiration* is a matter of *being* inspired. *Producing extraordinary results* is a matter of *being extraordinary,* and *being result-oriented. Fostering a great team effort* in the face of competitive battle involves *being a team player.*

Being is the context from which all of our thinking and actions spring, as opposed to *doing,* which is just a content that flows from the context. It is how we are being in any given moment that determines what's possible and not possible. How we are being shapes, limits, defines not only what we see as possible and achievable, but also the goals we set, the plans we make, and the actions we take. The way we show up at any given moment, and the way other people respond to us, are always a result of some way of being that is presently unknown to us.

There is a difference between saying you are a coach, teacher, or mentor and actually showing up that way. To be sure, other people will be able to tell the difference, and they will either eagerly listen to what you are saying or start debating you as a result. As Ralph Waldo Emerson said, "Who you are speaks so loudly that it drowns out what you are saying."

You and I have the power to actually choose who we are being.

The thing that's vitally important to understand is that you and I actually have the power to choose who we are being in the world. Most people don't know that who we are today is in fact a result of some declarations (or decisions) we make about ourselves based on past experiences and how we interpret them. "I have no choice but to be a top-down, command-and-control, kill-the-snake kind of manager." Once we make these decisions, we tend to forget that they are not based on fact, but rather on interpretation, and they go solid.

We have the power to choose who we are being because we have the power to see ourselves as a possibility again or as "fluid," rather than see ourselves as a solid bunch of predictable traits or behaviors. You might say, "Being a top-down, kill-the-snake kind of manager is not who I am; it's a decision I made about myself based on the conditions in which I found myself. If that's the case, perhaps I have other alternative possibilities, especially as the conditions may have changed. I'd like to explore some alternative possibilities such as being a Masterful Coach, teacher, or mentor."

We also have the power to choose who we are being because we have the power to not only declare possibilities but to speak and listen with commitment. When we declare our commitment to the possibility of showing up as a coach, teacher, or mentor, that possibility comes into existence just because we said it. The declaration of commitment does not automatically guarantee that we will show up as a coach and mentor, but it automatically does begin to alter our way of being and our actions. Let's explore this more deeply.

You Call Forth Who You Need to Be Through the Power of Language

There are two schools of thought to develop yourself as a leader, coach, and mentor. One is based on calling yourself forth through the "language paradigm"; the other is based on descriptions, explanations, and studying behavior through the "psychological paradigm." These two schools of thought are as different as night and day. Let's explore the "psychological" approach first, and then move to the "language" paradigm and calling forth.

The Psychological Approach. The traditional approach to teaching people how to lead, coach, or teach is to study the characteristics, traits, and behavior of people who show up this way. Next come the five leadership and coaching categories and twenty-five dimensions with all the prescribed attitudes and behaviors. Finally comes the 360-degree computerized feedback and analysis of gaps and strengths, presented in abstract training programs. This often leaves people bereft, thinking, "How do I get these characteristics and traits inside of me?"

This behavioral approach always reminds me of dissecting a dead frog to find out the secret of life, or how in an 18th Century laboratory there was the study of how to get rid of what the biologist Anton van Leeuwenhoek called "the bad humeurs" and bring in the "good humeurs." The approach is mechanistic and psychological in nature and founded on constructing leaders and coaches as you would build the insides of an old clock, and with the clockmaker, often an HR manager, in charge, not the persons themselves.

Today, an increasing number of leaders, managers, and HR professionals are realizing that this behavioral approach is fundamentally wrong-headed. They are increasingly beginning to realize that there is not a shred of evidence that even the best descriptions and explanations of leadership, coaching, or teaching make any difference. There is an increasing awareness that this approach produces a lot of information, yet has little impact on anyone's leadership or coaching ability.

The Language Paradigm. A new approach is beginning to emerge called the "language paradigm." As Martin Heidegger once said, "Words, like the chisel of the carver, can create what never existed before rather than simply describe what already exists. As a man speaks, not only is the thing which he is declaring coming into existence, but also the man himself."

You declare a new possibility for yourself that you can passionately engage in and come into the world to celebrate and express it.

The language paradigm has been talked about and explored by Fernando Flores.[2] The language paradigm suggests that we draw our identity from a "body of declarations" and commitments about the future. For example, two powerful commitments are

- *I am committed to the possibility of [being a certain kind of leader] and I will act to call that possibility forth into reality; and*

- *I am committed to giving up [a specific counterproductive behavior].*

This stands in contrast to the psychological paradigm, which says that who we are is a body of inherited characteristics and traits, as well as thrown behavior. Furthermore, the only way to change who we are is by understanding the past.

What we're saying is that you can declare new possibilities for yourself through the power of language and through the power of calling forth. That is to say, the power to choose who you need to be exists in your conversations, in your speaking and listening, not in grappling with your history.

When I declare the possibility of being a Masterful Coach, that possibility comes into existence just because I said it. When I take a stand for that possibility and begin to draw my identity from that stand, something powerful and profound happens. Suddenly, based on who I am as a commitment, I begin to see myself in a new way and begin to show up in a different way. I begin to discover the power of being my stand when I am interacting with direct reports, colleagues, and others.

This new way of being lives (or dies) in my conversations with people. I can choose to speak and listen from the stand that I am or from my moods. When I am being a stand for becoming a Masterful Coach, I *come from* a total commitment to causing people's success, even when I am aggravated, disappointed, or fed up with them. I listen from a commitment to unleash what people passionately care about. I speak from a commitment to bringing out the best in people, while providing honest and relentless feedback.

At the same time, I become aware of those times when I am not being my stand and am indulging myself in gossip, rumor, judging, and so forth. I can then use this self-awareness to remind myself of my stand and return myself to my commitment, adjusting my speaking, listening, and actions accordingly.

Three Powerful Declarations

The ability to stand inside a new possibility and call ourselves forth starts with making three powerful declarations of commitment. A declaration is a "speech act" that brings something into existence just because you said it. For example:

1. *I declare that what is possible for me as a human being is what I say is possible.* By making this declaration, you give yourself the power to choose what is possible in the future, rather than have that be determined by circumstance.

2. *Who I am is the stand that I take [to be a Masterful Coach].* In the past, you have said that who you are is your personality or automatic self, your winning strategy, your reactions. By making this declaration, you are saying that who you are is your commitment, and you are creating the possibility of a new way of being for yourself.

3. *The stand that I take is. . . .* When you take a stand, you are declaring your commitment to the possibility you have declared a reality and to making that the game you are playing in life with a passion.

PART TWO: MASTERFUL COACHING IS A MATTER OF DISTINCTION

Declaring the possibility and making a commitment to being a Masterful Coach generate a powerful new conversation within yourself and with others that begins to alter who you are being, while it at the same time shapes, limits, and defines your actions. It will soon feel as though you have stepped into a new domain with its own distinct governing values, body of knowledge, and operating principles.

For example, *being* a leader, manager, or consultant is different than being a Masterful Coach, teacher, or mentor. What are the distinguishing differences? We need to make these distinctions so we can be clear about who we need to be in the matter, and, as well, clear as to how to act. Making a distinction is the "speech act" of putting these differences into words. An example of these distinctions is that a Masterful Coach inspires and empowers people, whereas a traditional manager tends to command and control.

So the first step in mastering a new domain is to make the distinctions that are pertinent to that domain; the next step is to make them your own. Use language to declare a new possibility for yourself—*being inspiring, being empowering, being enabling*—and then take a stand for that possibility. When you take a stand, you agree to take a possibility and take actions that make it a reality. At the same time, you consciously and intentionally begin to draw your identity from the possibility you are standing for. This is made real through practice and study.

In a sense, making distinctions is really an *ontological exercise* that results in new ways of being, more than an *intellectual exercise* that merely defines new behavior. Making a new distinction can open up a new domain's possibilities for us as human beings, both telling us who we need to be in the matter and telling us the governing variables that will lead to effective action within those domains.

Seven Powerful Distinctions, Seven Powerful Transformations

The following seven distinctions (shown in Diagram 2.1) represent seven powerful transformations you need to make to become a Masterful Coach. These transformations are catalyzed first by distinguishing a new possibility for yourself as a human being and then by taking a stand to be a commitment to that possibility. This then alters the context that shapes, limits, and defines your actions. For example, *Who I am is a total commitment to the person I am coaching. Therefore, I will act as if I am committed to causing the person's success, no matter what. I will observe breakdowns and listen for what's missing that, if provided, will made a difference.*

DIAGRAM 2.1 *Seven powerful transformations for becoming a Masterful Coach*

1. **Be a Commitment to Making a Difference**

2. **Be a Total Commitment to the Person You Are Coaching**

3. **Be a Commitment to Honesty and Integrity**

4. **Be a Commitment to the Impossible Future the Person Is Creating**

5. **Be a Commitment to Transformation**

6. **Be an Activist**

7. **Be a Cheerleader**

Masterful Coaches stand in an inspired place.

1. Be a Commitment to Making a Difference

There are two fundamentally different places you can stand (or come from) in life. Which place you decide to stand in will largely determine whether you will be inspired as a human being or dejected and depressed. People who become Masterful Coaches make an existential choice to stand in the place that a difference can be made in the life of one individual, a team, or an entire organization. This is opposed to the other place people stand, which is resignation.

A Masterful Coach's inspiration does not come from being an enthusiastic, pie-in-the-sky or unrealistic dreamer. It comes from being inspired by great human beings who made a difference in situations that were difficult or impossible. It comes from being genuinely excited about the possibilities in front of you, from knowing that there is some part of yourself that is bigger than your circumstances. And it comes from being a monster of effectiveness, leaving behind a track record of successes.

Masterful Coaches not only stand in a place that a difference can be made, they speak, listen, and act from that place, never indulging in cynicism or allowing others to do so. When others give up on an individual or start to gossip, they say, "Transformation is possible." When others say, "It can't be done," they say, "So what? We're going to do it anyway." When the body of the organization says, "I give up. Forget it," they move themselves and others beyond that.

One of the ways Masterful Coaches inspire people to move beyond the "Forget it" is by putting exciting new possibilities on the table in the face of difficult facts and circumstances. Another way they do that is to introduce powerful ideas into people's thinking. A powerful idea is one that has the capability of shifting paradigms. I have seen that a distinction alone can have the power to catalyze executives to undertake a course of personal and organizational reinvention. For example, understanding that there is a difference between an Impossible Future and a predictable future, between creating the organization and reacting to it, and between being a knower and a learner.

Masterful Coaches put exciting new possibilities on the table and powerful new ideas into their thinking.

By introducing new ideas, Masterful Coaches not only inspire themselves, but also are an inspiration to others. A good example of this is the story of Jaime Escalante, a math teacher at an inner-city high school in East Los Angeles. Traditionally, the students from this school did not go on to college. It was not even considered a possibility because the students were unable to pass the aptitude tests. Everyone believed it was impossible for them to do this.

Escalante inspired, cajoled, pushed, wheedled, and needled eighteen students, who could not even do long division, to become math wizards. When the students took the college aptitude tests, they passed with flying colors. The testing board members were so surprised they thought that the students must have cheated. The teacher urged the kids to take the test again. Not only did they pass, but they also did even better than the first time.

Interestingly enough, their success not only created the possibility of their going on to college, but also initiated a growing trend at the school of students going on to further education. In the next five years, five hundred students from the school went on to college. Not one had ever done so before.

CALLING FORTH QUESTIONS

Think about a time in your life when you were really inspired or really inspirational. What was the source of that inspiration? Was it a leader, coach, or friend? Was it your own desire to make a difference? Was there a possibility that captured your imagination? Were you willing to take a stand for that idea? Were you willing to suffer the consequences in seeing the idea realized and still keep going?

Masterful Coaches stand in the possibility of the person they are coaching being extraordinary.

2. Be a Total Commitment to the Person You Are Coaching

Masterful Coaches not only stand for making a difference, but they do it by "being a listener" for people's greatness and by being committed to calling that forth. "I come into every job and put new possibilities on the table that either no one ever saw before then or they had said, 'It can't be done,'" says Bill Nahill, a leader I worked with. "I make it happen because I not only define new possibilities, but because I find great people in every job I come into. Curiously, they don't know they are great and the organization doesn't know they are great. I see my job as to bring that out of them, which requires a lot of commitment on my part."

Masterful Coaches are a total commitment to the person they are coaching. They stand committed to people being extraordinary, not just ordinary. Standing in the possibility of the person being extraordinary, they set forth big challenges that cause people to alter who they are being, their thinking, and their behavior. Nahill tells a story about a team member who asked him to go talk to a senior leader, "You can talk to him," the person said. Nahill responded, "I can talk to him because I knock on his door. You can talk to him too." The person learned to *be* big, to stop *being* small, and he soon became a candidate for a top leadership role.

Being a total commitment to the person you are coaching not only means being a stand for them and the goals and aspirations they passionately care about, but also it means standing with them in the face of breakdowns and providing what's missing. It means you coming from a place that everything is transforming, no matter how stuck or ineffective the person may appear. And it means going to bat for people when the world is displeased with them or wants to cancel their vote. To have a Masterful Coach on your side is a powerful thing, an awesome thing.

CALLING FORTH QUESTIONS

Recall a time in your life when a parent, teacher, boss, or friend showed up as being a total commitment to you. Recall what the person did that gave you the feeling of totally caring about you and totally believing in you. What did that feel like? What did he or she do to show support for you directly or with others that was "above and beyond" what was expected? Recall a time when you did the same for someone else in your life.

Masterful Coaches stand in a commitment to the truth.

3. Be a Commitment to Honesty and Integrity

Masterful Coaches often live on the horns of a dilemma. On one side, the coach naturally wants to create a good-spirited, positive, friendly relationship with the person being coached. This involves spending time with the coachee, enjoying real conversations that the person might have with no one else, expressing how much you believe in the coachee and what he or she is up to, and acknowledging progress. On the other side, for the relationship to also be powerful and profound, a coach must often provide potentially embarrassing or threatening information needed for growth and learning.

How do you do this without causing a blowup in the relationship? The inner dialogue goes like this, "If I tell this person I disagree with his views or give him this feedback, he may resent me and it could cause a blowup in the relationship. Yet, if I protect myself by withholding this information, the relationship will not be profound or powerful, and the person may eventually recognize this. What's the answer?"

The first answer is that, as a Masterful Coach, you need to be a commitment to the truth and you need to make that clear to the person at the outset. As Michel Renaud, one of our Masterful Coaches says, "I need to tell you that you can expect me to tell the truth." He then reminds people of this commitment at the appropriate time: "Remember I told you that I will tell the truth. I need to talk to you about something today. . . ."[3]

There is a way to tell the truth that is actually empowering to the person you are coaching and to the relationship. First, declare what you are both committed to at the beginning of the conversation. For example, "Bill, I'm here to support you in being the kind of extraordinary leader you need to be to realize your goals and aspirations." Declaring this commitment will support the person showing up learning as opposed to defensive.

Next, acknowledge your great belief in the person, as well as any progress being made, "Marina, you know how much I think of you and that I am committed to you." At the same time add, "Yet at the team meeting yesterday, I noticed some breakdowns and these reflect a few things missing in your leadership style that, if you had them, would make you an absolutely extraordinary leader." Then give the feedback.

Who is a role model for you in terms of honesty and integrity? How are you like the person or not like him or her? Where are you doing what you say you will do? Where are you not? Recall a time when someone gave you straightforward feedback that had a positive impact, even though it was embarrassing or uncomfortable. Remember a time when you wanted to give someone some straightforward feedback and did not have the courage to speak up. What was the barrier?

Masterful Coaches stand in the future people want to create and inspire them to act from it.

4. Be a Commitment to the Impossible Future the Person Is Creating

It cannot be repeated too often that Masterful Coaching is about creating futures, not filling gaps. One of the first things a Masterful Coach does is ask the person being coached what kind of Impossible Future he or she wants to create. For the coaching relationship to be powerful, it needs to be an Impossible Future that captures people's imagination and be one that they cannot realize on their own.

Once the Impossible Future is declared, two things tend to happen. The first is that people reduce the vision because they are afraid they cannot realize it, and the second thing they do is to get "sucked into the monster," as one CEO told me. They become weighed down by the incredible number of demands that are coming at them from the organization based on the present and things that happened in the past.

As a result, leaders often forget who they are as a commitment to creating the future, forget their promises, and come up with reasons and excuses. In so doing, they lose their power to create a new future. A coach, among other things, is an intervener and needs to give people back their power by returning them to themselves, to their commitment, and to being honest with themselves and others.

A coach's role, Veronica Pemberton says, is to "be the incarnation of the future people want to create." This means that a coach needs to stand in the future that the person being coached is committed to and look for ways to inspire people out of their day-to-day state of feeling overwhelmed and take action that will make the future a reality. This could take the form of in each coaching conversation declaring the vision and goals you are both committed to, keeping people focused on the plan, and taking the key actions necessary to translate vision into a reality.

CALLING FORTH QUESTIONS

Have you ever had a coach who was truly committed to you reaching an impossible future? What was it like to have someone stand totally behind you and believe in you? Who in your life do you need to give this kind of commitment to, a place that could really make a difference?

Masterful Coaches stand in a commitment to transformation, not just giving advice.

5. Be a Commitment to Transformation

It would never occur to most people to articulate an Impossible Future that takes them beyond their automatic self, their winning strategies, and their master programs. Further, even if they could formulate an Impossible Future, they would be incapable of realizing it based on who they have been in the past and what they have done to be successful, as well as their thrown behavior.

For example, I began coaching Bill Nahill, the leader mentioned earlier, based on a dilemma that could have been from the movie *Monty Python's The Meaning of Life.* "I am moving up the corporate ladder quickly, but is that what I really want? I have surpassed some of my financial goals, but is this all there is?" Also he had some concerns about his leadership style, based on some 360-degree feedback I had given him, even though he was a highly accomplished person.

He didn't have long to reflect about this due to his job circumstances. He became involved in declaring an Impossible Future—a humongous project that had the potential to transform the company, but that also required that he first transform himself. Let me explain: If Bill had an automatic self, it was to be charming, bright, optimistic, and competitive. His winning strategy was "give me a challenge that everyone has failed at and I will accomplish it." He was personally very effective, but sometimes left people feeling he was a bull in a china shop.

The coach had to be a commitment to *transformation,* to altering the ground of being (cause) that had caused Bill to show up the way he did with others, as opposed to *change,* which involves an alteration of behavior (effects). Being a commitment to transformation involves engaging people in a conversation designed to alter the context that shapes who they are being and thereby getting at the source of their behavior. This is different from simply telling them what they should or should not do. Being committed to transformation means "holding" that the person is transforming, even when he or she backslides, while addressing breakdowns and providing what's missing.

We started the coaching engagement with the idea of transforming Bill into more of a team leader and team player and his team into a "great group." This led to successful changes in behavior, but the real transformation was to come later when Bill proclaimed, "I figured out what I want to do. I want to be a coach and teacher." I asked him to explain. He continued, "I no longer want to be the person who takes on a big challenge and accomplishes things. I want to support other people in learning how to accomplish things."

This alteration in Bill's ground of being completely transformed his behavior. His project was not only a success, but the team also began to cook and almost every person in the team began to develop rapidly. Furthermore, it wasn't long before talented people throughout the organization wanted to be part of Bill's organization. "Want to develop faster?" Bill often asks talented people when he finds them. "Then fasten your seatbelt and let's go."

CALLING FORTH QUESTIONS

When you speak to people with a coach's hat on, do you tend to give advice and polite feedback? Or do you try to shift paradigms and give feedback that rips the blinders off? When you listen to people with your coach's hat on, do you just listen to their stories, or do you listen for the paradigms behind the stories that are likely to get them in trouble?

Masterful Coaches stand in a commitment to disciplined intensity.

6. Be an Activist

Think about the average company on any given day. People stream into the office, read *The Wall Street Journal,* make a phone call or two, and then head for the coffee and doughnuts. They then go to a meeting and voice arbitrary opinions, without making decisions or taking action. Nothing seems to matter very much.

Masterful Coaches are activists. They don't get stalled at the starting gate or bogged down in strategizing, planning, or preparing. For example, I have seen Roger Servison, Fidelity Investments' head of worldwide marketing, immediately translate vague reports and recommendations into actions. He focuses on the next, most meaningful step to take by asking himself, "What do we need to do to achieve the larger goal?"

Masterful Coaches know that an elephant can be eaten in small bites, even though the meal is huge! They forward the action by identifying the openings that will allow them to get a meaningful result in the shortest period of time and, at the same time, will allow them to learn something that will provide new opportunities for action.

Forwarding action means acting even when you are uncertain of the outcome. It means building rapid, rough, cheap prototypes to see what you can learn, then refining them and trying again. Like putting together a puzzle on a rainy day, you're never sure where the pieces go; you just start making connections. Some pieces fit together and some don't, but eventually the picture is complete.

When people work with a Masterful Coach, they are swept up by the "buzz" of purposeful activity that he or she creates, especially on a team. One of the characteristics of disciplined intensity is full participation—you are giving 100 percent, totally focused on the task, and strangely unaware of yourself. Rock climbers report that the hardest climbs are the most difficult to remember because there is never an opportunity to think about what they are doing. They generate disciplined intensity, calling themselves forth, making unreasonable promises and requests of others, bringing out "you're the best" in people 24/7 if they need to.

> Are you an activist, or do you tend to get bogged down in elaborate planning and preparations? Think about those times when you were the coach of a team (or were part of a team) that worked intensely and what you accomplished as a result. What was that experience like? What is the level at which you are willing to make demands of yourself and of others?

Masterful Coaches stand in a commitment to acknowledgement.

7. Be a Cheerleader

Masterful Coaches are not just masters of high performance and accelerated development; they are masters of human nature. They know that much of human life is a struggle for recognition. As William James once said, "The most intolerable state for a human being is the absence of acknowledge." Masterful Coaches are thereby very generous with acknowledgment, in contrast with most managers I have seen, who are incredibly stingy with it.

Masterful Coaches go beyond *challenging* people to set stretch goals and take action in the face of change complexity and competition; they also *support* people by standing on the sidelines acting as cheerleaders. They not only ask people to do things on the practice field that take them way beyond their comfort zones, but they also acknowledge their wins and gains and, in the process, give people a greater experience of themselves.

Masterful Coaches are not only a commitment to expanding people's ability to accomplish what it is they need to accomplish, but a commitment to do so in a way that expands their experience of themselves. They know the following three principles by heart:

1. Positive acknowledgment leads to a repetition of behavior;
2. Negative acknowledgment leads to unpredictable behavior; and
3. Absence of acknowledgment leads to negative behavior. "He who is wise, let him hear."

> **Are the people around you generous or stingy in acknowledging you? (Do you let it come into you or deflect it?) Are you generous or stingy in acknowledging people? What opportunities do you have to acknowledge people in the next sixty minutes, the next twenty-four to forty-eight hours?**

The Principle of Calling Forth

Calling forth is based on the notion of choosing who you will be and how you will show up in the world, regardless of how you are feeling, the people you are dealing with, or the circumstance you find yourself in. For example, recall a time when you had a big presentation to make and you were dead tired or in a bad mood. Did you run and hide your head under the covers? No! Did you call someone and make excuses? No again. Did you listen to sympathetic voices saying, "You can cancel"? Absolutely not! Instead, you stood and delivered, calling yourself forth through all of that.

Calling forth is not just about deciding to show up for a "big game." It involves declaring a new possibility, like being a Masterful Coach, and by standing inside that possibility, creating a new context for you to show up in the world. It involves taking a stand for the possibility and taking actions to make it a reality. And it involves drawing your identity from that stand (the commitment you are) rather than from your normal personality, position, or winning strategies.

It is important to point out that to declare a possibility in language and successfully call it forth, it needs to be one that you can be truly passionate about. It also needs to be one that you honestly believe you have the spark of potential to become, or it has to be some part of you that already exists but is not yet fully expressed. I can declare a new possibility for myself, such as being a great artist, astronaut, or tennis player, but if I don't passionately engage it or I don't believe I have the potential to realize it, I will not be successful in calling it forth.

Calling forth not only involves declaring a new possibility for yourself as a human being and taking a stand to be that, but it involves acting in a manner that will move the possibility to a reality. This often requires the kind of coaching, teaching, and mentoring to discover and express what is already within you.

For example, actor Robin Williams portrays this ability masterfully in the film *Dead Poets Society*. Williams coaches a student, whose self-image is meek and timid, to shout a barbaric "yawp!" from his belly. He then helps the boy to call forth his "poet inside" by visualizing Walt Whitman as a madman who is attacking him. The boy's poetry becomes striking and inspiring to the audience.

A SEVEN-STEP METHODOLOGY FOR CALLING YOURSELF FORTH AS A MASTERFUL COACH

Diagram 2.2 shows a seven-step methodology for calling yourself forth as a Masterful Coach. Let's look at each step.

DIAGRAM 2.2 *Calling yourself forth as a Masterful Coach*

STEP 1. Take a Stand for Being a Masterful Coach

Make the following declaration: "I am committed to being a Masterful Coach who inspires, empowers, and enables the people I work with to be the best that they can be." It's important to make the declaration public, which means that you agree to be your word and to be held to account.

You will discover that, once you begin standing inside this possibility, it automatically begins to alter your perceptions and how you think and interact with others. Once you make this declaration, act from the future that you have declared possible, rather than let old patterns take over. Try putting your coach or thinking partner's hat on at the next meeting and see how much it alters your behavior.

STEP 2. Declare Old Patterns You Are Committed to Giving Up

The journey to Masterful Coaching not only involves learning to step inside a powerful new frame, but it also means giving up or letting go of the old frames that lead to automatic ways of being, thinking, and behavior. For example, most managers live inside a frame that says, "Be in control, always have the answer, be right, and win." This is counterproductive to the declared possibility of masterfully coaching others. The next step then is to make a second public declaration that involves breaking the grip and excelling beyond this old frame. I am committed to giving up [list old patterns].

STEP 3. Scan Horizon for Coaches, Mentors, and Role Models

One way to break the grip and excel beyond old frames of reference is to identify coaches, mentors, and models who are a good match for you and your situation. Look within your group, organization, and community. Is there a coach, teacher, or friend who could serve this purpose? Once you identify the role model, it is important to observe him or her at work and ask questions about the characteristic you want to develop. You might ask, for example, "Where do you draw your inspiration from?" or "How do you convey inspiration to other people?" or "How do you stay inspired when circumstances are tough?"

STEP 4. Make Distinctions About Masterful Coaching that Will Guide You

The next step in calling yourself forth as a Masterful Coach involves making distinctions that will give you a powerful place to stand and come from. A coach, mentor, or role model can offer a powerful assist in making these distinctions and making sure you don't get off on the wrong track. For example, Masterful Coaches stand committed to being a *contribution* to themselves, others, and the planet, as opposed to merely being *successful* in conventional terms. If you bring it to every coaching conversation with coachees, this one distinction can make a powerful difference.

STEP 5. Step Up to Opportunities to Coach When Presented

I often work with leaders and managers who want to become Masterful Coaches. First, I work on getting their commitment to being coaches in place; then I create a shift in mindset. The next step takes into account the principle of "structure influences behavior." We ask people to coach a certain number of hours a week. We asked one client, a manager whom we will call the Home Depot "Do It Yourself" Man, to delegate much more and to coach sixteen hours a week. Then we monitored the impact it had.

It is important to do this kind of coaching on a friendly, informal basis and not in roles. It is the job of the person who has the opportunity to coach and can take on the job to ask: "Hey, do you need a coach or a thinking partner on that?"

STEP 6. Learn by Doing

People learn through study and practice, and by receiving meaningful feedback. You can learn by applying the guiding ideas, methods, and techniques you will learn in this book. It is important to not only set up a structure for coaching, but to also set up a process for receiving meaningful feedback. Ask people, "How am I doing as a coach?" "Is this conversation having an impact?" Or "On a scale of 1 to 10, how would you rate this coaching session?" If the answer is a "7," ask: "What would have made it a 10?" This will allow you to tease out new distinctions, as well as put in corrections: "I just got how this works."

STEP 7. Acknowledge Accomplishments

It is very important in the process of calling forth to acknowledge when you have shown up consistent with the new possibilities that you have declared. For example, if you said in your earlier declaration, "I am committed to the possibility of being a Masterful Coach who gives people the gift of my presence and acts as a thinking partner who draws out people's brilliance," find a way to acknowledge that. One good technique is to create an accomplishment journal in which you write these things down. Another is to share this with a coach, whose role is to act as your cheerleader.

The Power of Declaration in Becoming a Masterful Coach

- *I am committed to the possibility of being a Masterful Coach who inspires, empowers, and enables people to reach an Impossible Future.*

- *I am committed to giving up being a control junkie, know it all, or cop.*

- *I am committed to the possibility of paying attention to what's missing that can make a difference when there are mistakes or breakdowns.*

- *I am committed to giving up playing "here comes the judge" when there's a breakdown or mistake.*

- *I am committed to the possibility of being authentic with people.*

- *I am committed to giving up making hot issues undiscussable.*

CHAPTER THREE

COACHING HAPPENS IN CONVERSATIONS

The Power of Conversation

> *A human being cannot resist the temptation to express his personality and reveal himself; conversation gives him the opportunity.*

A conversation is a remarkable phenomenon generated between human beings. Wars are declared, grand social initiatives are promised, great scientific achievements are brought to fruition, and markets are created through a conversation—or rather through a network of conversations. When a new era dawns, such as the Industrial Age or the Internet Era, the old ordinary conversation is interrupted and a new extraordinary conversation is inaugurated that provides new ideas, fresh insights, and exciting new possibilities.

We have also in a very personal way experienced extraordinary conversations that have had a profound and powerful impact on our lives, conversations that interrupted the *old* patterns and opened our eyes to *new* horizons. These are conversations where we have been touched with exciting new possibilities, gained a greater appreciation of our own potential, or come to a revelation of our own foolishness. They are conversations where we somehow left *bigger* than we were before and inspired to greater action.

We have all had those kinds of extraordinary conversations that return us to ourselves and to our highest goals and aspirations. They have a certain spirit of light about them that is not only uplifting, but also—when such conversations happen—they seem truly magical. Yet these conversations often seem to happen by chance.

Masterful Coaching lies in the ability to consciously and intentionally be able to create the climate for such extraordinary conversations to occur. This book, and specifically this chapter, are about being able to discover and express your own ability to have such conversations with others on a consistent basis. It is about getting your hands on a powerful, repeatable, and proven technology that ensures that you will be able to have conversations with people that allow them to reinvent themselves and their organizations.

COACHING CONVERSATIONS ARE SPECIAL CONVERSATIONS IN OUR CULTURE

Coaching happens in conversations—in business, sports, in the performing arts. Coaching conversations are special conversations in our culture and they need to be distinct. First of all, a coaching conversation is not a conversation of chitchat, mere opinion, or advice. It is not a conversation where people indulge themselves in gossip and rumor or cynical comments. It is not even a conversation where people set reasonable goals, make plans, and seek to deliver on them through their Winning Strategies. And it is not a conversation where people listen for what's wrong with others or sit back and play "here comes the judge."

What then is a coaching conversation? It is a conversation in which you are burning with intention to have an impact. It is a conversation where you are speaking and listening from a total commitment to cause that person's success. It is a conversation where you extend people an "A" (see their greatness), even when they disappoint you or make mistakes. It is a conversation where you provide the kind of insightful feedback that rips the blinders off. It's a conversation where people see new possibilities and breakthrough barriers, showing up in an entirely new way. And it is a conversation where people walk away feeling inspired, empowered, enabled to act.

Masterful Coaches Have a Certain Way of Listening: Committed Listening

Masterful Coaches give people the gift of their presence—a high quality of time and attention.

Although people think Masterful Coaching automatically involves speaking—

giving advice or answers—it actually starts with listening. Masterful Coaches have a way of listening that we call *committed listening*. Committed listening starts with listening from a commitment to "give people the gift of your presence," a high quality of time and attention.

Yet it also involves listening from a commitment to absolutely bring out the best in people. This new way of listening is not transactional in nature, where people are given advice, tips, or techniques. It embraces, but goes beyond all this, and is actually transformational with respect to the person we are engaging with. Committed listening involves listening from a commitment to the coachee's greatness (highest and best self), even when the person is being a prisoner of pettiness and the rest of the world is fed up, disgruntled, and disgusted with him or her.

It involves listening from a commitment to unearth what people passionately care about and how that links into the extraordinary future they want to create for themselves and their organizations. It involves listening from who they are as a commitment and returning people to themselves, even when everything has fallen apart.

On a day-in, day-out level, committed listening involves taking into account that coaching is an activity characterized by a concern for the coachees. It involves listening to whatever the coachees' concerns are, "Tell me what is really on your mind." Are they upset with their boss? Are they muddled over a problem, a puzzle or dilemma, or confused? A good metaphor for the day in the life of an executive is a big ball of twine—a tangle of problems, dilemmas, puzzles, and emotional reactions. The coaching session is an opportunity to unravel it, and all people need is a place to start.

A Masterful Coach knows that committed listening is the foundation for all-powerful coaching.

As Michel Renaud, one of our coaches puts it, "I actually listen from a commitment that people are going to leave the conversation feeling freed up, clear, and empowered to act. I don't listen from the point of view that people need my answers, advice, or infinite wisdom. My point of view is that people possess within themselves the ability to resolve their upsets, do their own thinking, discover their own answers and the path forward. If I listen from that commitment, it's just magical."[1]

For example, a person may say, "My boss is a jerk." If you agree or disagree, the communication can get stuck with the person either going on and on or trying to justify his or her point of view. If you are willing to listen without agreeing or disagreeing, people will begin to see something that they didn't see before, which allows them to disengage from their reactive thoughts or feelings. You might hear, "You know what? I have been reflecting on this, and my boss really isn't that bad. I can see that I have really been upset with him and that I need to sit down with him and get clear about a few things."

It is much better for the coach to come to the table as a thinking partners rather than an arrogant "know-it-all." There is power in the coach and coachee coming to the table with a clear idea of the problem (or dilemma) they want to talk about, and having thought about the topic, but without dotting the "i's" and crossing the "t's," and then having a conversation. In this way, the coach and coachee create a partnership that is about discovering the answers together. This often leads to gaining a broader, deeper view of the problem or dilemma, as well as arriving at solutions that would never have been attainable on an individual basis.

Masterful Coaches don't just *listen to* what people are saying about what happened, but *listen for* the underlying beliefs, assumptions, and interpretations people make. Most people stand in a place that causes them to make arbitrary interpretations about people, situations, and events. For example, many managers draw their identity from coming out on top, being right, and getting power over others by *listening for what's wrong*.

Thus, when someone makes a proposal with a new, good idea, instead of hearing what's right in it and building on it, they listen for what's wrong with it. As coming out on top and being right represents a kind of payoff, this becomes an addictive cycle of interpretation that doesn't support people in being all that they are or all that they can be. Coaching is then about breaking the cycle of these addictive interpretations so that people are freed up. The kind of listening that we are talking about is transformational in nature. Diagram 3.1 illustrates what Masterful Coaches listen for.

A Coach Has a Certain Way of Speaking: Committed Speaking

One of the other ways the coach creates an environment for transformational conversations is through *committed speaking*. This involves speaking from a commitment to make a difference in people's lives. If you have listened loudly enough to people talk about their goals or problems, you will begin to

DIAGRAM 3.1 *Coaches don't just listen* to, *they listen* for . . .

- Who people are as a commitment and acknowledge it, even when they may want to give up.
- Who people are being in their listening that gets them in trouble, for example, "I'm right," "I need to win."
- Addictive interpretations, for example, people who listen for what's wrong.
- Attitudes or behaviors that will get people in trouble.
- Beliefs and assumptions people are taking for granted.
- Where people have jumped to conclusions or have gaps in their reasoning.

understand the background against which they are standing and from which they see the world. For example, they may see the world from the point of view of a generative leader who transforms roadblocks into opportunities or they may see the world from the point of view of a reactive manager who focuses on putting out fires.

Committed speaking involves speaking with the ruthless compassion necessary to penetrate illusions.

At the same time, given the place where you stand as a commitment to being a Masterful Coach and the background that you come from, you will see things that the person being coached doesn't see. Committed speaking involves speaking from a commitment to make a difference. For example, saying something that helps people see something they didn't see before that has the power to alter who they are being and what they are doing. This could take the form of making a distinction for a person (like being a generative leader versus a reactive manager) that expands people's horizon of possibility, or pushing them to break the grip and excel beyond old paradigms, or ripping the blinders off with regard to their own counterproductive behavior.

Speaking to leaders in a way that actually produces an alteration can be a real challenge. It is not just a matter of saying, "Look, to be an extraordinary leader or to build an extraordinary business, you need to do something new." It is more a matter of getting people to let go of an old "act" they strongly identify with, a personal (or business) Winning Strategy they have been successful with but which has become a limitation, or an incredibly righteous position about someone. People will often say, "Why should I change this? It's gotten me where I am today." Altering a point of view like this is always "an emotional process."

Committed speaking is also a matter of speaking with a kind of ruthless compassion that is necessary to open people's eyes and penetrate their illusions, "Look, you have a choice. You can step into the space of being an extraordinary leader, creating an extraordinary business by being a *contribution*. Or you can choose to continue with your 'act' of *kissing up to the boss* and your winning strategy of *kicking down at direct reports*. I know old patterns die hard. If you choose the former, I will support you 100 percent."

Bring the Background Conversation to the Foreground: Discuss the Undiscussable

Although most coaches sincerely intend to speak with candor and honesty or "talk straight," they may become cautious in order to avoid being uncomfortable. This can sometimes lead to sending mixed messages that prevent others from receiving the input they need to correct their errors and to learn. This pattern is heightened if the other person reacts with hostility to sincere attempts to give meaningful feedback. If you alter your communication as a result of this, you become an accomplice to the individual's, group's, or organization's defensive routines.

The reason we may be susceptible to doing this is that we have been conditioned to speak in ways rooted in certain social virtues—being nice, not upsetting people, minding our own business, and so on. One common organization defensive routine is to make potentially embarrassing or threatening feedback that is needed for growth and learning undiscussable. A coach has to be willing to discuss the undiscussable. Diagram 3.2 shows how coaching communication is different from social grease.[2]

Chris Argyris' left-hand column exercise is an excellent tool for learning to discuss the undiscussable in a way that does not create a "blow up" in the relationship. Diagram 3.3 shows an illustration of the left-hand column exercise, which shows a page divided in half lengthwise. On the right is everything that you said in the conversation and everything the person you were talking to said. In the left-hand column is everything that you thought but did not say. The idea behind the exercise is to become aware of what you have in your left-hand column that, if said, could make a difference in a coaching conversation.

DIAGRAM 3.2 *Social grease versus coaching communication*

SOCIAL GREASE	COACHING COMMUNICATION

Help and Support

Give approval and praise to others. Tell others what you believe will make them feel good about themselves. Reduce their feelings of hurt by telling them how much you care, and, if possible, agree with them that others acted improperly.

Increase other people's capacity to confront their own ideas, to create a window into their own minds, and to face their unsurfaced assumptions, biases, and fears by acting in these ways toward other people.

Respect for Others

Defer to other people and do not confront their reasoning or actions.

Attribute to other people a high capacity for self-reflection and self-examination without becoming so upset that they lose their effectiveness and their sense of self-responsibility and choice. Test this attribution.

Strength

Advocate your position and combine it with inquiry and self-reflection. Feeling vulnerable while encouraging inquiry is a sign of strength.

Advocate your position in order to win. Hold your own position in the face of advocacy. Feeling vulnerable is a sign of weakness.

Honesty

Tell other people no lies or tell others all you think and feel.

Encourage yourself and others to say what they know yet fear to say. Minimize what might be otherwise subject to distortion and covering up of the distortion.

Honesty

Stick to your principles, values, and beliefs.

Advocate your principles, values, and beliefs in a way that invites inquiry into them and encourage others to do the same.

DIAGRAM 3.3 *Sample of left-hand column exercise*

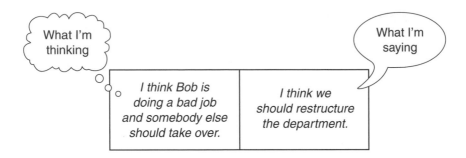

A SEVEN-CAP COACHING CONVERSATION SYSTEM

Masterful Coaches recognize that there are different types of coaching conversations. They choose the type to engage in depending on what is unfolding in the coaching relationship. They may also shift from one of these conversations to another in a coaching session depending on what is occurring. This is called "dancing with what is occurring."

There are seven distinct coaching conversations in Masterful Coaching— The Method™. I have noticed that, while Masterful Coaches use all seven, beginners or intermediates tend to get stuck in one type of conversation, such as giving answers or listening like a therapist. I have thus created the Seven-Cap Coaching Conversation System, first to assist people in distinguishing the different coaching caps they may wear and, second, to teach people how to develop the skills and capabilities to use them.

I have found that once people can distinguish among the seven different coaching caps they can become effective with using them fairly quickly. It is important to point out that, for the most part, you don't speak about these caps in your coaching conversation; you speak from them. Taking one cap off and putting another one on comes about as a result of your own external observations of your coaching interactions and your internal dialogue.

The Seven Coaching Caps outlined in Diagram 3.4 will support you in drawing the distinctions among the types of coaching conversations they represent, as well as help you to begin to act on them. The caps are numbered to provide a reference point, but they are employed in a non-linear way.

DIAGRAM 3.4 *Seven-cap coaching conversation system*

1. **Declaring New Possibilities Cap**

2. **Thinking Partner Cap**

3. **Drawing Others Out Cap**

4. **Reframing Cap**

5. **Teaching and Advising Cap**

6. **Forwarding Action Cap**

7. **Giving Honest Feedback Cap**

CAP 1. Declaring Possibilities

Masterful Coaches inspire people to pay attention to what they can declare, based on what's really possible versus what they can predict based on the past. There are always more possibilities than people may see for someone's career, a company's business model, or a path forward. People are blinded by their own lenses of perception, habits, or industry orthodoxies. If this is the case, brainstorm alternative possibilities. Then select the best ones. Keep declarations focused: "I am committed to the possibility of. . . [putting a man on the moon] [being the best leader in the company]."

- *Put this cap on* *when people show signs of resignation or say they have no choice but to pursue conventional options or don't see a path forward.*

- *Take it off* *when people see infinite possibilities but can't make any choices or when people can't buy into the "what" because they don't see a "how."*

CAP 2. Being a Thinking Partner

Leaders are often faced with problems, issues, and dilemmas to which there are no simple or obvious answers. As Einstein said, "The same level of thinking that got you into the problem won't be sufficient to get you out of it." If this is the case, find out whether the person would like a thinking partner. Begin by asking the person, "What do you think?" Then build on best ideas. Don't hesitate to offer new ideas, fresh perspectives, and innovative solutions. Question what you both may take for granted to make sure you don't jump to conclusions. Get the solution so it is 80 percent right, then iterate.

- **Put this cap on** *when the coachee is faced with human or business problems, dilemmas, puzzles to which there is no simple or obvious answer.*

- **Take it off** *when people need to move from thinking to action.*

CAP 3. Drawing Others Out

All too often, people think that being a coach or thinking partner is about telling people the answer. This can be a mistake because the coachee often knows more about the business than the coach does. Secondly, if you start by giving people the answer, you often wind up with a disempowered person who feels that he or she has nothing to contribute. Instead, start with the premise that the answer is within the person and it is your job to draw it out by listening for brilliance. Drawing out can also apply to putting feelings or reactions out on the table so they can be resolved.

- **Put this cap on** *when you sense people have the seeds of a brilliant idea, but are expressing it in an inarticulate or vague way, or when you feel you have been providing people good ideas and they are not responding, or when people feel misunderstood by you or others.*

- **Take it off** *when people are interpreting things in a disempowering way, have jumped to conclusions, or are making assumptions that cannot be validated by directly witnessable data.*

CAP 4. Reframing Thinking and Attitudes

This cap is very useful after drawing people out. For example, good questions to ask are: "Will the way you have framed the problem give you the results you want?" "Do you really think you can shrink your way to greatness with this company or do you think its time for a growth strategy?" This cap is the key to doing transformational work. How is the person seeing him- or herself (the role) now? How do people need to see themselves differently? How is the person thinking about the problem? How does his or her thinking need to shift? What is the lens or filter through which the person speaks or listens? How does it need to change?

- **Put this cap on** *when you pick up red flags like a wrongheaded way of looking at the problem or solution, limiting beliefs and assumptions about themselves, others, and the situation, crazy thinking, poor attitudes, or disempowering interpretations.*

- ***Take it off*** *when people have a more inspiring, empowering, accurate inter-pretation of reality or when people have the right mindset on the problem or solution and are ready to get on with it or when you feel a how-to tip or technique is now appropriate.*

CAP 5. Teaching and Advising

A coach is different from a therapist. The difference is the coach often has a teachable point of view that he or she feels very passionate about and wants to communicate. "We need leaders at every level," "We need excellence. Good enough isn't good enough." This cap is often put on to make distinctions that open up new categories in people's minds. For example, a powerful dis-tinction is that there is a difference between compliance and commitment. The teaching and advising cap is also used to offer practical advice. Give advice that is: (1) caring and candid, (2) practical, (3) wise, and (4) well-timed, meaning when people are open to hearing it.

- ***Put this cap on*** *when you have a teachable point of view to put out to an individual or group, when making a distinction would create greater clarity or power for people, or when people solicit your wisdom or advice.*
- ***Take it off*** *when people start to debate everything you say or when you hear lots of "yes but's," or when you feel you have made your point. Often at this time it is appropriate to try on the Drawing Others Out Cap.*

CAP 6. Forwarding Action

Masterful Coaches focus on interacting with people with regard to their goals and problems in a way that takes them beyond an answer and brings them to a moment of true insight. They follow this by taking those insights and forward-ing action. If you have come up with some powerful insights, then the actions to take will usually fall out of them. I conclude almost every coaching session with a thirty-day action plan. The idea is to come from the point of view that there is always a path forward and let's discover it. Focus on small, high-lever-age steps that move the ball forward without overwhelming people.

- ***Put this cap on*** *when people have had enough strategizing and theorizing and are ready to act, when they don't see an opening for successful action, or when you have clearly identified what's missing in the situation and the question "what's next?" is on the tip of your tongue.*

- **Take it off** *when doing the same thing better doesn't produce different results. This could lead to putting on the Declaring New Possibilities Cap and brainstorming alternative courses of action, or putting on the Reframing Cap and looking at the issue from a new perspective or seeing where you have a blocked mental model.*

CAP 7. Giving Honest Feedback

Most people have sincere and honest intentions with respect to results and in their relationships with others. Yet we all suffer from the phenomenon of blindness. We cannot see ourselves as others see us, detect our strengths or gaps, or recognize the unintended consequences of our actions. Thus, putting on the Giving Feedback Cap is essential to helping people become more aware. It is important to make sure that any assessments you make are based on witnessable observations, as opposed to arbitrary judgments. An assessment is just an opinion, but opinions can make a difference. Make a positive assessment first, a negative assessment second; finish with a commitment to review the feedback.

- **Put this cap on** *when you are creating a leadership development plan and you need to assess strengths or gaps, or when you have created business plans and people's actions are leading to unintended results either in the business or with people.*
- **Take it off** *when people are not open to feedback, or when it is time to get back into action.*

A SUCCESS FORMULA FOR POWERFUL COACHING CONVERSATIONS

We have talked about committed speaking and listening. We have introduced you to the Seven-Cap Coaching Conversation System. Now let's put it all together. In our work, we have discovered a successful formula for having coaching conversations that is proven and repeatable. It starts with a set of generating principles and then moves toward a specific transformational technology.

Think of the following generating principles as the background conversation playing in your mind, which you are continually bringing to the foreground of your conversation with the coachee:

1. Your passion and enthusiasm for the conversation matters;
2. The individual you are speaking with matters;

3. Who you are in the conversation matters (Are you being a stand for transformation or just being a stand for looking good or trying to please?);

4. Creating a shared context matters ("This conversation can have an impact"); and

5. Being clear about the intended result and holding yourself accountable to delivering it matters—in other words, closing all escape hatches.

Then apply the step-by-step formula outlined in Diagram 3.5.

DIAGRAM 3.5 *A success formula for powerful coaching conversations*

---

1. **Source a successful coaching conversation by being prepared.** *What are the purpose and goals? Who do you need to be? Who does the coachee need to be?*

2. **Declare your commitment at the beginning of the conversation.** *"This conversation can have an impact. Here are the purpose and goals."*

3. **Dynamically use the Seven-Cap Coaching Conversation System.** *Dance with what's occurring. Decide which cap to put on and take off.*

4. **Make sure the person leaves the conversation with greater clarity, and power, and with an opening for action. Check in, get feedback, and adjust.** *What's missing that, if provided, will make a difference?*

STEP 1. Prepare for Every Coaching Conversation so that It Turns Out Brilliantly

According to one of our coaches, Veronica Pemberton, "The first thing you need to do before every coaching conversation is to 'center yourself' by preparing powerfully." She goes through the following pre-coaching ritual before every conversation.

Get clear on the purpose, goals, and intentions. Start your preparation by taking out a blank sheet of paper and writing down the purpose of the meeting and what your goals and intentions are. For example, is it to challenge people to go beyond predictable goals and create an impossible future? If so, write it down. Is it to break the grip of resignation by unearthing people's passions? If so, write it down. Is it to have a breakthrough in self-expression? Is it to review the accomplishments of the last six months or follow up on a thirty-day action plan? Write down all the results you want, between five to ten items.

Get clear on who you need to be in the conversation. Next you need to *center* yourself, to come from a powerful *ground of being* in the coaching conversation, in order to be effective with the person and to produce desired results. Our normal, everyday ground of being that involves Winning Strategies such as "looking good," "trying to please others," or "accommodating clients" will not be sufficient to push people to stretch themselves, break the grip of paradigms, rip off the blinders. Also, our fears, self-doubts, and insecurities can get in the way.

A coaching conversation is not a walk in the park. You not only need to think about who you need to be in the matter, but also be very grounded in this. The reason is that anything can happen in the conversation because people are unpredictable. If you are not centered in your ground of being and people don't respond to you the way that you thought or something unexpected arises, you will tend to fall back into your old Winning Strategies or defensive routines.

Being the author of your ground of being is not a matter of declaring new possibilities for yourself as a human being out of thin air or simply writing down some affirmations. It's a matter of declaring who you need to be in the matter, based on who you are as a commitment and who the other person is as a commitment within the context of the coaching relationship. You have to be willing to declare things that are already true on some level that represent the best things about your relationship.

For example, you might start out by saying, "Joe, let me tell you where I stand with you and where I am standing in this conversation. I am totally committed to you and your future. Further, I know you stand with me in that commitment, as well as to having a powerful partnership together. Sometimes that means challenging your views, other times supporting them." Now that you have created a shared context, you might continue, "I have done my homework and this is why I think you now need to stretch your definition of yourself and your business model."

The point is, if you are present to who you are as "a body of commitments" and who the coachee is as "a body of commitments," you won't react to something odd that he or she might say. If the person says, "I totally disagree," instead of taking it personally, you might say, "Okay, you see things differently. Please tell me what leads you to that view."

All you have is who you be.

Once you are clear about who you need to be in the conversation, write down some positive affirmations about that. For example, *I am a Masterful Coach. I am an extraordinary listening for this person. I am profoundly committed to this person and what he wants to accomplish. I am a committed speaker and listener who is able to address this person's concerns. I am a commitment to transformation and a coach who can extricate people from the reality in which they are lodged.* This pre-work helps to call yourself forth in a manner that is consistent with producing desired results.

Get clear on who the coachee needs to be. You also have to take into account that, as a coach, you may have a point of view about a person or you may hold some prejudices or carry a chip on your shoulder, which creates a context for how you speak and listen to people and consequently how they show up. So part of your pre-work is to center yourself in who the person being coached needs to be in the conversation, so that you can be a clearing for desired results, rather than an obstacle. Think about who the coachee is as a body of commitments, rather than as a bunch of inherited characteristics, traits, or thrown behaviors.

When you are clear about who the other person is as a commitment, you can call that forth in the conversation. You do this by making a declaration: *"Pam, I know you are totally committed to an extraordinary future for the business, and totally committed to reinventing yourself in the process."* Your intention in making this declaration is to bring out the best in Pam so she will receive the communication. For the declaration to be powerful, as mentioned earlier, it has to be true on some level and you have to believe it.

Next write down a number of declarations (affirmations) about the person that represent the highest and best self within the context of what you will be creating together. For example, *Sam is totally committed to an extraordinary future and is totally committed to an extraordinary coaching relationship with me. Sam is really on the verge of a transformation, even though it may look otherwise. He is a listening for me, even when he disagrees. He is an activist regarding goals and priorities we set.* You will be amazed, if you prepare yourself in this way, how much more effective your coaching conversations will be.

STEP 2. Declare Your Commitment at the Outset

This can take the form of saying: "I am totally committed to this conversation making a difference for you."

I am sitting in an executive conference room on the 52nd floor of a New York skyscraper with Stanley Clarke, senior vice president of Thompson Corporation PLC, a big financial service company. Clarke, a British ex-patriot in a dark gray Savile Row pinstripe suit, has called the meeting to discuss one of his vice presidents, Ben Bennett. "He has a serious leadership issue and, at the same time, he has a record of great results. However, I am strongly leaning toward removing him from his role." Clarke has spoken to Bennett several times about the leadership issues. "What incites me to a cool rage is that he won't acknowledge he has a leadership issue."

Just then the phone rings. It's David Korkosz of Masterful Coaching. He has been working with Bennett for three months now. Korkosz has been asked for his comments on Bennett's progress.[3] He thinks Bennett is transforming, but there is a negative listening for him in the organization due to years of his authoritarian behavior. Korkosz thanks Stanley Clarke for the opportunity to speak and then begins with a powerful declaration: "First of all, I'd like to say that we are all here because we are committed to the Thompson Corporation having extraordinary leadership and to being an extraordinary company."

This declaration of commitment is intended to create a sense of shared purpose that will support Clarke, Korkosz, and myself in rising above his emotional reactions. Clarke sees where Korkosz is coming from, smiles warmly, and nods in agreement. "I'm interested in gaining your perspective."

Next, Korkosz makes another very powerful declaration: "I am personally committed to this conversation making a difference for you."

You and I possess within ourselves the ability to transform who we are being at all times and under all conditions. This ability lives in our conversations, in our speaking and listening.

As David speaks these words, a light goes on in my mind, my ears perk up, and I come to the edge of my seat. What a powerful way to begin a conversation, I think to myself. Only a Masterful Coach who stands in the possibility of making a difference would ever think of beginning a conversation like that. It would never even occur to most people in corporations to begin a conversation in this way.

By making a public declaration of commitment that the conversation make a difference for the person, the coach creates a powerful new context that actually alters what's possible in the conversation. Coming into that conversation from that context immediately alters the coach's everyday way of being in the world.

When you say, "I am committed to this conversation making a difference for you," it alters your way of being, as well as your speaking, listening, and actions.

Instead of showing up as, for example, being competitive or needing to be right and win, you show up as *being* a powerful contribution. It not only alters your own speaking, but the listening of the person you are speaking to. The person lets go of the need to compete or be right, drops suspicious listening, and also shows up as a contribution.

In the case above, the coach spoke to Clarke's listening without divulging any confidentialities. He provided insight into the fact that Bennett acknowledged his leadership issues and, secondly, was working very hard to address them, even though the listening in the organization hadn't caught up to it yet. Clarke then agreed to stand in the possibility that Bennett could actually be an extraordinary leader. Further, he agreed to coach him on calling himself forth as such.

STEP 3. Put the Seven-Cap Coaching Conversation System to Use

Make use of the Seven-Cap Coaching System as you begin to have coaching conversations. Think about the purpose, goals, and intentions of the conversation and then think about what kind of conversation cap you will need to put on to have that conversation. For example, if your purpose is to enroll people in what is the opportunity in coaching for them, as well as to think about their goals and aspirations, the first cap you might put on is a Declaring New Possibilities Cap.

The next step is to then use self-awareness as a resource to determine whether the kind of coaching cap you have on is working or not working. If it is not working, it is time to change caps. For example, if the coachee wants to express what is really on his or her mind and you are wearing the Teaching and Advising Cap, the conversation will start to break down and you will experience the person tuning you out.

It is also important to recognize when one cap has served its purpose and when it is time to take it off and put on another cap. For example, it might be better to put on the Drawing Others Out Cap and listen rather than continue to wear the Teaching and Advising Cap after you have made your point. Then, after listening for a while and hearing people express a point of view that is laden with limiting beliefs and assumptions, you might choose to take off the Drawing Others Out Cap and put on the Reframing Cap. Following that you might choose to put on the Forwarding Action Cap.

STEP 4. Make Sure People Leave the Conversation with Much Greater Clarity, Power, and Readiness to Act

One way to judge the effectiveness of a coaching conversation is by how people feel when you are finished. If people are masterfully coached, they will come away from the conversation in three ways:

1. They will feel inspired by a newfound freedom to be who they need to be to get results as well as feel okay about the way they are.
2. They will feel empowered by new possibilities that they did not see before that will make them more effective.
3. They will see a clear path forward and be ready to jump into action.

Let's use a metaphor to describe this. People are like goldfish in the water. Just as the water is invisible to goldfish, people's environments are largely invisible to them. They don't see that, given the corporate climate they are in, they have given up and adapted to the absurd. They don't see that their goals have slipped off the radar screen given the incredible number of demands coming at them. And they don't see that, given their Master Programs and Winning Strategies, they will never accomplish the results they want, no matter how hard or intelligently they try. They see what the others do to cause relationship issues, not what they do themselves. They feel frustrated, confused, and powerless. All of this constitutes the "water" in which they live.

Check in with people and get feedback: "Is this conversation making a difference for you?"

The purpose of a coaching conversation is to extract people from the water by allowing them to become aware of it so that they can declare new possibilities for themselves and their company that take them beyond resignation, break the grip of Master Programs and Winning Strategies that are leaving them stuck or ineffective, or help them complete incomplete relationships that are causing them to suffer. Thus, when people go back to the water, you notice that they are clearer, freer, more powerful, and that their actions are more in line with where they want to go.

How do coaches take people out of the water? They do it by providing a perspective that allows people to see things differently and act differently, "Let's step back and put your relationship with the CEO (boss) in perspective. Is it that he doesn't listen, or is it that you come to the table with a decision that he won't listen?"

They also pull people out of the water by making provocative statements or asking questions such as, "I like your business plan, but what beliefs or assumptions do you need to question that you have taken for granted?" They do it by returning people to themselves, their promises, and to action when they are upset. They do all of this with wisdom, compassion, and humor for the lessons each of us needs to learn in life.

Speak from a commitment to make a difference, reflecting on what's missing in the view of the world. Keep it up until the light goes on in people's eyes.

Finally, Masterful Coaches are good at getting feedback for themselves. They will ask several times during the conversation, "Is this conversation working for you?" If the answer is "Yes!!!" and people are feeling fired up, have greater insight into their situations, and are ready to act, great! If the answer is "No," the conversation isn't working and people feel confused, stuck, or ineffective, don't take it personally. Instead Masterful Coaches reflect on what's missing that, if provided, will make a difference and then take a different tack. They repeat this cycle until they see the light go on in people's eyes.

When You Stand Committed to Making a Difference

- *You prepare for the conversation in the first place. What can you say that will be life-altering?*

- *You listen from the point of view that others have sincere and good intentions, even though their perceptions may be distorted or their thinking off-base.*

- *You focus on your shared commitment to an extraordinary future rather than become a prisoner of pettiness: "We are all here for. . . ."*

- *You listen for people's authentic concerns and validate those concerns rather than sitting in judgment of them.*

- *If people see things arbitrarily or hold things crookedly, you don't make them wrong; you provide them with the background they are missing.*

- *You discipline yourself to put ideas (make distinctions) into people's thinking that will shift paradigms.*

- *You translate those ideas into actions that can be taken in the next thirty days.*

CHAPTER FOUR

MASTERFUL COACHING IS TRANSFORMATIONAL

Triple Loop Learning

Nothing happens without personal transformation.

I have chosen to focus a great deal of my work with Masterful Coaching on empowering executives of corporations to make a difference in their world. The reason for this is that executives are not only in the position to set inspiring goals and come up with revolutionary strategies, but they also create a context in an organization that will impact the lives of dozens, hundreds, if not thousands of people. At the same time, the multi-domestic corporation is perhaps the single most influential organization in the world today. Yet the lessons mentioned here actually apply to leaders and managers at all levels in every kind of organization. So please read this extrapolatively.

In my view, leadership coaching is about inspiring, empowering, and enabling leaders to create an Impossible Future, which they can passionately engage in. This Impossible Future must be big enough to embrace all of their other accountabilities and be one that they can commit to as the game they are playing in life. In my view, most leaders need a Masterful Coach to create the business to realize an Impossible Future, not so much to *run the business* and achieve a predictable future.

At the same time, on a more day-in, day-out, down-to-earth level, leadership coaching involves expanding people's ability to accomplish what they need to accomplish (the hard stuff)! In either case, coaching gives the leader more power. According to Tracey Goss, "Power is the velocity at which you take a possibility and turn it into a reality."[1] Yet the power to expand the magnitude of the goals you set and increase the velocity by which you achieve them can only happen if you are willing to participate in your own personal process of transformation. There are three guidelines for Masterful Coaches to keep in mind in doing transformational learning.

1. As Masterful Coaching is transformational in nature rather than merely transactional "information," people need to make a free and informed choice to participate.

2. People need to see that who they are as leaders and persons is not something solid, but something that is fluid and pliant, in a process of becoming.

3. People transform who they are by surfacing, testing, revising beliefs and assumptions that have been successful for them. This is always an emotional process.

TRANSFORMATIONAL LEARNING: LIFE AS A NARRATIVE

One way of looking at life is as a story that we tell about who we are. This story is our existential autobiography. As Jermone Bruner[2] has pointed out, "The self is not a thing, but a point of view that unifies the flow of experience into a coherent narrative, a narrative striving to connect with other narratives and become richer." The way we tell our story about who we are or what happens to us in our lives and work is not just based on facts and events, but on how we interpret things.

For example, you may think of yourself as a great leader because you are in an executive position in an organization, when in fact you are not leading at all and are just pursuing predictable goals and plans. Or you may believe that you are not a leader because of something that happened in the past that led you to conclude that you don't have leadership qualities. Or you may think that when your boss calls you and asks you questions about what you are doing in your area, his intention is not to act as a thinking partner in the way he says, but to meddle in your business.

It is important to understand that you and I do not just have a story; *we are our stories.* Our stories shape, limit, and define our way of being, the way we think, and the way we interact with others. It is by using our story about ourselves as a reference point that we decide how to act in a rational way in any given situation. Masterful Coaching involves helping people surface, question, and redefine their stories when the current story is called into question or breaks down.

"Some people enter our lives and leave almost instantly. Others enter and remain, forging such an impression on our hearts and minds we are changed forever."

—Anonymous

The Best Gift Is a Good Example

George Jones is a manager of a Global 1000 telecommunications company in the Asia Pacific Region. He has viewed himself as one of the best and the brightest—a good leader and solid manager, yet not a real change agent who could carve out a new reality. He set a goal for himself and his group of $500 million in earnings. He did the Masterful Coaching Workshop and he realized that, while he thought this was a stretch goal that represented an inspiring Impossible Future he and others could be really excited about, it was actually a predictable goal that could be achieved by following his and his company's Winning Strategies.

He had not engaged a Masterful Coach before because of the story he told about who he was: He could succeed based on his natural talent and ability without coaching and because he saw his goals as a stretch but within his grasp. "I don't need a coach to accomplish this. I can achieve it by being the leader I already know how to be, and by doing what I (and my organization) already know how to do." He had also resisted coaching because he had always viewed it as something that was remedial. He had received feedback that, while he was very bright, he tended to dominate the conversation with his views and opinions and needed to improve his listening skills. Yet all of that had suddenly changed.

He had looked at that picture of the journey to creating the Impossible Future (Diagram 1.1 in Chapter One), and it was as if he had been struck by lightning like St. Paul on the way to Damascus. According to Jones, "It came through to me so clearly that it would be much more exciting to me and to my organization to declare an Impossible Future that would require that I not only stretch my definition of my business, but also stretch my definition of myself as a leader."

Jones was struck by a definition I had shared about the difference between a goal and a possibility: *Possibilities are a future to stand in and bring into the present by acting from.* Leaders declare possibilities without evidence or proof that they can be realized and without knowing the path to the result. For example, "Man on the moon in ten years." By contrast, *goals are something that we try to get to from the present based on past successes.* Today's companies must meet their growth earnings goals or be penalized by Wall Street. As a result, many businesses automatically set predictable goals that will almost happen automatically.

Jones created a powerful partnership with a Masterful Coach from our Swiss office, Hans Peter Hartmann, and set an unreasonable expectation for himself and his business of "a 15 percent increase in earnings per year." He declared this as a possibility that he would stand inside and take committed action to realize. At the same time, he set some more conventional goals that he would report on to corporate and to Wall Street analysts.

Jones knew that, to reach this goal, he and his group would have to step into new territory. They would have to become *game changers,* to reshape the future of their industry, and *game growers,* to expand the pond by creating new customers and increased share of wallet by acquiring more business from existing customers. This was distinctly different from doing what he and his company had always done as *game players,* being the fast, efficient, low-cost producer.

As soon as Jones took a stand for the possibility, Hartmann began to work with him on the question: "Who do you need to be as a leader to realize this?" According to Hartmann, "I knew that for Jones to deliver on this goal, he was going to have to be a different kind of leader. He would have to create a context wherein he invested in relationships with direct reports and others he wanted enrolled in the vision of the future, as well as develop the listening skills that would create a context where people came up with new good ideas and put them to use." Jones made a sincere attempt to alter his behavior in both of these areas and made some dramatic improvements in a short period of time.

Another area where Jones went to work was on his conservative nature that sometimes got in the way of showing the excitement that he actually felt about things. So the coach also worked with him on expressing himself completely. Hartmann said, "It was essential that he break through his automatic self and learn to be the kind of leader who could excite and energize his organization. Showing excitement became a coaching project that we took on for the year. Some things take quite a bit of time to alter or change."

Next Hartmann worked with Jones to shift his mental model of being a manager, from being *a rule follower* to being *a rule breaker* and *rule maker* who blazes a new trail not just for his company but his industry. The company produced a commodity, "telephone terminals," and the Winning Strategy was to "run the factories full" and "run them cheap."

To create the kind of gains in growth and earnings Jones was seeking would require creating an elastic business model that was grounded in core competencies but, at the same time, not constrained by them. Jones and his group ran a CollabLabTM to explore creating a more innovative environment and specifically to explore ideas for growing the business by expanding the pond and creating new customers, as well as gaining greater share of wallet with existing customers.[3]

The coaching continued over the course of the year with a view toward challenging and supporting Jones on staying centered on the Impossible Future he had taken a stand for, as well as who he had to be in the matter. This consisted of making sure the Impossible Future stayed a priority and that he did not get swept along by all the demands that come with running a big company.

The coach focused on supporting Jones as a leader to continue to inspire his organization to make the Impossible Future a reality. He also focused on forwarding powerful action against the plan, honestly acknowledging breakdowns, and providing what's missing that would make a difference. To make a long story short, it was highly successful.

COACHING LEADERS—TRIPLE LOOP LEARNING

Context is the background against which you are standing that shapes your perception of reality, your identity, thinking, and behavior.

Embedded in the story of George Jones are many of the guiding ideas, tools, and methods that we at Masterful Coaching use to coach leaders and managers at all levels. What I would like to do in the rest of this chapter and the following chapter is take the implicit knowledge in this story and make it explicit so that you begin to apply it to your coaching relationships.

I would like to explore more deeply one of the most important guiding ideas behind this work, which is what we call Triple Loop Learning. It is a model that allows you to enter into the learning system of people and support them in reinventing who they are as leaders in the process of producing extraordinary results.

Triple Loop Learning lies at the core of Masterful Coaching—The Method™. It allows coaches to bring about breakthroughs for people and breakthroughs in results. It allows for fundamental shifts in thinking and attitude. It provides the guiding ideas (or mental models) that shape how a coach thinks and interacts with people. People don't talk about guiding ideas in a coaching session; rather they speak from them.

Masterful Coaching—The Method starts with declaring powerful new possibilities for the business and then translating these into goals that take people beyond what they already think and know based on industry orthodoxies or past experience. It also involves declaring new possibilities for the leaders in light of what they want to achieve that take them beyond their old management styles. As leaders move from strategic planning to action, they inevitably produce unintended results, either in their relationships with others or in their business dealings. Learning involves correcting mistakes and producing intended results for the first time.

A Masterful Coach will get to the source of the breakdown and make use of one or more of three learning loops: *triple loop*—altering people's way of being; *double loop*—altering people's mental models and thereby their thinking and actions; and *single loop*—tips and techniques. The coach provides people meaningful feedback that allows them to see where their view of things or their actions lead to unintended results. Diagram 4.1 is an illustration of the Triple Loop Learning Model.

DIAGRAM 4.1 *Triple loop learning*

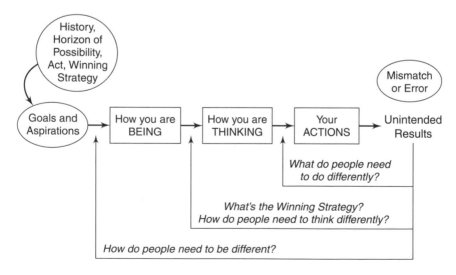

Masterful Coaches are not only highly skilled in providing feedback that removes the blinders from people's eyes, but also in making new distinctions that open up new possibilities for them or allow them to think differently and act differently. These can be life-altering. For example, "Do you want to compete with your direct reports or be a contribution?" "Do you think you will reach your goals by being a rule follower or do you need to become a rule breaker and maker?" (See Chapter Ten.)

MASTERING THE DEFINITIONS AND DISTINCTIONS OF TRIPLE LOOP LEARNING

There are certain definitions and distinctions that are essential for getting started with Masterful Coaching and Triple Loop Learning. These distinctions not only provide the coach a set of guiding ideas for going about their work but also, in many cases, the coachee as well. These distinctions make it possible for the coach and coachee to get on the same wavelength and have a more powerful conversation. These distinctions are (1) context; (2) history; (3) horizon of possibility; (4) Winning Strategy; (5) Master Programs; (6) automatic self; and (7) transformation. We will explain the last first.

Transformation

Coaching people to create an Impossible Future always requires personal and organization transformation. Transformation involves intervening in who people are being (triple loop), which in turn influences their thinking (double) and behavior (single). The way you are being at any given time—an inspired leader or dull manager, excellent or mediocre, an activist or analyst—determines what is possible and not possible. When a *transformation* occurs, something powerful happens in who people are being that is beyond a mere *change in behavior.* The person who is there now was not there before; the person who was there before does not exist.

Context

Context is the background against which people are standing that determines their perceptions of reality. It is this background that determines what they see as possible and achievable. It is this background from which people draw their identity and formulate their thinking and attitudes. Masterful Coaching is about intervening in the context so as to produce a profound alteration. For example: What is the context that determines what people see as possible and achievable? How do I intervene in that context so that they can create an Impossible Future? What is the context from which they draw their identity that results in them "playing small"? How do I intervene in the context so that they show up bigger?

The context that you come into the world from is made up of your history, your horizon of possibility, Winning Strategy, and automatic self.

History

Our context (background) consists of our history, Winning Strategies, and automatic self. We are all born into a certain historical community, grow up in a certain family, work in a certain industry, as well as experience successes and significant failures. All of this leads to thrown ways of being, attitude, and behavior. This applies to both individuals and companies. Leaders typically get stuck in the one right way to manage based on their history—command and control, laissez faire, whatever. Companies get stuck being a "One Strategy Wonder"—Xerox, photocopies; ATT, long distance; Intel, chips. Masterful Coaching is about helping people to distinguish themselves from their history so that they can stand free in the present and create a powerful new future.

Horizon of Possibility

Our horizon of possibility is set by our personal and cultural history. What we see as possible and achievable is not just influenced by facts and events, but by interpretations we make. For example, in coaching government leaders in Quebec, I observed that people did not aspire to the top leadership positions. When I asked why, people told me, "My grandmother told me I was born to eat a small loaf of bread." Companies have the same tendency to narrow their horizons of possibility as a result of limiting attitudes and beliefs they have inherited from the past. Masterful Coaching is about expanding people's horizons of possibility. This involves making powerful declarations and dismantling limiting beliefs and assumptions.

Masterful Coaching is about intervening in people's context so as to produce a profound alteration in who they are being.

Winning Strategy

Our Winning Strategy is often a compensation for what we see as not possible. For example, "I'm afraid to lead, but I will follow." "I don't know how to grow the business, but I can cut costs." Your Winning Strategy is the source of your success, but it is also the source of your limitation. Masterful Coaching often involves getting people to declare an Impossible Future that takes them beyond their Winning Strategy. This is different from trying to improve a Winning Strategy. To appreciate the distinction, ask yourself, "What have I done so far to be successful? Where does that limit me in taking my success to the next level? Am I willing to put aside the success I have become in order to create an Impossible Future?"

Master Programs

These are the master paradigms inherited by all human beings that tend to shape, limit, and define our thinking and behavior. Diagram 4.2 illustrates our master paradigms, based on the work of Chris Argyris.[4] Each one of these paradigms produces a variety of action strategies. These could also be looked at as generic Winning Strategies.

DIAGRAM 4.2 *Master paradigms and action strategies they produce*

Master Paradigm	Action Strategy
Stay in unilateral control	Pursue your own agenda
Maximize winning, and avoid losing	Unilaterally advocate your position, suppress inquiry but don't upset others
Seek acknowledgment, avoid disapproval	Look good, try to please others
Be invulnerable	Act like you know it all. Don't show any emotions
Avoid the appearance of incompetence	Cover up mistakes and cover up the cover up

Automatic Self

We don't design our history, horizon of possibility, Winning Strategy, and Master Programs. They design us. They show up in something that I call our "automatic self." Our automatic self determines that we set goals to compensate for what we believe is not possible. Our automatic self manifests itself by making sure that who we are and everything we do are consistent with our personal (or company) Winning Strategy. It includes our automatic thrown ways of being around the boss or direct reports, automatic ways of thinking based on industry orthodoxies, automatic responses to dealing with risk, disagreement, conflict, and so forth.

The Process of Personal and Organizational Transformation

Declaring an Impossible Future is the most powerful way to start the process of personal and organizational transformation.

The fact is that our automatic self, horizon of possibility, Winning Strategies, and Master Programs are like a box, and once inside the box, like all human beings, leaders and managers cannot think or act outside the box. It is not possible inside that box to create an extraordinary leader, nor is it possible inside the box to create an extraordinary future for the company. The only way to break out of the box is transformation or Triple Loop Learning.

As mentioned earlier, transformation involves intervening in the context that shapes who we are being and therefore our thinking and our actions. In my experience, there are only two ways to alter the context, and both are valid. One way involves making a powerful declaration of possibility that moves you beyond your history, horizon of possibility, and then standing inside that possibility. When people see a new possibility for themselves, they more readily embrace change.

The other way to intervene in the context has to do with shifting the particular perspectives, beliefs, and assumptions that constitute the context—or reframing their mindset. This is usually an emotional process. People don't just have their perspective; they become their perspective. People don't just have their beliefs; they become their beliefs. People don't just have their Winning Strategy; they become their Winning Strategy. Intervening in these, even with the best intentions, is likely to produce defensive reactions.

Although both approaches are valid, in my view the most powerful way to intervene in the context is to inspire and empower people to declare an Impossible Future that they cannot achieve through their automatic self, old Winning Strategies, and Master Programs. This work not only involves declaring an Impossible Future as possible, but encouraging people to take a stand for the possibility and to transform that into a reality.

Coaching people to transform into extraordinary leaders usually involves asking them to stop identifying with their automatic selves and to start identifying with their Impossible Futures. A question we often ask leaders is: Who are you when you are being your stand? An inspiring leader, an empowering manager, a coach and teacher? This usually involves people declaring new possibilities for themselves and again taking a stand for those possibilities.

Coaching then involves working with people through a process of Strategic Planning in Action to actualize their Impossible Future. As people make committed attempts to perform, they produce unintended results. Coaching then involves providing ongoing feedback based on the Triple Loop Learning. Use the questions at the end of this chapter to guide you in which loop to use.

RUT STORIES AND RIVER STORIES

When engaging in a coaching conversation, rather than just talking about Triple Loop Learning, a Masterful Coach asks people, "What's really on your mind?" They then listen to the stories that people tell, knowing that, as Ralph Waldo Emerson once said, "Everything you say reveals you." The stories that people tell about everyday events often reveal the context that defines who they are, as well as their horizons of possibilities and the Winning Strategies that are the source of their success and limitations. They also reveal their arbitrary interpretations of the reasons for unintended results.

Therefore, a Masterful Coach pays very close attention to these stories and views them as an opportunity to foster personal transformation. There are basically two kinds of stories that people tell—rut stories and river stories.[5] Rut stories keep people stuck in old ways of being and old thinking patterns, which results in inaction. River stories are stories of personal growth and transformation, stories of growth and learning. Imagine that you are your story (or stories). To a great extent what determines whether your story becomes, in Shakespearean terms, a comedy or a tragedy is whether you become enlightened and transform your rut story into a river story.

For example, let's say you have a story about yourself that says you are a good leader who is authoritative and smart, who likes winning. You pride yourself on taking the contrarian view and being right a lot of the time on people and business issues. You have also collected a lot of evidence over the years that your approach works: "Just look at my results." However, you also have received some coaching and 360-degree feedback from people at work that says you are a stiff, humorless dictator who always has to be right and make others wrong. Your son, by the way, also tells you you're a jerk for always trying to run his life.

If you could look at that coaching feedback as an opportunity or gift rather than be crushed by it or become defensive ("They just don't understand"), then that might be the first step in transforming yourself. You might say to yourself, "There is something about my leadership style and my whole story about myself that is actually getting in the way." You start to alter your point of view, seeing leadership in some other way than being an authority, being smart, always being right, and so forth.

Then one day you wake up and realize that you no longer have to draw your identity (self-worth) from being on top, from being right, or from needing to win. You can be influenced. You no longer need to have the answers—you can say, "I don't know." You can become an inquirer. You then begin to develop a new narrative about yourself that is about being a learning leader, about being an inquirer, about drawing others out, and with that, you transform your rut story into a river story.

Recognizing River and Rut Stories

You'll recognize rut stories when people talk about what's happened and make interpretations about things that represent an inaccurate, disempowering, and distorted view of reality. Rut stories often come from giving up and saying "Why bother?" in order to compensate for what's not possible, from blaming others instead of owning up to unintended results and learning the lessons we need to learn, and from taking things personally that aren't personal. These stories often have a self-reinforcing pattern.

For example, someone has a story that says, "My boss doesn't listen to me." The person goes to the next meeting with the boss with a "Why bother?" attitude and puts the point of view across without any passion, barely getting the boss's attention. The person then comes away from the meeting saying, "It was just as I thought; the boss didn't listen," blaming the boss for the fact that he or she didn't get the message across.

River stories are generally those of personal growth, self-renewal, and transformation. When people tell a river story, they speak with clarity, authenticity, and vulnerability regarding their growth edges, learning places, and breakdown spots. These stories often reflect that people have had "a revelation of their own foolishness," which has allowed them to learn the lessons they need to learn in order to take the next step in their lives. For example, they might say, "You know the problem was me, not my boss. I came to the table from the decision that my boss wouldn't listen, and therefore didn't express myself. I am now working on a breakthrough in self-expression."

While river stories are born out of a commitment to learn and grow, rut stories develop when people use defensive reasoning to protect themselves.

For example, people distort reality in order to save face, collude to avoid talking about any topic that could cause upset, and cover up errors by blaming others. These defensive stories and actions become so ingrained that people are hardly aware of them. They lead to unintended results, limited learning, escalating errors, and individual and collective illusions.

How do you transform rut stories into river stories? How do you speak and listen in a way that penetrates collective illusions? How do you break the grip of defensive reasoning when its self-sealing logic is leading to disaster?

Transforming Rut Stories into River Stories

One thing is clear: Transforming rut stories into river stories is not like a chat around the office water cooler. It involves engaging people in coaching conversations where you are dealing with them on at least three different levels of human experience:

1. Strengthening people's intention to create something in their lives that is not just an extension of the same old story;

2. Surfacing, testing, and revising limiting beliefs and assumptions that lead to unintended results; and

3. Using emotional energy as a source of transformation and letting go of physical blocks.

The methodology shown in Diagram 4.3 will help you transform rut stories into river stories.

DIAGRAM 4.3 *Transforming rut stories into river stories*

Listen for beliefs, assumptions, and meanings in people's stories.	"What are the unintended consequences of this story?"	"What are other ways to view what happened?"
Recognize and interrupt the rut story	Understand nature of the rut story	Create a river story
Name and identify rut story.	Step back from the story; observe facts and inferences.	"What are new ways of being, thinking, and acting?"

1. Recognize the Rut Story and Interrupt It

There are many times when people will go on and on with a rut story. I've found that the key is not just to pay attention to the plot line of the story, but to the structure of interpretation that people bring to it. As soon as I see that people are looking at things crookedly in their minds or speaking in a way that reflects limiting beliefs and assumptions, it automatically throws up a red flag for me that they are telling a "classic" rut story.

Diagram 4.4 outlines some classic rut stories. Let's look more closely at each of these classic rut stories.

DIAGRAM 4.4 *Rut stories and their consequences*

The "I need other people's approval" story	People's intention to look good replaces intention to be good.
The "I'm afraid to lose what I have" story	People play it safe, take no risks.
The "artful victim" story	People give away their power and can't create what they want.
The "tranquilizing" story	People cover up incompetencies; no learning occurs.
The "Why bother?" story	We know what we're talking about; we have twenty years' experience.

> **The "I Need Other People's Approval" Story.** People may not broadcast this story aloud, but they often tell it to themselves, constructing a whole series of pretenses and defenses in order to look good or gain other people's approval. The consequence is that the intention to look good often displaces the intention to be good (to perform and to create workable relationships).
>
> **The "I'm Afraid to Lose What I Have" Story.** This story is often told by people who put off their visions, dreams, and aspirations in order to seek or keep their security. They often complain about their lives not being satisfying but, at the same time, they create lots of reasons to justify standing still. These people are

generally non-players in the workplace, even though they may look like they are playing. The consequence is that they often spend their whole lives getting ready for everything to fall into place, only to discover that, like a seed, they have gone past their expiration date.

The "Artful Victim" Story. This story is probably the most common. It involves people skillfully using defensive reasoning to create an open-and-shut case as to how other people or circumstances are doing them in. The consequence is that they often get stuck in this story, forfeiting all their power to other people or the situation, and then are unable to create what they want.

The "Tranquilizing" Story. Whenever people do not achieve a result, are incompetent at a task, or do something that gets them into trouble, they usually come up with a set of reasons and excuses. The purpose of the explanation is to tranquilize them and make them feel better about themselves. The consequence of doing this is that people do not highlight their own incompetence (which leads to limited learning), errors are covered up (which leads to more errors), and reality is distorted (which leads to individual and collective illusions).

The "Why Bother?" Story. People who tell this story say that they cannot create what they want because their possibilities and choices are limited. "I don't have the time." "I don't have the authority." "It's not in the budget." Oftentimes, this story is a cover-up for wanting to stay in their comfort zones or for not wanting to take responsibility. This often betrays an underlying attitude of resignation. The consequence is that people get stuck in this story and lose the ability to see the possibilities and options that they actually have.

When I hear people telling their particular version of a classic rut story, I intervene very aggressively: "Wait a minute. I think you are telling a classic rut story here and, in the process, digging a hole for yourself."

Intervening not only means interrupting the story in a literal sense, but more profoundly, speaking and listening with a strong intention to penetrate the illusions under which people may be operating. This involves breaking the grip of their existing structure of interpretation—frames, beliefs, and assumptions.

Coach: I am getting the impression that you are telling an "approval seeking" story. It seems that you want to accomplish certain things that are very important to you, but it appears that you are designing your actions to be reasonable and nice and perhaps to make yourself look good, rather than to create what you want.
Coachee: Well, maybe you have a point, but I need approval to get my goals accomplished.
Coach: Let's dig into this.

Coach: You say you don't have enough time to create the strategic plan for your division because you are always in meetings. This could be an example of what I call a "tranquilizing story"—something you give as an explanation.
Coachee: Well, it's true.
Coach: Do you really need to go to all those meetings? Let me make a provocation. Is the problem really that you can't say no but you use the meeting story to justify not having enough time to create your plan?

Your job as a coach is to point out the difference between a rut story and a river story, as well as teach people to inquire into and reflect on stories in a manner similar to that illustrated above. After a time, people will intuitively understand whether or not their opinions, assumptions, and beliefs are going to help them produce the results they want: "Wait a minute. I hear myself telling a rut story. I'd like to step back and look at that for a moment."

2. Understand the Nature of the Rut Story

Often when people are telling a classic rut story, they are not even aware of it. In effect, they are frozen into their story. At this stage, you need to say something that creates a meltdown or unfreezes the story and creates the readiness to change. By identifying and naming the story, you help people become aware of it. By making people more conscious of the unintended consequences of their stories, you set the stage for them to extricate themselves from them.

Coach: I hear you telling a "why bother?" and an "approval seeking" story about your efforts to introduce Business Concept Incubator to spur innovation and growth and Six Sigma to improve processes. You say you are not sure the CEO supports it and without that, you won't get the resources or budget. You sound resigned and ready to give up.
Coachee: I could do something, but first I need to have the CEO's approval as well as resources and support. I do feel like giving up.

Coach: Do you realize that if you give up, you automatically forfeit your ability to create the future that you want in the company or the difference you want to make?
Coachee: Yes, that is true, but I am blocked in.
Coach: There may be other ways to look at it. Instead of focusing on what you can't do, why not determine if there is anything that you can do to enroll the CEO or to start small with the resources you have right now, something you can create now that might bring a success.

3. Create a River Story by Seeing Things in a New Way

Coaching people to revise their stories often involves helping people to see that they are the authors of their stories. They may not have freely chosen what happened to them in life or work, but they constructed what the story meant to them, and thereby bear the consequences of it in their lives.

It's important to emphasize that people get stuck in their stories when they interpret who they are or what has happened to them and see things in an inflexible or rigid way. This leads to them being ineffective in their relationships or their actions, and to a great deal of suffering.

By coaching people to see who they are and their experience of what happened to them as partially a matter of their own interpretation, they free themselves up from their stories. This involves using a technique called "fluid framing." You might say, "How you see yourself or what happened is one possible interpretation. What are other possible interpretations that would be more inspiring, more empowering, more accurate?" This allows people to revise their stories and develop a new point of view about themselves, others, or the circumstances.

Another way to assist people in revising their stories or being more flexible with their interpretations is to help them take a second look at their observations of what actually happened and the assessments they made about it. Observations are based on directly observable data; assessments are the judgments (inferences) made about those observations. Normally, people do not distinguish between the two and get into trouble when they take assessments as fact, when in reality they are only interpretations.

Assessments are often heavily influenced by the tendency to take things personally, blame others, or explain things away. Asking people to distinguish between their observations and assessments can help to put a crack in this structure of interpretation.

Coach: On what observations are you basing your assessment that the VP doesn't like you and doesn't encourage others to cooperate with you?
Coachee: I know they are under the gun to complete their own projects, but they come late to meetings.
Coach: Do you see that you went from that observation to the assessment that it was personal and to the conclusion that they didn't want to cooperate?

Or

Coach: Is what you are saying about the other group a fact or an interpretation?

Once people begin to step back a bit from their stories, the next step is to generate alternative interpretations. As your job as the coach is not to provide people with a better belief system than the one they already have, it is important that you encourage them to come up with a different interpretation. However, it would be foolish to forsake your wisdom, intuition, and insight. If you want to offer advice, it is better to say something like, "I have a belief that . . ." or "One possibility might be that. . . . What do you think?" rather than, "I think this is how you ought to look at it."

Coach: How else could you look at this?
Coachee: I see that I have to include other people's points of view a lot more in my reality.
Coach: What else?
Coachee: I also see that I tend to point a finger when something goes wrong, rather than to hold up a mirror.

Sometimes these everyday incidents can reveal the part of a person's existential narrative that is most limiting but causes him or her to suffer. Doing this work will often open up big cracks in the person's Master Program and give you the opportunity to do the inner healing work that needs to take place for personal transformation. As people expose their thinking, it's important to give them permission to express their emotions.

Emotions can be a powerful source of transformational energy, and expressing them can help people to let go of a point of view that keeps them stuck, helping them to see something they didn't see before. There are appropriate ways to elicit emotions, even though the cultural environment in business doesn't always encourage it. The coach might say, "I welcome your emotions about this." Another simple approach is to say, "Tell me about your emotions as you speak." When people get things off their chests, they often drop defensive reasoning and the wall of arguments they have constructed to protect themselves. This can suddenly create an opening for moments of true insight.

> **Coachee:** *I have been holding a lot of this inside. Now that I've got this fear and anger off my chest, I am starting to see that I go to the table already assuming he won't listen and thus don't put my ideas across.*

It's important to acknowledge people for their vision, courage, and commitment as they open up new possibilities for themselves.

> **Coach:** *Your commitment to your extraordinary future and to personal and organizational transformation is really inspiring to me, and I am sure it will pay off in terms of results.*

THE MYTH OF ICARUS

In Greek mythology, Icarus, seduced by his own power after putting on wax wings, flies too close to the sun. As he does, his artificial wings melt and he falls into the sea and dies.

There is a good lesson here for all of us that gets to the heart of this book. Like Icarus, many of us have great strengths that seduce us. These strengths often lead to our early successes. But eventually we become so enamored of them or overly reliant on them that we cover up our weaknesses or we fail to recognize the need to change something that seems natural and right. To expose our weaknesses or to change something with which we have been successful and then to do something new is difficult, especially if we are full of pride. It requires not only a commitment to change, but to learning.

Coaching is having both the toughness and the compassion to skillfully intervene in people's learning processes. A successful coaching relationship is always a story of transformation, not just of higher levels of performance. It's a story that takes people beyond their immediate passion and pride and helps them to come to grips with the fact that, to reach what is really possible and achievable for them, they must be willing to fundamentally question who they are, what they do, and why they do it.

To challenge and support someone else in his or her story of transformation goes beyond doing something for others and extends to ourselves. To have someone invite us to participate in his or her transformational learning process is not just an opportunity but also a gift, a gift to the human spirit. It's the opportunity to look up from what we are trying to accomplish and the mundane aspects of daily affairs and to see the hidden meaning behind all that we do. It's learning not only to recognize who other people are and what they are magnificently capable of, but also to know ourselves at the same moment.

When to Use Triple, Double, or Single Loop Learning

- *Triple Loop Learning. Is the issue a matter of intervening in the context that shapes who someone is being that manifests of the person's automatic self— for example, dominating versus empowering, suppressive versus innovative? Make new distinctions that shape the person's way of being.*

- *Double Loop Learning. Is it a matter of intervening in the mental models that caused someone to be blindsided by company or industry orthodoxies? Reframe mental models and provide more empowering and accurate interpretations.*

- *Single Loop Learning. Is it a matter of people knowing who they need to be in the matter and what is required is an act of courage—getting them to jump into action and do something different? Give a tip or technique that guides people's actions.*

CHAPTER FIVE

COACHING EXECUTIVES AND LEADERS AT ALL LEVELS

A Powerful, Step-by-Step Model

The power of a Masterful Coach and a talented leader with a burning desire to achieve is damn near infinite.

I can say without exaggeration that the power of Masterful Coaching and a talented executive or leader who is burning with desire to achieve personal and organizational aspirations and, at the same time, has an attitude of curiosity, humility, and learning is damn near infinite. I have seen people transform from "RTB" (run the business) managers, to incredibly generative "CTB" (create the business) leaders in less than a year.

I have seen people expand their vision and create an extraordinary future that they previously never would have dreamed of or even dared to imagine. And I have seen people accomplish breakthrough goals that were difficult or impossible. Interestingly enough, this can only happen as a result of breakthroughs for people and transforming certain aspects of corporate culture.

I realize that those who can only compare Masterful Coaching to traditional leadership education or management training may find such claims provocative, difficult to believe, or even disingenuous. I stand by them nonetheless, as do the hundreds of leaders who have experienced it.

The difference between Masterful Coaching and leadership education is like the difference between riding an Apollo rocket ship up into space and spending a day at Disneyland with two tickets to Space Mountain. This claim is not based on theory or an egotistical need to prove that my way is better, but from actual practice and from personally experiencing the results that are produced on both sides of the fence.

Then what makes the difference? Masterful Coaching has been designed as a step-by-step method that aligns personal and organizational ambitions and aspirations; it takes place over a period of a year or more, rather than in a three-day classroom experience; it is grounded in the real work "situation," unlike abstract training programs; it provides real-time feedback, not a 360-degree computer printout; and finally it is transformational, not transactional. I would like to introduce you to the five-step executive coaching model, but before doing so I will provide an example.

TAKE 'EM OUT AND SHOOT 'EM

Jim Nokes, executive vice president of Conoco, is standing in front of the DS (Downstream) 100 meeting, a group of leaders gathered together in Houston's Sofitel to hear about his ideas for the new Conoco DS. The flash of his smile and the glint in his eyes radiate a warmth that could take the chill off a Kansas City winter morning—his ancestral stomping grounds. He learned business by osmosis from his father—who brokered agricultural products across the Midwest with a down-home charm and the skill of a high-flying Wall Street trader.

To describe Nokes is to engage in a dialogue of opposites. He has a Napoleonic bearing and drive to win, but at the same time is humble and unassuming. Nokes, named by the press as Mad Dog, was charged with saving Conoco's North American Downstream operation and subsequently achieved $450 million in real improvement. He speaks with a kind of Harry Truman good-humored, no BS candor, and demands it in return. One of his best qualities as a leader is that he is quick to point out his own learning edges, chuckling about his own mistakes. This makes him a lesser God that people can identify with.

He is at the hotel in Houston to talk about his vision of an ambitious future, and his new "global ground rules." To make sure everyone knows he means business, he starts off with a story about John Wayne. He says, "Wayne is the trail boss on a cattle drive. It's been a long, hard ride and two of the hands decided to pull out. Wayne says, 'You signed on to see us through to Abilene, you gave me your word, and if you don't keep it, you'll pay the consequences.' The men tug at their gun belts, spit in the dust and say, 'We're leavin.' Wayne, wanting to set an example for the rest of his trail hands, pulls out his six-shooter and plugs both of them."

Nokes is building up to his next comments, "I am going to talk to you about my vision and global ground rules for Downstream. I expect every leader in this room and beyond it to not only sign up for these, but to sponsor them, and those that don't . . . well, they are not going to be around." Then all of a sudden, almost in mid-tracks, he stops and says, "Wait a minute, that's the wrong story. That's a story about command and control. We're here to talk about inspiring, empowering leadership. . . ." He chuckles. The people in the room, most of whom Nokes has endeared at one time or another with his strong will and also his humility, break up in laughter. The event is a home run.

Nokes and I had begun working about a year earlier. He had been in his executive vice president role for a year, a promotion received as a result of his talent and ability and also as a result of saving the North American Downstream organization from being sold off. He had turned one of the companies "marginal assets" into an incredible money machine that produced lots of cash. Nokes was struggling when I met him to discover the difference he could make in his executive role.

At the time that I began working with Nokes, he had not carved out a new vision for DS, but tended to just keep "operating," which often meant getting in the hair of his direct reports—Richard Severance of North American DS, Rick Hamm of European DS, and George Pazkowski in the Asia Pacific region. I felt Nokes was like a sleeping giant, someone used to the hue and cry of business combat on the front lines of the oil industry who had fallen asleep one night and awakened in the plush executive offices in Conoco's Houston center, where it is so quiet you can hear a pin drop. The alarm clock was now ringing inside his heart and soul and he was itching to sink his teeth into something mighty big.

One day we sat in his executive suite meeting room at his golden table and he said, "I'd like to show you my goals for the year. What do you think of them?" I looked at the goals and they actually looked pretty darn good. "They're a good set of goals and priorities, Jim, and could make an impressive agenda for the year, but let me ask you a question: 'Are you passionate about them?'" Just then there was an interruption and Nokes had to leave the office for a few minutes to talk to his senior executive assistant and confidant, Josette George.

I don't know what words were exchanged, but Nokes came back in the room and said, "I'll tell you what my real goals are, the ones that I can be really passionate about. I'd like to become CEO and transform Conoco, creating a phenomenal business success." That moment was, in Jean Paul Sartre's terms, a self-expressive, existential act. As Martin Heidegger[1] once said, "Words don't just describe or explain, but rather, like the chisel of the carver, they can be used to bring something into being. As a man speaketh, not only are his words coming into being, but also the man himself."

From this point on, having declared his Impossible Future, Nokes would be like a different man. At the same time, I sensed that to become CEO and transform the company he would first have to transform himself. I eased into this issue with a question, "To reach these goals, is this going to take a radical change of your leadership style or an incremental improvement?" Nokes shot back without even skipping a beat, "It's going to take a radical change." He was going to have to show up completely differently.

I then suggested we do some 360-degree feedback to get a line on who he was being and how he was showing up today. This was a first step in plotting out a leadership development plan. In the next few weeks, I collected feedback from the CEO of the company, Archie Dunham, his colleagues on the Conoco management committee, and most of Nokes' direct reports. When I walked into his office to present him the feedback he chuckled and said, "Give me the bad news." I told him, "Jim, if two people call you a horse, saddle up."

The feedback from the CEO and colleagues all said the same thing. It was essentially this: "We all think Jim is a great guy. We all know Jim is the kind of leader who knows how to save the day by fixing an operation and producing great financial results, by running full and running cheap." So far so good. I continued, "What we don't know is whether he can be an inspiring leader who can create a positive vision for Conoco and DS, as well as carve out a new reality in which the vision can happen." At that moment, the scales fell from Nokes' eyes. He was blindly pursuing a Winning Strategy of getting results, which had actually been perceived by others as a source of strength, but also a kind of limitation.

It is said in the Bible that "change can come in the twinkling of an eye," and that's exactly what happened in Nokes' cases. It took about ten seconds for Nokes to "unfreeze" his leadership style and begin to "transform" and "refreeze" it. In the coming weeks, I began acting as Nokes' conversation partner, drawing out his thoughts on both the leadership breakthroughs he wanted to achieve, as well as on business breakthroughs. This took the form of a global vision for Conoco Downstream and a set of global ground rules by which he and his direct reports, the Downstream Leadership Team, would carve out a new reality for the company.

There are a couple of things I noticed that are worth mentioning here. Until the time that this transformation occurred, Nokes was at the effect of what the CEO, Archie Dunham, said and did. He wasn't the type of person to set his sights on looking good or making impressions but, at the same time, a lot of his speaking and listening seemed to take place inside a container about how this or that would play with Archie. Once Nokes took a stand and decided to be the author of his own destiny, it didn't seem to matter all that much anymore. He said, "We're shooting for a billion dollars in earnings in Downstream. And we are going to have to have the courage to be innovative. If you can be innovative, you can't be shut down. I don't know how Archie will feel about it, but we are going to do it anyway."

To get to a billion dollars in earnings Nokes defined three games for him and his team to play: (1) being a *game changer*—who invents new products and new markets; (2) being a *game grower*—who comes up with powerful new ways to increase today's business from new and existing customers: and (3) being a *game player*—who looks for ways to strengthen the business's foundation.

In the game change category, Nokes observed that Conoco had been making its money off oil for the past one hundred years. He felt the company had to at least have a viable alternative, especially with the vagaries of the oil market. He championed a new division of the company with a billion dollar plus potential called Cevolution. It was in the midst of producing a breakthrough product called carbon fiber (a byproduct of residue found at the bottom of the oil barrel) that could be used to create a powerful, stronger, lighter future in batteries, autos, building products, as well as in conductives. In the game grower category, he began to tell his managers, "The game is not just to manage people on their numbers, but to get every growth idea that people have out of their heads." In the game player category, he sponsored Six Sigma quality. He saw this as a way to make sustainable real improvements while taking cost out. Savings in year one were $80 million, while creating a small cultural revolution around process improvement.

He began to coach and to extend much more trust to his direct reports, who had accused him in their feedback of sometimes being either too hands-off or alternatively too meddlesome. What was most interesting about this was that it allowed him the time and space to become more of a learning leader and certainly more reflective. I noticed a dramatic rise in his level of insight into complex issues. One day I said to him, "Has your IQ just shot up about 100 points since we started this work together or have I just gotten to know you better?" He said, with a mixture of pride and humility, "I hope it is both." Over the coming months, Nokes made extraordinary progress. I continued to challenge and support him in every way I could. (The story of how Nokes began to transform his worldwide organization is continued in the next chapter.)

MASTERFUL COACHING FOR LEADERS—THE METHOD™

We are now ready to take an in-depth look at the Masterful Coaching model that the Jim Nokes story has begun to illustrate. As outlined previously, the model is focused on helping leaders declare an Impossible Future, while at the same time reinventing themselves and their organization. Masterful Coaching for Leaders–the Method has an important structural component. It is based on meeting face-to-face with the leader you are coaching once a month (as a minimum), supplemented by a mid-month coaching conversation phone call. The monthly coaching session allows the coach and the leader to set goals, make plans, and establish monthly priorities and key actions. The mid-month phone call allows the coach and the coachee to continue to operate in the same world.

Diagram 5.1 shows the five-step model. Let's look at each step in more depth.

DIAGRAM 5.1 *Masterful Coaching—The Method™ for Executives*

STEP 1. Enroll leaders in an extraordinary coaching relationship.

STEP 2. Coach the executive to design an Impossible Future for themselves and their organization.

STEP 3. Gather and provide 360-degree feedback—*To reinvent the organization, reinvent yourself first.*

STEP 4. Engage in Strategic Planning in Action with the executive and the team.

STEP 5. Coach executive effectiveness through monthly follow-up on goals, priorities, and high-leverage actions.

STEP 1. Enroll Executives in an Extraordinary Coaching Relationship

The first step is to get to know each other so as to establish a human relationship. Ask personal questions that get the other person to tell you his or her story or narrative, personal goals and aspirations, current role, and background. Share your own narrative in an open way. This will help to establish chemistry with the person.

Next sound the tone of leadership coaching by sharing experiences you have had in coaching or being coached by others. As you tell these, begin to weave in the following distinctions that will serve to map the territory of coaching for the person you are speaking with. Masterful Coaching is about (1) creating an extraordinary future versus filling gaps; (2) accomplishment versus therapy; (3) transformational learning versus transactional learning; and (4) action not psychology.

It is important to emphasize that a Masterful Coach "chooses" the person being coached because the coach is genuinely excited about the person and genuinely believes in what the person is up to. If that is the case, the next step after mapping the territory of coaching is to enroll people in Masterful Coaching. The enrollment process starts here and never stops.

Enrollment involves eliciting people's voluntary emotional commitment. I often ask people: "How often do you have someone who is a Masterful Coach (and an extraordinary human being) come up to you and say, 'I am going to devote the next day, month, or year to being a total commitment to causing your success as a leader, manager, and human being'?" The answer to the question is "never!"

Enrollment involves unearthing what people are passionate about, drawing out the leadership and business challenges they are facing. I often say to people, "You might reach your goals today on your own. My observation is that coaching gives you the *power* to reach goals and aspirations that would otherwise be impossible. It also empowers you to do this at a much higher rate of *velocity,* and to avoid stepping on landmines in the process."

After that I ask people, "In light of the leadership and businesses challenges you are facing in this job, what do you think is the opportunity in coaching for you?" I give people a chance to talk about the opportunity and to enroll themselves. Then I say, "It sounds like you are a definite yes to coaching. Is that true?" Or "It sounds like you are a definite no." Or "If you are a 'maybe,' perhaps you have more questions."

Once people are enrolled, the coach says, "If we want to have extraordinary results, we need to design an extraordinary coaching relationship, not just one that is good." This starts with creating a 50/50 partnership. It is not just about how the coach comes to the relationship; it is about how the coachee comes to the relationship. This is a good way to begin to create clear expectations. This sets the stage to talk about the structure of the coaching relationship. For example, "We will meet monthly and speak every week by phone, for example, Monday mornings at 7:30 a.m."

Talk About What a Coach Bringing 100 Percent Looks Like

- *Standing in the future you want to create and being totally committed to your success*
- *Challenging and supporting you on your goals, priorities, blind spots*
- *Speaking to you based on a commitment to the truth*
- *Empowering you to deliver on your commitments*
- *Being a cheerleader for your successes*

Talk About What Bringing Their 100 Percent Would Look Like

- *Something at stake, for example, goals, projects they passionately care about*
- *An attitude of curiosity, learning, and humility*
- *Asking the coach to be a thinking partner; being a request for coaching (help)*
- *Listening versus debating what the coach says*
- *Keeping their word on monthly priorities*
- *Following through on practice assignments*

Designing an extraordinary coaching relationship must be done in an ongoing way with rigor and intention.

Designing an extraordinary coaching relationship is not a one-time event, but an ongoing process. The coaching process can generate leadership and business breakthroughs in three to six months; afterwards people tend to rest on their laurels and start to go into a holding pattern. One of the first things I do as a coach is to look for when that energy is in the relationship. Red lights go on if I feel they are not playing a "big game," or the person's head isn't in the game. Red lights also go on if I feel I am bringing more energy to the relationship than they are. More red lights go on if the person is not really listening for what I have to say.

The coach absolutely needs to address this honestly, rather than smooth it over: "I am totally committed to you causing your continued success, both with your leadership and business breakthroughs. I know we have made real progress since we started, so I want to ask you a question: 'Do you think we still have an extraordinary coaching relationship or just a good one?' I am concerned because I have observed a few things that are missing."

The coach then addresses the issues: "Let's both honestly look at what's working, what's not working, and what's missing." For example, "Instead of talking to me about the goals and aspirations you are reaching toward, you come to our sessions and only want to talk about what you have already achieved. Sometimes I have the feeling that you are debating me rather than being a listening for what I have to say. Also you are making far fewer requests for coaching from me then before. Do you have any requests of me? I have one or two for you that I think would take this relationship to the next level."

STEP 2. Coach Leaders to Design an Impossible Future for Themselves and Their Business

Once people are enrolled in the coaching relationship with respect to their immediate leadership and business challenges, the next step is to design an Impossible Future. The intent is to take the discussion you began in Step 1 regarding the leader's goals to a whole new level. I have found that people will passionately engage in an Impossible Future, if it aligns personal and organizational ambitions, and will realize it through the dance of imagination, intellect, and capital.

I usually present the diagram (1.2) on creating a possible future rather than a predictable future to show that in most cases leaders articulate goals and aspirations for themselves and their organization based on their personal (organizational) "Winning Strategy" and their history. As a result, they are often unaware of the fact that even their so-called stretch goals are actually predictable goals that involve doing the same thing better. As mentioned earlier in the story about George Jones, the light often goes on in people's eyes when they see this. They also see that they are actually bored with the game they are playing.

I then work with people on designing an Impossible Future that will give the leader a "big game" to play, one that is exciting and energizing. In most cases, talented leaders are playing a "small game" that doesn't make any difference in their world. For example, "Shrink headcount" or "Cut costs by 5 percent this year." I have found that the key to empowering people to articulate an Impossible Future and big game is to release their personal and organizational aspirations (ambitions) that they have never previously dared to articulate.

DISCOVERY PROCESS FOR
DESIGNING AN IMPOSSIBLE FUTURE

- *What do you passionately care about?*

  Draw out passions in both their personal and business lives.

- *What is your greatest personal (organizational) ambition?*

  For example, "To be an inspiring leader who transforms the company culture" and "To become the future of our industry."

- *Declare an Impossible Future possible and take a stand to make it a reality.*

  Create a focused declaration: "To become CEO," "To transform the company," "To lead a revolution in our industry."

- *What would be your greatest leadership challenge? Business challenge? Team challenge? Are you up for that?*

To set the stage for designing an Impossible Future, I often make a distinction between being a *generative* leader who creates something that never existed before and being a *predictable* leader who manages what already exists.

At this point, I come back to it, "You will never realize your Impossible Future unless you step into the space of being a generative leader and step out of the space of being a reactive manager."

This means the person needs to stay centered on creating the future, rather than just reacting to the incredible number of demands that most leaders have coming at them. This leads to a discussion of how the leader is going to manage his or her time and attention in the coming months. To support this, I make a distinction between doing what makes a difference, what's important, and the trivial.

Most managers cannot distinguish between what makes a difference and the important. To help them to become more aware, I go through their time schedules with them and identify activities spent in each area. I then give them a homework assignment to create a month's schedule with 60 percent of the focus on things that make a difference and 40 percent on the important. I also show them the Pyramid of Accomplishment diagram, which illustrates a mental model for time management. (See diagram 5.2.) Interestingly enough, many leaders see that they are spending more time in community meetings that have little effect on the business than they are in any of the four sections of the Pyramid.

DIAGRAM 5.2 *The pyramid of accomplishment*

**Masterful Coaches set priorities
according to the pyramid of
accomplishment**

*Masterful Coaches
use this mental model
for time management.*

*The more levels of the
pyramid you handle, the
more you will accomplish.*

Creating
the Future

Creating High
Leverage Relationships

Coaching Individuals
and Teams

Running the Business Producing
C&E, Control O&O

STEP 3. Gather 360–Degree Feedback and Create a Leadership Reinvention Plan

To reinvent the organization, you have to reinvent yourself first.

Creating an Impossible Future requires personal and organizational reinvention. Our automatic self, Winning Strategy, Master Programs, and so forth are insufficient. I often start this process by asking the following question: "Do you think that creating your Impossible Future will require a radical change in your leadership style, or more of an incremental change in your leadership style?" In most cases the answer is, "I think it will require a radical change in my leadership style."

This allows me to introduce the notion of getting some 360-degree feedback (from boss, colleagues, direct reports, and family) on who they are being as a leader today and whether that is sufficient to create an Impossible Future. I make a point of saying, "You have become very successful by being who you are today and the way you are now, and you don't *have to* change anything. At the same time, now that you have put a stake in the ground for an Impossible Future, you may *choose to* change (transform) something about yourself."

I then ask coachees to give me a list of people they would like to participate in the 360-degree feedback process. I want to emphasize that this method is based on doing in-depth feedback interviews, not computerized checksheets. We have found that this leads to being able to give much more meaningful feedback than the often-used computerized feedback form, which I find relatively useless and which easily becomes a "numbers game."

In the interviews, it is a good idea to ask questions to get people to talk about the person, rather than giving them a list of leadership attributes to rate the person on. For example, one business unit leader we know got a great feedback report using a computerized approach based on five leadership categories, with twenty-five dimensions, but was then summarily fired within a few months for lack of business performance without ever being aware of how that was actually showing up.

The questions to ask are these:

What are this person's . . .

- *Possibilities and potential?*
- *Strengths?*
- *Gaps?*

- *Winning Strategy and biggest blind spot?*
- *Derailers?*
- *Developmental steps?*
- *Next most appropriate job?*

After doing the feedback process, I prepare to have a conversation with the leader that will catalyze the reinvention process. I carefully review the feedback, looking for patterns and paying attention to what has been said here by people that will give insights that will make it possible to have a life-altering conversation with the leader. For example, "You are an inspiring, charismatic leader, but sometimes your Winning Strategy of needing to be right and win, as well as finding what's wrong with others, gets people defensive."

I present the feedback by doing what Ben Zander does with his students at the beginning of the year, extending them an A for the class.[2] "I am totally committed to you and what you are up to. I believe you have the potential to be an extraordinary leader and create an extraordinary future. At the same time, there are some patterns that show up in this feedback that I want to address with you that, if you could take it in, it would make all the difference in the world." This is preparation for hitting people with a hammer.

I tell all coaches at Masterful Coaching to keep in mind the model of *Unfreeze, Transform, and Refreeze* while delivering 360-degree feedback. It is extremely important to present the feedback with enough "heat" that it unfreezes the leader's certainty in his or her automatic self, Winning Strategies, behavior patterns. If you don't generate enough heat to unfreeze this certainty, you will be fighting it for the rest of the coaching engagement. I sometimes use the term "demolition process" to describe the unfreezing phase of the feedback.

> **You invent the Impossible Future by declaring an ambitious aspiration and declaring that fulfilling that future is the game that you are playing in life.**

The Reinvention Paradigm

Once the feedback is presented, I give people time to digest it and then engage in a transformational conversation with them using the *Triple Loop Learning method*. The idea is

- *To inspire them to make some new declarations about themselves consistent with the Impossible Future they want to create and*

- *To dismantle limiting beliefs and assumptions that lead to their automatic self, Winning Strategies, and so forth.*

Often at this point I show the reinvention paradigm, shown in Diagram 5.3, which illustrates the process of declaring and taking a stand for a new future and then looking at who you need to be as a leader to actually make that happen.[3]

DIAGRAM 5.3 *The reinvention paradigm*

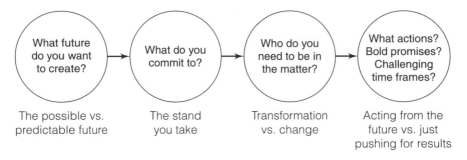

Reinvention Paradigm

You invent the Impossible Future by declaring an ambitious aspiration and by declaring that fulfilling that future is the game you are playing in life.

What future do you want to create?	What do you commit to?	Who do you need to be in the matter?	What actions? Bold promises? Challenging time frames?
The possible vs. predictable future	The stand you take	Transformation vs. change	Acting from the future vs. just pushing for results

I am careful in this process to continue to validate the person by extending an A and to not crush him or her or make the person "wrong." (If that happens, people will become defensive: "Hey, this automatic self is fine!") I might say something like, "You are charming and disarming, but also somewhat intimidating to colleagues and direct reports. Do you think those two ways of being (sets of behavior) will be enough for you as a leader to realize your Impossible Future? Think about your Impossible Future and ask yourself, 'Who do I need to be in the matter?'"

Or I might say, "Your Winning Strategy of being a know-it-all, needing to be right and win, finding what's wrong has allowed you to create some great business results for your company in the competitive market you are in, but it often results in your crushing new ideas that are put forward to you by people and creates a disempowering environment for people around you.

To realize your Impossible Future, you are going to have to stand apart from this Winning Strategy, or at least recognize when it becomes an obstacle and gets in the way. You need to become a 'clearing' for new, good ideas, for bringing out the best in people, and for whatever else is missing to realize your goals."

This usually results in creating some new declarations, which become the basis of a leadership reinvention plan. It's important to keep the plan focused on two or three areas that represent high leverage for the person. My experience is that, while the 360-degree feedback may reveal many strengths to build on and numerous areas for improvement, it is better to keep the coaching effort focused on those aspects that are most high leverage. I have discovered that over the course of the year, as the person strives to step into new territory as a leader, the same one or two old patterns will come back to bite him or her. Work on these.

Pick one or two areas for a leadership breakthrough project and focus on that as a project for the entire course of the coaching engagement. For example, being a learner, rather than a knower; having a breakthrough in self-expression; showing up as a leader; being a coach and teacher rather than a command-and-control or kill-the-snake manager; or jettisoning some disempowering attitudes or behaviors. Brainstorm as many ways as possible to succeed with that project. Then choose the best ways based on the coachee's personal style and the effectiveness of the approach. This could include monthly practice and reflection assignments.

One good technique is to ask the coachee to keep a leadership breakthrough journal, a diary recording any successes that resulted in the person showing up differently between sessions. You can review these along with the 360-degree feedback at each coaching session.

To Realize My Impossible Future
- *I am committed to the possibility of [new position, new way of being]*
- *I am committed to giving up [automatic self, Winning Strategies, attitudes and behavior]*
- *My leadership breakthrough project is . . .*
- *My key monthly actions are . . .*
- *I will keep an accomplishment journal*

STEP 4. Strategic Planning in Action with the Leader and His or Her Group

Now that the stage is set for the person showing up as an extraordinary leader, the next step in realizing the Impossible Future is to set the stage for some extraordinary business results. This starts with doing the Strategic Planning in Action (SPIA) process with the leader and his or her direct reports. This process involves looking at three questions:

1. Where are we now?
2. Where are we going?
3. What's missing that will make a difference?

This process allows people to set meaningful goals and monthly priorities that become the basis of coaching people in real time on their real business issues and concerns. Do this entire SPIA process on flip charts. Wallpaper the entire room with them.

QUESTION 1. Where Are We Now? The "What's So" Process

The best and fastest way to plot a course to an Impossible Future is to be clear about where you stand today. We do this through the "what's so" process. The what's so process is about facing reality. Imagine for a moment that you are interested in buying a house. Before you finalize your decision you will take a walk around the house, going through all of the rooms, as well as examining the basement, the attic, the garage. By the time you're through, you'll have a pretty good idea of this house, where it needs work, and if it is something you are interested in.

The what's so process is like a walk around the house. You ask the group to look at how it is right now in their business, starting with the environment the company is operating in. For example, ask, "What are five portents of change that have already occurred that will alter the future of your industry? Which one of these is your company or group creating?" If people have nothing to say, it tells you the company is a *rule follower* rather than *a rule maker* and *breaker.*

Then the group takes a look at each aspect of the business, noticing: (1) what the accomplishments are; (2) what's working; (3) what's not working; (4) what's missing that, if provided, would make a difference; and (5) the opportunities. These are not opportunities presented from a compelling future, but those opportunities that have been revealed by taking a really close look at today's situation.

By the end of the process, all participants will have viewed the business from multiple perspectives. You will have tapped the knowledge of each and every person in the room and people will be totally grounded and aligned in the present state of affairs. Standing in a thorough examination of the present, people are not only able to powerfully *envision* the future, but also to then *create* the future.

The "what's so" process is also an excellent way for new leaders of a group and coaches to get grounded in the business or big game. Without this reality base, you may wind up coaching the leader on the 50,000-foot level of the business or on "touchy feely" issues.

"WHAT'S SO" INQUIRY

Start by taking an overall look at the business and then divide the business into four or five other categories (for example: business strategy, finance, R&D, marketing, sourcing, customer service, and so on) to inquire into. Ask the following questions in each category. Move beyond interpretations to actual facts by digging into what people are saying:

- *What are the facts?*
- *What are the accomplishments?*
- *What's not worked? Or has worked?*
- *What's missing that, if it were provided, would make a critical difference?*
- *What are the opportunities given by the "what's so"?*

QUESTION 2. Where Are We Going? Set Breakthrough Goals and Priorities for Year

At this point, I tell the leader and his or her team, "We know what the Impossible Future we stand committed to is. And we have a much clearer idea about where we are now with respect to that as a result of the 'what's so.' The 'what's so' process has also revealed opportunities that we were not aware of. Now we are ready to set some key breakthrough goals and priorities that move us from where we are to where we want to be. The idea of a break-through goal is that it represents a spearhead for the Impossible Future. The goal should be *challenging* enough that it forces people to use their imagination and not be blindsided by orthodoxies and, at the same time, be *attainable*. It is very important to not only set yearly goals, but also a thirty-day action plan that tells people what to go to work on.

Where Are We Going?

- *State the Impossible Future—the vision or strategic intent.*
- *Identify three key mandates that will translate vision to a reality, for example: inspired organization, game growing ideas, business integration.*
- *Create a breakthrough goal for each category looked at in the "what's so." Ask each group to come back with a plan to make the mandate a reality in their own area.*
- *Make sure someone has the "A" or accountability for each goal.*
- *Paint a picture that reveals the conditions of satisfaction for reaching each goal.*
- *What will success look like? How will we measure it?*

QUESTION 3. What Is Missing That, if Provided, Would Make a Critical Difference?

Now that the leader and his or her group have looked at what's so and set some goals, the next step in the Strategic Planning in Action process is to identify what's missing that will make a difference. The idea is to ask: "What is missing that would allow this goal to be realized?" I tell coachees that what's missing is not always obvious. It's something that we have to create and discover together. I might say: "Let's paint a picture of the vision, and then create a *structure for fulfillment* that would allow us to realize the vision." For example, in order to realize the vision of innovation, what's missing might be a new customer interaction model that generates new good ideas, a website to back this up, a new reward and recognition system, and so forth.

> **What's Missing? Inquiry**
> - *Review the flip charts with all the "what's so" and goals, then brainstorm what's missing that, if provided, will allow you to reach those goals.*
> - *In most cases, what's missing is not obvious, like "more resources," but rather new ideas, fresh approaches, innovative solutions.*
> - *Condense the list of what's missing into the most high-leverage items.*
> - *Translate what's missing into small, breakthrough projects that have a beginning, middle, and an end.*
> - *Create a "structure for fulfillment" for the project to succeed.*
> - *Create a thirty-day action plan with specific accountabilities.*

STEP 5. Coach Leader Effectiveness Through Rigorous, Active, Monthly Follow-Up

The last step in the leadership coaching process involves working with leaders to achieve a quantum leap in effectiveness. This involves coaching them to stay centered in their stand for their Impossible Future and to take actions that will make it a reality rather than something that is swept along by other people, circumstances, and events. It also involves coaching people to align others in their goals and plans, as well as learning how to drive results over the line so that something is actually accomplished. As Peter Drucker[4] pointed out after fifty years of counseling executives, "I have not run across a single 'natural' leader who was born effective. Executives need to learn to be effective."

Four issues that lead leaders to be ineffective frequently come up in the coaching process:

1. Leaders' time is not their own—in other words, they have endless demands coming at them.
2. Unless leaders take a stand to change the reality in which they live and work and stay centered in making that happen, the flow of events tends to determine what they work on.
3. Leaders are only effective if people make the vision their vision.

4. Leaders exist within organizations, which can become their entire universe; they often don't see portents of change for their industry or deeply understand their customers' concerns.

It's my observation from coaching many leaders that they set ambitious aspirations, sail through the process of Strategic Planning in Action, and then start to drift. The role of a Masterful Coach is to intervene in this drift so that people focus on who they need to be as leaders to create the Impossible Future. It also means intervening so that people make their mandates and goals real through committed speaking, listening, and action. This involves getting people to make as many promises as possible and then rigorously following up so as to create a context wherein people expect to be held to account for their word.

A play-by-play process for this step might look like this:

- *At the beginning of the monthly coaching sessions, declare what your commitment in the meeting is. "I am here to support your commitment to being an extraordinary leader and to creating an extraordinary future that makes a difference for your organization." Then create a space for the coachee to discuss whatever is on his or her mind or anything the person would like to bring up in the session. Give yourself the space to do the same. This can lead to an hour or more of conversation on emerging issues and opportunities.*

- *Initiate a new conversation on how it is going with the coachee's leadership and business breakthrough. Start with discussing how it is going with the leadership breakthrough. This is done with the "what's so" process and takes about thirty minutes: "What's been accomplished with respect to your yearly leadership goals and key projects this month?" "What's working? What's not working? What's missing?" This often leads to new possibilities and openings for action.*

- *Next, look at how it is going with the business breakthrough and yearly goals overall, which is followed by a "what's so" process on what has taken place over the past month: "What's been accomplished with respect to your yearly business goal and key projects this month?" "What's working? What's not working? What's missing?" If you are stuck, look for new openings for action together.*

- *Follow with an investigation into goals, priorities, and key actions that the person agreed to take the previous month. I say to the coachee, "You promised to do this, this. and that? Did you do those things?" (Sometimes it may feel somewhat awkward to hold a leader accountable to his or her promises, but you need to look at it in terms of supporting and challenging the person to experience a breakthrough in personal effectiveness.) In the early part of the coaching engagement, the answer to those questions is often, "No. I didn't do it." I then ask, "Why not? Did you think it wouldn't make any difference." Again, the answer is often, "No, I think it would make a difference. But I don't like doing that kind of thing," or "I wasn't in the mood," or "I just didn't get around to it;"*

- *Then talk about standing in their commitment to an Impossible Future and honoring their word as themselves by delivering on promises. We distinguish this from standing in their commitment to being in their "comfort zone" and honoring their moods or preferences as themselves. Interestingly enough, we observe that many leaders don't do what they said they were going to do the following month, so we repeat the same kind of dialogue with them. By the third month, they fully expect to be held accountable for their word and begin to consistently deliver on their promises.*

It is very important in this process to *coach* people, *not manage* people. Says Veronica Pemberton, "I sometimes check in with people to remind them of their commitments and follow up on this to see whether it happened, but I never hover over people to make sure they do something, and I never act like a school teacher who wags her accusing finger at people who didn't do their homework. I want to create a context in the relationship where people expect to be held accountable for their word, but at the same time, I don't want to make them wrong, which can put them on the defensive and polarize the relationship. I always want to leave the ball in their court."

Follow Up and Follow On—A Brief Summary

- *Support the leader in declaring his or her commitment to take a big step forward in being an extraordinary leader who realizes an Impossible Future for the company.*
- *Briefly review progress on leader's leadership breakthrough, goals, projects; then briefly review business breakthrough, yearly goals, projects, and so forth.*
- *Do a "what's so" for the last thirty days. Accomplishments? What's working? What's not working? What's missing? What's next?*

- *Follow up—hold people to account for their word with respect to last month's thirty-day action plan. Make sure you are both complete with this.*
- *Create a thirty-day action plan for the next month that includes things that were dropped out from the previous month, but that are still meaningful.*

PART II

TRANSFORMING GROUPS

A Masterful Coach is someone who can not only transform an individual, but who can transform people in groups. Over the years, I have discovered that this is far more than a straightforward task. It is not just a matter of creating a shared vision, formulating a concrete plan, and giving feedback on the right set of behaviors. It is a matter of learning to recognize and disperse the subtle, but powerful, defensive routines of the group, which can provide a strong undercurrent that washes away everything else you are doing.

Chapter Six, "Reinventing the Organization," provides a five-step model—Masterful Coaching—The Method™—for leaders to use in coaching people in groups to produce both breakthroughs for people and breakthrough results. The Method follows these five steps: (1) Stand for Something—An Impossible Future, (2) Be Your Stand, (3) Create a Powerful Context, (4) Generate an Alignment of Wholes, and (5) Act from a Stand that the Individual Matters.

We will revisit Richard Severance, president of Conoco's North American Downstream operations, to see what he did to create an Impossible Future and transform the culture of his organization. There will be examples of other exemplary leaders who used the Masterful Coaching methodologies to transform their functional organizations or small groups.

Chapter Seven, "Building Shared Understanding," will focus on a fundamental skill needed to create a shared vision and make it a reality. Although many people in groups tend to think that this starts with a strategy session, it actually starts with the group developing the skill to transform unproductive conversations into a productive dialogue. This chapter takes into account that most managers tend to have strong egos and a need to be right and win. The result is that they tend to be passionate advocates of their own views, while not so passionate in inquiring into the views of others. This chapter will provide strategies for balancing advocacy and inquiry in groups. It will also show that breakthroughs are rarely the product of blind genius but rather the product of creative collaboration among groups that are made up of crazy combinations of people. You will learn five keys to mastering the art of creative collaboration.

Chapter Eight, "Recognizing and Dispersing Posturing and Defensiveness," shows that in order for a group to articulate and realize a shared vision, learning is essential. However, groups frequently enact what Chris Argyris of Harvard calls "organization defensive routines" that prevent learning. You will learn how to recognize and disperse organization defensive routines so that a group can begin to have really powerful, generative conversations.

Chapter Nine, "Go for Results Now!" addresses a key question: How do you take a big project that is bogged down in endless planning and preparations and get people into action so that it can be implemented? This chapter will show you how to spearhead a breakthrough in large projects by bypassing elaborate planning and preparations and going for a result now. It is based on the work of Robert Schaffer, as outlined in his book *The Breakthrough Strategy*. We have used the principles and techniques he offers in coaching numerous leaders and managers with great success to create their Impossible Futures.

CHAPTER SIX

REINVENTING THE ORGANIZATION

Being the Source of a New Future

Creating a new future doesn't just happen. It needs to be powerfully sourced.

In my experience, most CEOs and executives are experienced in the art of the deal, not in the art of creating organizations that stand out from the crowd. Instead of priding themselves on creating an extraordinary leadership culture, building competitive organizations, and grinding out results, they pride themselves on being heroes or hellions who pull off a multi-billion-dollar mega-merger or acquisition. It's a sad fact of life that most of these deals fail to bear fruit.

To me what distinguishes an *extraordinary* leader or manager from an *ordinary* one is the ability to realize an Impossible Future that people didn't dare to dream or even imagine. This starts with their setting unreasonable expectations, and involves reinventing both themselves and the organization. It is not that extraordinary leaders aren't also experts in the art of the deal; it is that they see this as part of a much larger process of transformation.

Jack Welch, the legendary former chairman of GE, is an excellent example of the kind of extraordinary leader I am talking about. Welch in his time presided over the mega acquisitions of RCA, NBC, and Honeywell and racked up an extraordinary record of financial results. Yet Welch, a tough competitor, defines himself not by his strategies, deals, or numbers, but by creating a culture of extraordinary leadership and a boundaryless organization. According to Welch, "By far my overriding passion is people." He says his biggest accomplishment was creating a "people factory."

Warren Buffet refers to Welch as the Butch Harmon (Tiger Woods' coach) of CEOs. Scott McNealy, CEO of Sun Microsystems, an impressive company in its own right, confesses to being an "unabashed Jack groupie" and to looking up to Welch as his coach and mentor. Companies like Allied Signal, 3M, and Home Depot regularly snap up GE executives mentored by Welch.

Yet when Welch became chairman of GE, he defined his Impossible Future as being "Number 1 or Number 2 in every GE business." Standing before the Wall Street analysts for the first time at New York's Pierre Hotel, he said that he wanted GE to become "the most competitive enterprise on earth." His objective was to put a small company spirit in a big company body, to build an organization out of an old-line industrial company that would be more high-spirited, more adaptable, and more agile than companies that were one-fifteenth GE's size.

It's a well-known fact in business circles that Jack Welch either reached his vision or came damn close. What's less well known is how much time Welch spent, almost 70 percent of his time, on what he called "my passion, which is people." As he puts it, "When all is said and done, what I do for a living is coach and teach people." What's also even less well known is that Welch had many coaches and mentors himself before and after getting into the chairman's job.

It started with his mother, who specialized in tough love or "kisses and kicks," and included many teachers and bosses. In Welch's own words, "It seemed like I found a coach and mentor in every school and every job I had," including Reg Jones, his predecessor, who one day came into Jack Welch's office, gave him a hug and said, "Hello, Mr. Chairman." His coaching and mentoring continued through GE's transformation.

GUIDING PRINCIPLES OF ORGANIZATION REINVENTION

In order to realize an Impossible Future, you need both personal and organizational reinvention. You can do a lot to further personal reinvention, but if you do not also reinvent the organization, people will tend to get caught up in organizational ways of being, thinking, and behavior that are counterproductive. Reinventing an organization holds certain risks for companies because it involves reinventing the things that have made both individuals and the companies successful in the past.

There are a few overall guideposts that we at Masterful Coaching use for coaching leaders in the process of organization reinvention.

GUIDING PRINCIPLE 1. The Person at the Top Must Make "Sourcing" an Impossible Future and the "Reinvention" the "Big Game"

An Impossible Future that represents the reinvention of an organization doesn't just happen; it needs a leader who can make it happen. The leader's role is to "source" the Impossible Future (an act of creation), not to be a manager who operates the status quo. The leader must be burning with intention to make the Impossible Future happen. Over a year, a minimum of 60 percent of the leader's time and attention needs to be spent in energizing the organization with regard to the transformation process. The coach supports the leader in being "at source," finding the path forward, and holding the course.

GUIDING PRINCIPLE 2. All Key Leaders of the Reinvention Must Reinvent Themselves with the Help of a Masterful Coach

Nothing happens without personal transformation.

The goals, Winning Strategies, and culture that exist in the organization are a direct reflection of the ways of being, orthodox thinking, and behavior of the leaders who are in place. Therefore, it is essential that all executives who will play a key role in the Impossible Future and the organization reinvention engage with executive coaches. The executive reinvention process is thereby the catalyst for the organization reinvention and vice versa, which accelerates the whole process. To involve a critical mass of leaders in the reinvention process at all levels, a team coaching process can be used. (Our approach is called *Action Coaching™.)*

GUIDING PRINCIPLE 3. Coaching the Reinvention Starts by Breaking the Grip and Excelling Beyond Organization Winning Strategies

The organization reinvention mirrors in many ways the personal reinvention process. For example, company leaders are asked to look at "who the organization is today" in light of new possibilities and the opportunity spaces that are emerging in the business environment, rather than just looking at "what have we done in the past." The company's Winning Strategies are examined and questioned, including the business model, cultural norms, and the unwritten rules that govern people's behavior.

GUIDING PRINCIPLE 4. Leaders of the Reinvention Must Not Only Communicate About the Impossible Future, but Must Act from It

The CEO and direct reports need to be coached to stand in the Impossible Future and communicate from that future, as well as to act in the present to make it a reality. They must see that they have the opportunity to play the "Big Game" every time they speak and listen. This starts with generating a new conversation that alters the context and becomes the vision, climate, and spirit of the company. Action is defined as engaging in conversations designed to bring the reinvention about, not merely engaging in a "go do" loop to produce a result. This includes designing high-leverage projects, as well as making powerful promises and requests.

GUIDING PRINCIPLE 5. Leaders Foster Powerful and Effective Action by Continually Looking at What's Happened, What's Missing, and What's Next

When breakdowns occur, look for what's missing rather than who is wrong.

Creating an Impossible Future requires a clearly articulated vision, a well-thought-out structure for fulfillment, and effective and powerful action. This involves coaching people to investigate what needs to be reinvented to achieve the vision (for example, the purpose, the processes, the culture, the people) and then inquiring into what's missing (that's essential) that needs to be produced. This provides an opening for powerful and effective action. The coach also helps people to understand that when people are going for a breakthrough, breakdowns happen. They don't allow people to indulge themselves in "Who is right?" and "Who is wrong?" This line of thinking doesn't move anything forward. Rather than allow people to indulge in these interpretations, a Masterful Coach asks: What happened? What's missing? and What's next?

MASTERFUL COACHING—THE METHOD™ FOR ORGANIZATIONAL REINVENTION

In addition to the guiding principles, I have developed a five-step model for coaching leaders to reinvent their organizations (Diagram 6.1). Masterful Coaches follow the model step by step to help ordinary managers become extraordinary managers.

DIAGRAM 6.1 *Masterful Coaching—The Method™ for reinventing organizations*

1. **Stand for Something—an Impossible Future**

2. **Be Your Stand: "It Starts with Me"**

3. **Create a Powerful Context**

4. **Generate an Alignment of Wholes**

5. **Act from a Stand That the Individual Matters**

COACHING STEP 1. Stand for Something—An Impossible Future

Human beings are often thrown into a world with a prevailing set of conditions that diminish the human spirit. In the political or social or economic sphere, these conditions might be hunger, poverty, or persecution. In the sphere of the business and organizations, it might be autocratic leadership, paralyzing bureaucracy, a worn-out, burned-out business model, or one that provides little opportunity for personal (or business) growth.

In the normal course of events, most people bury the fact that they passionately care about these things and resign themselves to their future being a continuation of the same old story. They say something like, "Things shouldn't be this way, but I can't make any difference in the situation, so why bother?" In effect, what they do is submit to the agony of defeat and take themselves out of the game of making the impossible happen. There is nothing left to do but wait for retirement.

Masterful Coaches inspire people to take a stand that a difference can be made, from themselves, out of nothing, and in the absence of proof.

What people then do is to develop a Winning Strategy to compensate for what they believe is not possible and accommodate themselves to their resignation. This usually involves withdrawing to some safe territory where they can keep their heads down and shoulders back. Even efforts to make a contribution become an accommodation of their resignation. In organizations there is often an all-pervasive climate of profound resignation that restrains the human spirit. The following are some examples of Winning Strategies that are often used to compensate for the resignation people experience.

- *I would like to be an executive in another field, but I am stuck in this job with a pair of golden handcuffs. I will just have to "settle" and make the best of it.*

- *I can't deal with the CEO or the corporate culture. I am going to focus on my business unit, where I have control.*

- *We can't grow because we are in a commodity business in a mature industry. We need to focus on squeezing more juice from the lemon—cut costs!*

- *I will set some reasonable "stretch goals" that don't require fundamentally questioning the strategy of the executive management team.*

- *Coaching my direct reports would be a major project, and I can't fire them, so I put up with them or make some gestures to develop them.*

One of the most powerful things a Masterful Coach can do to transform an organization is simply to acknowledge this climate of profound resignation, which has the possibility of motivating company leaders to recognize and do something about it. Another thing a Masterful Coach can do is to inspire leaders to reach beyond their Winning Strategies and dare to take a stand that a difference can be made. This is the first step in transforming a climate of resignation into a climate of possibility, and thereby unleashing the human spirit into action.

Only by taking a stand can leaders realize an Impossible Future or give birth to a new culture.

The Principle of Taking a Stand

Taking a stand is a declaration of commitment to call something forth, for example, an Impossible Future that most people cannot or would not dare to dream or even imagine. It is a declaration that is made without evidence or proof. There is no need to justify taking a stand to make a difference and no surefire prescriptions to follow in making it happen. There is a commitment to make bold promises and to take action so as to fulfill them. For without action, the possibility you have declared will never become a reality.

Your role as a Masterful Coach is to inspire people to unearth what they passionately care about, so they can begin to formulate that into a vision. It is also to empower people to stand in an inspired place rather than a resigned place. And it is to enable people to generate exciting new possibilities that are powerful enough to transform their organization and that they dare to take a stand for.

The key is to encourage people to pay attention to what they can declare as possible, rather than what is predictable based on industry averages, present circumstances, or past experience. To do this, people must step into the reinvention paradigm. This starts with three very powerful declarations:

1. I declare that what is possible is what I say is possible.
2. I declare who I am is the stand that I take.
3. The specific stand that I take is. . . .

The following are some examples of stands that people might take.

The Stand That I Take Is. . .

- *To be true to myself and what I passionately want my work to be.*
- *To transform the organization from a culture of resignation to a culture of opportunity.*
- *To be the future of our industry—catching the wave of the next technology rather than being blindsided by change.*
- *To grow our business by 150 percent in three years and increase earnings 15 percent a year.*
- *To stretch our definition of our business and ourselves to reach our goals.*
- *To provide a great customer experience every time.*
- *To coach the people in my group to reach the next level of effectiveness.*

Taking a stand is about making your world match your word, rather than your word match your world.

Coaching leaders to take a stand starts with engaging them in questions and being a committed listener who draws them out. Some people may come to these answers quickly, but my experience is that people do not give themselves the opportunity to even think in this way very often, and it may take having several conversations over a period of time for them to awaken the inspiration and imagination to create an Impossible Future that they want to stand for.

Coaching Questions That Stimulate People to Take a Stand for an Impossible Future:

- *What do you passionately care about? What really matters to you as a human being, leader, and manager?*

- *Have you gained some idea of the Impossible Future you want to create? Take your best shot at a vision. Are you ready to stand for that?*

- *What specific opportunities do you have in front of you for making a difference, which the timing is right for, if only you dared to take a stand?*

- *What's the "big game" that you want to play beyond what's predictable or business as usual? Are you ready to toss your hat into the ring?*

- *What would be worth accomplishing so much that it requires reinventing your entire self?*

Taking a Stand for an Inspired Organization

I have written about two executives at Conoco, Jim Nokes and Richard Severance. One of the executives on both of their teams was a bright, fast-track manager named Carin Knickel. About the time that I was working with Nokes and Severance, Knickel called me and asked me if I would be interested in coaching her. She told me she was a person who had a huge commitment to personal growth and learning. I responded by saying, "But if you want a coach, you need a game. What's the Impossible Future you're standing for? If you want me to coach you, it has to be a really big game, one that you are really passionate about. What's the big game you want to play?" Knickel was a bit stumped.

Knickel called me back a few days later and said, "I want to create a *totally* inspired organization," in the service of her business unit's goals around the Impossible Future. I thought this was pretty amazing, given that she was working in a one-hundred-year-old energy company, which tended to be higher on the resignation side than the inspiration side.

Knickel also said she was taking a stand as a leader "to be a Masterful Coach who brings out the best in people." She also committed herself to make a qualitative contribution to creating a "coaching context" that would produce extraordinary leaders and deliver unprecedented results. She then went to work on making her commitment real through action—co-designing with me a new coaching program for herself and her business unit (team) called Action Coaching™.

Her inspiration inspired many leaders in the company and hundreds of people to clamor to become involved in this yearlong Action Coaching program. This wasn't one of those big corporate rollout affairs from on high, but rather came about naturally as a result of people feeling the excitement about what the program promised and the results it started to produce.

Knickel not only dramatically improved her leadership and coaching skills, but also became a rallying point for herself and other leaders to create a context of leadership and coaching throughout the entire organization. The program was based on setting breakthrough business and leadership goals that would really make a difference and then coaching people to achieve them over the course of a year (not in three days in the corporate "sheep dip"). This program had a significant impact on transforming the culture from one of resignation to one of inspiration and opportunity.

The following year her job changed to being vice president of Conoco Cevolution, an organization that had come up with a breakthrough carbon fiber technology. I asked her, "Now what's your game?" Her response: "I am still totally committed to creating an inspired organization. I am still totally committed to becoming a Masterful Coach, and now I am going to take a stand for leading a revolution in the materials industry." She is well on her way to doing it, and by God, nothing is going to stop her.

COACHING STEP 2. Be Your Stand: "It Starts with Me"

Taking a stand is usually understood on the surface as what happens when an individual sees an opportunity to make a difference and declares a powerful commitment to act in a way that matters. On a deeper level, taking a stand is a powerful act of transformation. The transformation comes about as a result of an *ontological system* where their stand (or commitment) becomes the context for who they are and their speaking and listening and actions. This is different from the *psychological system,* where people's past is the context of who they are—the basis for understanding cause and effect.

Taking a stand is a defining moment that can transform people and the world in which they live and work.

Let me explain how this works in a coaching context. As people take a stand for an Impossible Future they can passionately engage in, it naturally leads to designing a "big game." This game becomes the context for who they are and everything that they do. As they play the "big game," they begin to increasingly draw their identity based on their commitment rather than the identity they built up around their Winning Strategy. They begin to relate to themselves, not just as the CEO, VP, or manager (that is, their position), but also more importantly as the Impossible Future and reinvention process.

Soon other people begin to see them not just as the person at the top, but also as this Impossible Future. Their stand shows up in who they are and in everything they do. It shows up in speaking from their commitment to bring out the best in others as opposed to speaking from their reactions. It shows up as listening from their commitment for what's missing that will make a difference rather than listening for what's wrong. It also shows up in their daily actions—making powerful promises and requests and rigorously following up rather than letting things slide. In so doing, they begin to set the tone for everyone else in the organization to show up differently too.

Extraordinary leadership is simply the result of ordinary people taking a stand for something currently impossible in their reality and then acting to make it happen.

Martin Heidegger says that who you are as a leader creates a "clearing," an opening in the forest that shapes the way others will show up around you. You can be a clearing for people to show up as daring and bold leaders, reinventing the organization, or a clearing for showing up as predictable managers trying to fix the organization and improve on the probable.

When you are being your stand for an Impossible Future, you create a clearing for what you are standing for. When you are being your commitment to stand in an inspired place as a leader rather than a resigned place, you create a clearing for others to move beyond resignation and show up as inspiring leaders. When you passionately speak your commitment to a vision of an extraordinary organization, it creates a clearing for others to speak their commitment to a vision of an inspired organization. When you listen from your commitment to produce what's missing to create an inspired organization, you create a clearing for others to do the same

> *When you are being your stand, you create a new clearing in the culture for the Impossible Future you are standing for to come to pass.*

Taking a Stand Creates a Clearing for What You Want to Show Up

In Heidegger's terms, leaders are often remembered for the new clearings they create in the culture as a result of being their stands. For example, Jack Welch created a clearing for GE to create an extraordinary leadership culture with a boundaryless organization, driven by competitive zeal. He was able to do this because he was the personification of daring and bold leadership, boundaryless behavior, and unrelenting competitiveness. As Welch says, "The person at the top sets the tone." Your level of commitment to the vision becomes other people's level of commitment. Your own level of enthusiasm and energy becomes everyone else's level of energy. Your level of creativity and drive is emulated by everyone else.

It's my experience with Masterful Coaching that few executives really stand for something; even fewer know what it really means to *be* their stand. I tell executives that although *being your stand* may sound like jargon, it is actually much more familiar to us than we might think. It simply means "being our word" rather than our automatic self, moods, and preferences. We have all had an experience of speaking, listening, and acting from *being* a body of commitments rather than from being our automatic self, moods, or preferences.

To make this real for people, I use some practical, down-to-earth, everyday examples that people can relate to. For example, we all know the difference between being our stand to eat a healthy diet and exercise five times a week, and waking up in the morning and being our reasons and excuses. We all know the difference between being our stand to speaking to our children out of a commitment to be a good parent and role model and lecturing, brow beating, and controlling. Similarly, we all know the difference between being our stand to devote our time and attention to the reinvention and getting sucked into the incredible number of demands coming at us.

Return people to their stand when they are in reaction by asking them to take a deep breath and press the reset button.

Another way to help people master this distinction is to ask them, "Who are you being when you are not being your stand?" In most cases, people will realize that they are being their automatic self, their Winning Strategy, and their thrown attitudes and behaviors. There can sometimes be a fine line between being an inspired visionary who takes a stand for a leadership and business breakthrough and a manager who makes others fear him or her. Part of a coach's role is to tear the blinders off and allow people to see when they have crossed over that line. It is also the coach's role to point out that, while being your automatic self is just that—"automatic"—being your stand takes coaching, study, and practice.

To review, once you have coached executives to take a stand for an Impossible Future and the reinvention, the next step is to coach them to *be their stand*. This starts with asking them, "Who do you need to be in the matter?" Answering this question becomes the basis for creating a leadership development plan. This consists of picking one or two leadership breakthrough projects to work on for the next year. Then, have monthly conversations to assess how they are doing in terms of their leadership breakthrough. Ask: What happened? What's missing? What's next? (Diagram 6.2).

DIAGRAM 6.2 *Forwarding powerful and effective action*

COACHING STEP 3. Create a Powerful Context

Ordinary leaders think in terms of creating a vision of the future, yet often fail to create a context that will allow the vision to become a reality. Extraordinary leaders think in terms of creating a context that will become the vision, climate, and spirit of the company. The context is the environment that shapes, limits, and defines who people are being in the company. It defines what people see as possible and achievable and even what they see. It determines the way strategy is developed and the way goals are set. It determines how planning is done, decisions are made, and actions are taken.

Coaching executives to create an Impossible Future often involves creating a shift in context that alters the content of the organization. If you think of context as a bowl, what's inside the bowl is the content (Diagram 6.3). The surest way to change the content is not by putting in new content, but to change the context (the bowl) that ultimately shapes the content that is there. When you shift the context, you automatically begin to alter the content. For example, if you want to create innovation in an organization, you need to create a context for innovation. If you want high performance, you need to create a context for high performance. If you want leadership and coaching, you need to create a context for this.

DIAGRAM 6.3 *The context is the bowl; the content is what's in the bowl*

Malcolm Gladwell has written in his book *The Tipping Point* that human beings are not just sensitive to changes in context, but they are exquisitely sensitive to changes in context.[1] His research into how our social epidemics spread has shown that creating a shift in context follows certain key principles that any Masterful Coach and leader can powerfully and directly apply.

Masterful Coaches inspire people to see that their organization is the context they create for it.

Shifting Organizational Context

First, the shift in context must have someone who is the source of that change. Second, a shift in context comes from a big idea that generates a new conversation, and thereby alters the old conversation. Third, a shift in context comes about as a result of small, focused actions that make a big difference. Finally, a shift in context does not happen gradually, but in one dramatic moment—a shift in corporate culture can come on a few years rather than over decades. The "tipping point" is the moment of the critical mass, the threshold, the boiling point, where the context shifts and the content along with it.

To use a simple example, in the 1960s, Martin Luther King, Jr., and others took a stand for the idea of civil rights—that all people are equal under the law. The idea was big and contagious and was spread by opinion shapers and movers such as Ralph Abernathy, Robert F. Kennedy, Lyndon Johnson, and others. The focus for a while was to change the context through civil rights demonstrations. The civil rights movement reached the tipping point, however, in one dramatic moment when Rosa Parks, a black woman in Montgomery, Alabama, refused to move to the back of the bus.

You bring a company culture to the tipping point with a passionate few, a teachable point of view, and focused initiatives.

Create a "Sourcing Document" That Generates a New Conversation

In coaching executives, I often spend several days with them on creating a shift in context. I tell them that a shift in context doesn't just happen, it has to be powerfully sourced, and they need to see themselves as 100 percent responsible for making this happen. I then work with them on creating a "sourcing document" or reinvention manifesto. This includes their stand for the Impossible Future, who they need to be in the matter, their teachable point of view (guiding principles), as well as small, high-leverage focused initiatives they can champion to make sure the organization reaches the tipping point.

This sourcing document has three purposes: (1) It provides the executive with the necessary "sourcing material" to generate a new conversation in the organization, and break the grip of the old one; (2) It provides a way for other leaders in different parts of the organization to keep the conversation going; and (3) As conversations disappear, it ensures that sourcing material doesn't get lost. Leaders involved in the reinvention are asked to read the sourcing at a minimum weekly.

In coaching Jim Nokes of Conoco to create a context, I started by asking him to define an ambitious aspiration for himself and his organization—a clear, power goal that represented "true north."[2] This led to him declaring his stand for "creating the greatest downstream business in the world" a vision that captured people's imagination. The next step he took was to put a stake in the ground by making a commitment to a billion dollars in earnings (triple the earnings at the time). The idea was not just to please Wall Street, but to create a pull for a kind of cultural transformation in the company—one that would transform a hard-to-turn supertanker into a cigarette boat.

He asked each of his direct reports to define a big "new" game for their organizations—one based on being a rule breaker and maker, not rule follower. Each business unit of the company was to play in each of the following three arenas: (1) *Being game changers* who come up with innovative business concepts that could revolutionize the industry; (2) *Being game growers* who find ways to grow the business by getting a greater share of wallet from new customers or existing customers; and (3) *Being game players* who run a tight ship through continuous improvement. The only game the company was playing at the time Nokes took this stand was that of being a game player.

*Coach people to develop a teachable point of view that will create a
mindset that allows for and pulls for the vision.*

Articulate a Teachable Point of View That Alters People's Perceptions

I also talked to Jim Nokes about not only being clear about his leadership
mission, but his teachable point of view (TPOV). This is a powerful tool for
generating a new conversation that becomes the vision, climate, and spirit of
the company and for breaking the grip of the old conversation. I pointed out
that when leaders powerfully articulate a teachable point of view they directly
intervene in the organization context so as to alter how people are being,
their thinking, and behavior across the board.

I often use examples to make the point. Roberto Goizueta, when chairman of Coca-Cola, created a new context to help reach his goal of growth:
"Think share of stomach versus share of market." The enemy was not Pepsi,
but coffee and tea. Andy Grove created a new context at the highly successful
Intel to not become complacent when he said, "Only the paranoid survive."
Jack Welch created a new context at GE with a teachable point of view based
on "boundaryless behavior."

It is important to not only coach leaders to develop a powerful teachable
point of view that can alter people's perspective, but to also couch it in language that people can't get out of their heads. Slight changes in phrasing or
presentation can give an idea what in advertising is known as "stickiness." For
example, remember Wendy's famous tagline "Where's the beef?" Goizueta's
TPOV, "Share of stomach," became one of those ideas at Coca-Cola. In the
same sense, "The boundaryless organization" had the same sticky quality at
GE and fueled both the transformation of the corporate culture, as well as
international initiatives.

At Conoco, Nokes wanted a teachable point of view with bite. He trans-
lated this into a set of six global ground rules. One of the main ideas behind
Nokes taking a stand for such an ambitious future was to generate a new conversation around creativity, innovation, and risk. He liked to say, "It's business
concept innovation *and* incremental improvement—not either/or but
both/and." Previously, if you asked someone in the company to be creative
and innovative, he or she would have responded not by creating a new business, but by being innovative within the context of running the business and
incremental improvement. Now they could spread their wings and fly.

It is also not only important for the person at the top to have a powerful

TPOV, but to communicate it with commitment, passion, and zeal. It takes one person to generate the conversation, but inevitably it requires the assistance of others. Gladwell calls this the "law of the few."[3] You need people with the personality, enthusiasm, and connections to spread the word. The idea is to "get the sourcing over the line," in other words, so that it exists in the minds and hearts of the average worker, independent of the originator.

Diagram 6.4 shows some examples of teachable points of view that create something new as opposed to prevailing points of view.

DIAGRAM 6.4 *Examples of teachable points of view*

New	Prevailing
• *Be a generative leader who creates what never existed before*	• *Be a predictable manager who improves what already exists*
• *Strategy is revolution, the rest is tactics*	• *Use strategy to compete heads up with the competition on price*
• *Collaborate across boundaries to achieve the impossible*	• *Maintain a functional organization*
• *Be fanatical about quality*	• *Of course, we believe in quality products*
• *Someone somewhere has a better idea*	• *We know what we're talking about; we have twenty years' experience*

Create One or More Powerful Initiatives to Ground the New Context in Action

Along with a vision of what is possible, clear goals that represent "true north," and a teachable point of view, designing an organization context usually involves four to five powerful initiatives that provide the leader a practical and immediate legacy. This is a way to make the vision a reality and to put it on everyone's monthly, weekly, and daily agenda.

As you will recall earlier, Malcolm Gladwell said there were three to four key factors to creating a new social epidemic or context. You need: (1) a big sticky idea that people can't get out of their heads; (2) a few people with the personality, enthusiasm, and energy to act as a contagion and spread the idea; and (3) small, high-leverage actions that can make a big difference. Let's focus here on the last point as a means of bringing something to the tipping point.

Gladwell uses the example of street crime in New York City subways. In the early 1990s, there were thousands of "fare jumpers" a day who didn't pay, the subways were covered with graffiti, and muggings as well as murders were common.[4] The situation came to the attention of the national press when Bernard Goetz shot four would-be assailants in the subway, because one of group snickered, asking him for $5.

A new subway police chief, William Bratton, was brought in. During the first week, Bratton entered the subway to see the turnstiles jammed and a derelict holding the slam-gate open, taking tokens from passengers. Bratton said, "What the hell," and gave him his token. Another derelict was sucking a token out of the jammed turnstile with his mouth and tongue.

Bratton decided to create a shift in context by launching two initiatives. The first was to clean up the graffiti, train by train. The second was to place plainclothes police people in the subway stations who would immediately arrest fare jumpers and hold them handcuffed on a platform in a daisy chain. Bratton said that these two issues—graffiti on the subways and fare jumpers—created a context that attracted more serious crimes. Everyone told Bratton he should take a stand against muggings and other violent crimes, but he remained steadfast in his views. Bratton was proven right, when less than a year after launching the initiatives, subway crime declined dramatically—almost to nil.

In coaching executives to create a shift in context for their organizations, this is a very useful example. The point to get across is that you don't have to change everything; you just have to launch a few focused initiatives that make a difference. I worked with Nokes to design some initiatives for his global downstream organization.[5] This is a rough list of what that looked like:

- *A commitment was made to have high-impact players in every key leadership job, primarily through coaching people on significant leadership and business challenges.*

- *Each business unit leader was expected to play all three games—game grower, game changer, and game player.*

- *An Innovation Collablab™ was held that served as an incubator for both transformational and incremental innovation—ideas with bottom-line impact.*

- *Six Sigma as a way to achieve real improvement and lower costs was implemented across the company with $180 million in cost savings.*

Earlier I gave an example of how I coached Richard Severance of Conoco to empower him to transform the climate of resignation in his part of the company to a climate of opportunity.[6] Together with Severance, we created four powerful initiatives with the idea of engaging the hearts and minds of the average person. The first involved creating extraordinary leaders (as opposed to command-and-control managers) that were Masterful Coaches. An ABCD performance management model was also introduced—not just a high leadership standard to aspire to but also designed to weed out old school autocratic managers who diminished people and suppressed new, good ideas.

Then to create a climate of opportunity where the average person could make a difference, we implemented two other initiatives: a business incubator, which was intended to spawn innovative business ideas, and a Six Sigma deployment model to provide people in most of the major sectors of his organization an opportunity to make a contribution through a project-oriented, process-improvement approach that produced extraordinary financial results.

The combination of Severance's vision of the Impossible Future, the transformed leadership paradigm that replaced command and control with empowerment, together with the opening for new business ideas and Six Sigma, had a significant impact in bringing the organization to the tipping point and creating a shift in context. The climate of resignation was soon transformed into a climate of opportunity.

COACHING STEP 4. Generate an Alignment of Wholes

The next coaching step has to do with the CEO (person at the top) aligning the entire organization around the vision and teachable point of view and initiatives that have been set up. Nine times out of ten, what happens is that the CEO begins a huge rollout program to all the minions of the organization, in all the far-flung corners of the world.

While this approach has some merit, it is insufficient. The CEO's message may be inspiring, but is often drowned out by conflicting messages sent by local leaders who are pursuing their own agendas. There is also quite often a tendency to cherry pick the ideas people like from the change agenda.

Another more powerful approach is what I call an "alignment of wholes." The CEO "sources" leaders at every level to re-create the Impossible Future and reinvention process in their respective organizations, while leaving some room for translation and adaptation. The notion behind it is, if you look into one of the parts of the organization, you see the whole.

The approach I coach leaders to use is quite the opposite from having the CEO jump on the corporate plane and roll out the new vision and values statement in hopes that it will stick. It involves bringing the top one hundred or so leaders together and spreading the gospel, but also impressing on them their role in this process. "My job is to source this vision into the organization, and your job is to re-create the sourcing in your organization. I am speaking about the vision, teachable point of view, and initiatives we have undertaken."

This is where the sourcing document provides these top dozen to hundred or so leaders a very powerful tool in terms of inspiring, empowering, and enabling them to re-create the context. I coach executives to ask their direct reports and others to read this sourcing document or "reinvention manifesto" at a minimum of once a week.

Each leader of the reinvention returns to his or her team and creates a version of the sourcing document. It includes all of the things that the original sourcing document had in it, plus those things that the local leader and the team want to put in it to make it their own. For example, "We see our role in making the Impossible Future of the company a reality to be. . . . We promise to re-create the teachable point of view of . . . with every breath we take. And we promise to elicit people's commitment to participation in the reinvention initiatives."

To ensure that this happens, I coach executives to give each group three mandates for the year. For example:

"Dear Business Unit Manager. This year I am asking every group in the company to achieve something that represents a quantum leap with respect to (1) innovation, (2) Six Sigma, and (3) Masterful Coaching. I intend to follow up on what you are doing with each of these mandates in the near future."

The purpose of the follow-up is not just to stay in alignment and coach people on following through with their promises, but also to generously recognize and reward people for their contributions in sourcing the Impossible Future. Jack Welch of GE was famous for sending handwritten notes that both challenged people to "step up" and also acknowledged them.

COACHING STEP 5. Act from a Stand That the Individual Matters

In the normal course of events, people at various levels of an organization or society know what the issues are that need to be addressed to move the company to the next level. Yet they often have the attitude of, "What can I do, given the leaders who are in place or difficult facts or circumstances we are in?" Another common attitude is, "I am just a small potato." As a result, the average person often defers any responsibility for change to someone or something beyond him- or herself. If leaders at higher levels collude with this behavior, there is little hope of transforming the organization.

Thus it is essential to coach executives to take a stand to treat each and every individual as absolutely essential for the realization of the Impossible Future, and to act from that stand. Think in terms of transforming the organization, one person at a time, and see yourself as 100 percent responsible for bringing this to pass, even when people are a pain in the neck.

Let's say you are coaching someone who says he gets along great with the CEO and the people at the "coal face," but that his direct reports just don't "get it" with respect to the vision and are a nuisance, questioning everything about the reinvention process at every staff meeting. He implies: "These people are jerks." Instead of agreeing with the person that the direct reports are a bunch of jerks or for that matter disagreeing with him, try this, "You know what? I think you are not being your stand with your direct reports, which is to transform the organization by seeing the greatness in each person. If your listening for them was that 'You are the greatest, the most brilliant, the most committed,' they might show up entirely differently. In fact, I can guarantee, as your coach, that if you were on board for these people, they might really produce some miracles."

Look for teachable moments to establish that every person can make a difference, and that everyone must try.

Leaders set a context by respecting the dignity of each person and having a teachable point of view that everyone can make a difference regardless of level in the company. The idea is to inspire and empower managers, individual contributors, executive assistants, and secretaries to step up and play a bigger game that will give them a greater experience of themselves.

For example, Jim Nokes' executive assistant, Josette George, became one of the most powerful change agents in initiating the Conoco transformation through orchestrating three context-setting gatherings for the top one-hundred leaders and a CollabLab on creating a culture of innovation, as well as providing coaching and support for the executives with whom she frequently interacts. She doesn't wait for someone to tell her to do something to make a difference: "I always come from the principle that whose job it is to make a difference is the person who has the opportunity." When she sees an opportunity, she jumps into action without being told or asking permission.

In addition to setting a context with your teachable point of view, challenge and support people to break the grip of cynicism and see the opportunities they have to make a contribution, whatever their level in the organization is. You can do this by making powerful promises and requests of people that require them to take action they would never otherwise take. Consider how, for example, John Nelson, a CEO I coached at the Norton Company, started a transformational leadership program.

One day Nelson saw a manager named Joe on the elevator and asked how the leadership initiative was going in his organization. Joe said that people were really taking the lead in his organization, but that there was no one taking the lead in the relationship between his organization and the next one. As they got off the elevator, Nelson said, "Why don't you take the lead on that, Joe?" Nelson later shared with me that he could tell from the look in Joe's eyes that it would never have occurred to him to take the lead in that situation. Yet that's just what Joe did and it had a significant impact on the level of collaboration in the organization.

Instead of letting people off the hook with a resigned, "What can I do?," coach people to answer a question with a provocative question: "What *can* you do? What can you do with your existing authority and resources?" One of the things that is important to recognize here is that everyone wants to make a difference; they just don't see the opportunity. You can give them that opportunity by launching initiatives that capture the organization's imagination, whether Masterful Coaching, a business concept incubator, Six Sigma, or making the shift from products to services.

CHAPTER SEVEN

BUILDING SHARED UNDERSTANDING

Mastering the Art of Creative Collaboration

Why is it that the individual IQs of the group members average 130, while the collective IQ is about 13 as evidenced by the quality of their dialogue?

Why is it that the annual round of strategic planning sessions hardly ever creates the opportunity for people to fundamentally question the strategy?

Why is it that so many people in cross-functional groups cancel out people from other areas, even though everyone is sincerely committed to cooperation?

Why do we criticize others before we even try to understand them? Speak instead of listen?

We have seen what it takes for a Masterful Coach to inspire an individual to invent an Impossible Future, to impact the person's thinking and begin the process of organization reinvention. Yet to realize an Impossible Future, a Masterful Coach must also impact how people in groups think and interact together, if the reinvention is to work. This involves coaching people to be able to engage in a real quality of dialogue that builds shared understanding that perhaps leads to something new. It also requires creating forums for strategic conversations to take place that go far beyond the yearly planning and budgeting session. Yet herein lies the rub.

Let's imagine a typical monthly meeting of the executive group in your company. First, imagine that the person at the top has made a really arbitrary decision that has "ticked off" people and has created an undertone of cynicism amongst participants. Second, it's a meeting with the same five people who have met for the last three years. It is inevitably the same old conversation, rarely a new conversation with fresh insights. Third, the people in the room are the authors of the current strategy or business processes so there is rarely an opportunity to question the strategy. "It's the same old planning and budgeting session as last year."

Or consider another major issue in building shared understanding around emerging issues or opportunities: Every member of the group suffers from "the smartest man in the room" syndrome, which means they are used to dominating the conversation. Each tends to be a very passionate *advocate* of his or her own opinions, but very poor at *inquiring* into others' views or questioning what they themselves take for granted. At the same time, hot issues that could lead to open conflict are covered up with a kind of superficial congeniality and made undiscussable. People suffer at every meeting they go to. They can't even talk about it. They just put up with it, while asking under their breath, "Why do I have to spend all this time in meetings?"

Their Winning Strategy is to "be smart, be right, and win." They are unaware of how they listen for what's wrong in what others are saying, as well as how their own paradigm paralysis leads to individual or collective illusions. Further, they are unaware that they are unaware.

Coaching people to drop the "smartest man in the room syndrome" and to be collaborative creates a clearing for dialogue.

Let me cite my own example. As leadership development trainer in my earlier career, I was used to standing up in front of a room and having all the answers, and so I tended to dominate the conversation with what seemed to me like the simple and obvious answers. Later, as I became involved in executive coaching, the issues I took on became more complex and I realized that, in many of the business situations people faced, there were no easy or obvious answers.

As necessity is the mother of invention, I discovered that the key to coming up with a brilliant solution was to drop the smartest man in the room syndrome and become a collaborative person. I naturally reached out to others as "thinking partners," taking on an attitude of curiosity and learning. I quickly discovered by gathering thinking partners that two heads were better than one, and that more than three or four heads were often even better.

It became evident that the key to brilliance lay in gathering different views and perspectives until my understanding became broader and deeper and I was led to a moment of true insight. If people could build shared understanding in groups, it would often lead to surprising, thrilling, breakthrough solutions.

COACHING GROUPS TO TRANSFORM HOW THEY THINK AND WORK TOGETHER

How does this apply to coaching people in groups? First of all, at least one of the leaders has to take a stand to transform how the group thinks and interacts together. Second, the person must see again that, if you want to reinvent the organization, you have to reinvent yourself first. Again, the executive(s) has to put aside the smartest man in the room syndrome and take a stand to be a collaborative person.

This can start with some declarations, for example, "I am committed to the possibility of being a collaborative person who sees other people's truth as one valid point of view, rather than the enemy. I am committed to giving up always needing to prove that I am right and to always having all the answers."

Third, altering how a group thinks and interacts involves coaching people to hold a different type of meeting where people discuss not just the "what" of the conversation, but the "how." Throw out some simple, but thought-provoking questions like: "What's your experience of sitting in a typical meeting with this group?" "What works about our conversations with each other? What doesn't work?" "What's missing?" Coach people to transform combative conversations into a productive dialogue.

Fourth, it is important to coach people to create some new models of conversation that are more effective than their old ones. For example, physicist David Bohm wrote that there is a difference between discussion and dialogue.[1] In a discussion, people's intention is to advocate their own views and beat down others' views, which often leads to an incoherent conversation.

Encourage Dialogue Rather Than Discussion

In a dialogue, the intention is to gather divergent views and perspectives so as to build shared understanding (or construct a shared mental model), which perhaps leads to something new. Bohm described a dialogue as a "free flow" of meaning in the group, whereby people give their opinions, but at the same time they are willing to be influenced by others. He believed that dialogue should not even be limited by a topic.

In coaching generative leaders and teams that are "up to something" to engage in powerful conversations, I introduce the difference between dialogue and discussion. Building on this, I also introduce a new model called a "collaborative conversation." A collaborative conversation has the spirit of a dialogue in that it brings together divergent views and perspectives in a free and open exchange, yet it is much more focused. It is not just a process of building shared understanding, but also a process of shared creation. Its purpose is to (1) reach a goal; (2) solve a problem; or (3) discover something new.

You can help people to understand this by distinguishing the difference between a *cook alone* and a *cook together* school of conversation. In the *cook alone* or *potluck* model of conversation, the idea is that you bring your ideas and opinions to the table and I bring mine—take it or leave it. In this potluck model of conversation, all you get is a lot of different dishes that contain people's finished opinions and assumptions.

In the *cook together* model of conversation, people bring their different views and backgrounds along with all the ingredients of their thinking and enter into a shared creative process. Instead of serving up finished products, people take their raw ideas, cook them together with others' thoughts, question the reasoning process, and perhaps come to a new idea or insight.

You can also coach people in groups to expand their ability to think and work together by distinguishing the different evolutionary stages of a collaborative conversation. You can move people to a higher level of conversation by first helping them to be aware of what stage of conversation they are in and asking them to take more risk in speaking with more authenticity and vulnerability and to empty themselves of biases toward other people or views.

Stages in Evolution of a Collaborative Conversation
- **STAGE 1. Polite discussion.** People communicate diplomatically to avoid open conflict, while at the same time sending mixed messages.
- **STAGE 2. Rational debate.** People put issues on the table, arguing the different sides rationally and suppressing their emotions.
- **STAGE 3. Chaotic discussion or war.** People realize they have both intellectual and interpersonal conflicts that are not easily resolved and that could lead to a blowup.
- **STAGE 4. The spirit of dialogue or embracing the enemy.** People start to communicate with authenticity and vulnerability and empty themselves of biases toward other people or views.
- **STAGE 5. Collaborative conversations.** Building shared understandings that lead to exciting new possibilities and opportunities not attainable on an individual basis.

Give People the Experience of a Collaborative Conversation They Will Never Forget

I am standing in the Forest Pines Hotel Conference Center in the Humberside area of Northern England. A group of street dancers called the Eurythmics are drumming on plastic buckets as they stomp their feet and whip the crowd into a frenzy. Gregg Goff, managing director of ConLim, who has on occasion met with the likes of Tony Blair to discuss energy prices, steps out from behind the scenes with two large poles in either hand. He and the Eurhythmics start pounding in a percussive rhythm to a quarter beat. Changing the game, changing the game, changing the game, changing the game—until the crowd is roaring.

This is the beginning of a two-day CollabLab with the theme of "The Customer, Changing the Game." The CollabLab is one of the methods we use at Masterful Coaching to assist executives to powerfully launch and accelerate the process of organizational transformation. It gives people the experience of having a powerful collaborative conversation around a specific issue or opportunity that results in the process of shared creation. The power of the CollabLab is not in the coach providing the group answers, but in the constant pulling apart of perspectives and putting them back together again in new configurations.

The CollabLab Compresses Time and Alters How a Group Thinks and Interacts

The CollabLab is nothing like a yearly strategic planning and budgeting session that leads to "better sameness." Nor is it a presentation by a "Big Eight" consulting firm, where you are deluged with hundreds of PowerPoint slides by people who have done your thinking for you. Nor is it a typical three-day training program where the troops are put through the proverbial "sheep dip." It is a fast-paced, powerful process that is stimulating, engaging, and profound.

In the CollabLab an extraordinary combination of people are gathered together. For example, you might bring together veteran executive VPs and young high flyers, MBAs and technology geeks, marketing experts and engineers, anthropologists and software designers, research scientists and artists, salespeople and customers. The group has the task of actually creating something together in the session, rather than engaging in the normal business planning mode where people come together to talk about what they are going to do later, separately back at the office. In the CollabLab people invent new strategies that revolutionize their industry, shift corporate culture, dream up advertising campaigns complete with mocked up ad copy, develop rapid prototypes of new products, and reinvent organizational processes from a blank sheet of paper.

Part of the power of a CollabLab is that people achieve goals in a few days that would normally take weeks or months. This is made possible by masterfully coaching the process and skillfully employing its seven accelerators. The coach works with a design team to do things like (1) define the topic of the session, (2) pick attendees, and (3) design the exercises. For example, in an exercise called "Back to the Future," people are asked to imagine that it is now 2010 and a major business journal is coming to interview them. They now have a totally inspired organization. The company has transformed from [fill in] to [fill in]. They have launched a product revolution in their industry and their customers love them. How did they do it?

The Seven Accelerators of the CollabLab

1. *A Big Significant Goal.* Pick one that inspires commitment and collaboration. (A one-sentence problem statement keeps discussion focused.)

2. *Research.* Advanced topic research allows the coach to introduce "new information" that reveals possibilities and breaks paradigm paralysis.

3. *Juxtapositions.* Juxtapose multiple talents and perspectives in the event so as to light creative sparks and unfreeze biases.

4. *Focused Dialogue.* Define the problem so as to generate possibilities, design a solution, and do a deep dive.

5. *Tools and Techniques.* Brainstormers, metaphors, rapid prototyping, ladder of inference, toys.

6. *Rapid Prototypes.* People actually create something together in the session versus talk about what they will do later.

7. *Seven Iterations.* Each iteration takes half as long and doubles the output of the previous iteration.

The Masterful Coach's Role in a CollabLab Is Powerful, Yet Subtle

Most companies set stretch goals, but often fail to reach them. The reason is that they have a confining network of mindsets, policies, rules, and regulations that constitute a giant "hairball" they are caught in. The role of the Masterful Coach, metaphorically speaking, is to get people to "orbit this giant hairball." To do this, the coach must creatively, collaboratively, and iteratively unleash the collective intelligence of the group and each participant to ensure the best solution to the issues at hand.

This might involve doing some up-front *discovery work* (R&D) and introducing some "new" information that jars loose paradigms and allows the group to discover a much wider universe of possibilities than would otherwise be considered for solving the problem at hand. Three examples of what this might look like are

1. You are competing heads up with the competition on price. Here's a list of companies (for example, Starbucks, Virgin Atlantic, Disney Cruise Lines) who all did something to make the competition irrelevant.

2. Here is how the two best companies in your industry run their business. Why don't you do it that way?

3. Your customers say they want what they want when they want it, or they will leave. Dream up twenty-five alternative possibilities for giving it to them.

The coach must also design and orchestrate the process so that people in groups are able to bring order to the wider range of possibilities. One way to do this is by asking people to create a set of *solution specification criteria*. This provides a platform for designing a solution that becomes the basis of effective action. The intention is that people leave the CollabLab with a fully developed collective work product, as well as an action plan to test it, and get feedback from which they can do another iteration.

The coach's role not only involves designing and orchestrating exercises according to a fairly intense schedule, but observing what is happening in the group, making assessments, and then intervening appropriately. For example, to ensure that the group's biases don't prevent certain people or points of view from being listened to, the coach might add an exercise that helps people to "step inside my frame of reference." Or the coach may also introduce additional tasks to make sure the group doesn't come to closure too early. Or they may move the group along when there is nothing further to be gained. They act as a coach one minute, then a scribe, then an artist, then a Socratic questioner.

THE COLLABLAB™ PROCESS—A THREE-STEP MODEL THAT WORKS EVERY TIME

I vividly recall one CollabLab I did with the Estee Lauder cosmetics company with the purpose of "reinventing the brand" so as to increase market share and sales. I spent two weeks researching the history of the company, including its dynamic founder Estee Lauder. I spent time hanging out in Filene's department store in Boston, Harrods in London, and some key boutiques in Paris. I saw why the brand needed to be reinvented. For the most part, the Estee Lauder cosmetic sections of the stores were seldom visited by women under forty-five or fifty. What I still needed to learn was "Why?"

I started off the CollabLab by showing a film of Estee Lauder, who was a woman of today if ever there was one. Estee was an ambitious, entrepreneurial person, as well as a great wife and hard-working mom, who saw cosmetics as way to bring a little luxury into her own life and those of other women like her. After showing this film, the group began to discuss the undiscussable.

The first thing they discussed was that the company had an autocratic management style and that they had never dared to open their mouths before. The executive VP who sponsored the event encouraged people to continue to speak out, which led to people discussing other undiscussables. There were a lot of strong feelings that Elizabeth Hurley, the model in all the brand's ads, was not someone that they believed women could identify with. "She looks like she rolled out of bed looking glamorous and sexy without any makeup on at all."

This introduction to the CollabLab was just the beginning of two days of very insightful, rigorous, creative, and inspiring conversations that launched the reinvention the Estee Lauder brand. I will go further in the Estee Lauder story as well as the Conoco story as I introduce you to the CollabLab process.

The CollabLab is based on a number of different conversational recipes that provide both a meta-structure for the whole event (usually two to three days) and other conversational recipes that are used to stimulate the best creative and analytic thinking from both individuals and the group. The CollabLab process varies, yet is in large part an amalgam of three to four conversational models which I discovered in writing the book *Mastering the Art of Creative Collaboration*. One of these models is the "Open Space" concept pioneered by Harrison Owen.[2] Another, which we talked about in Chapter Five, is the "Strategic Planning in Action" model from the Hunger Project,[3] and a third is the "Scan, Focus, and Act" model introduced by the Meta-Systems Group in 1983 and developed further by Matt and Gail Taylor into a conversational process.[4]

In preparation for the CollabLab, it is crucial to work with the sponsors of the event to come up with a one-sentence definition of the problem to be solved. In general, edgy is better than fuzzy and leads to generating new possibilities. In the Conoco Europe CollabLab, for example, the strategic goal was to double the business (which included fourteen hundred gas stations throughout Europe). The problem statement was "One more Euro" [per customer visit]. In the Estee Lauder CollabLab, the problem statement was simply to "Put a new face on the brand" (and reflect that in all the advertising and in store merchandising). In some CollabLab sessions, the original problem statement dissolves as new perspectives are gained and a new one is created.

After the problem is defined, there are three distinct phases:

Phase 1. Generate Possibilities.

Phase 2. Design a Solution with WOW!

Phase 3. Do a Deep Dive—Build Out the Solution.

PHASE 1. Generate Possibilities

People in the group broaden their perspective by creating a rich shared information pool, then explore a wide range of options.

Once the problem statement is clear, the next step is to discover alternative possibilities for solving it. This starts with scanning the horizon with the view to seeing the issue from as many different perspectives as possible. Companies on the fringe of your industry might be a source of ideas, or you might look to leading competitors in your own or unrelated fields, or observe customers' shopping habits to detect unmet needs and wants.

Soon people find themselves in a richly diverse shared information pool that interrupts the old conversation they have around the office every day, which leaves them with very few options. This leads to a new conversation in which alternative possibilities and fresh insights begin to emerge. To accelerate this part of the process, we use brainstorming, based on the premise that the best way to get a good idea is to get a lot of ideas. It's important to point out that, if the generating possibilities process is too short, the brainstorming will tend to get stuck in the same old boxes.

Generating possibilities starts with scanning the horizon to learn about portents of change in your industry, your competition, and your customers.

In the Estee Lauder CollabLab, we broke the group of thirty or so people into three subgroups. One team began brainstorming possibilities for putting a new face on the brand. The group came up with a large list of fascinating and intriguing names of possibilities for new models. Another group came up with possibilities for a new ad campaign that would appeal to today's women. A third group began brainstorming in-store counter displays.

By contrast, in the Conoco CollabLab the group started from the premise of "one more Euro" [per customer visit to a gas station] and asked the question, "While I am here, I might as well. . . ?" The brainstorm generated ideas that started with banking services through ATM machines that not only dispensed money, but also lottery tickets and locational services such as directions to local stores or nearby restaurants. Then came ideas like an optometrist corner or Disney toys for cranky kids in the car. And finally, a slew of convenience items that would create a warm, inviting ambiance—fresh baked goods right out of the oven, fresh flowers, gifts, wine, fruits and vegetables, or even steaks and chops.

PHASE 2. Design a Solution with WOW!

The majority of design solutions developed earlier are discarded in favor of those that meet a set of specific design criteria and that have WOW!

In this phase, people begin to focus on those possibilities that will result in the best resolution of the situation. The majority of possibilities generated in the previous phase are discarded in favor of those that will become part of a real design solution. This is done by asking a group to come up with a set of *solution specification criteria* (usually three to five) that they will build a solution around. The design criteria must express people's desires and needs, as well as constraints.

The desire to design a solution that meets desires and needs, but also addresses limitations, sets up a "creative tension" that produces new ideas, fresh approaches, and innovative solutions. In the Conoco CollabLab, the solution specification criteria were: (1) "one more Euro," (2) new offerings would have to be compact as the Conoco Jet stations had limited square footage, and (3) the solution needed to combine high-tech, with high touch.

Soon people began thinking in terms of a *Mini Mall that sold gas* rather than a *gas station that sold convenience items.* Fresh baked goods, flowers, wines, and toys became part of this model, as well as the ATM machine with locational services. At the same time, many other items were discarded, especially those that took up a lot of space.

In the Estee Lauder CollabLab, the group settled on a four-point set of solution specification criteria for reinventing the brand:

1. The solution needed to build off the strength of the brand's heritage (as inspired by the film of Estee Lauder).

2. It needed to put a new face on the brand that today's younger, married with children, working women could identify with.

3. It must emphasize not just luxury, but also a certain "quality of life."

4. It must be executable.

The group created lots of possibilities for putting a new face on the brand in the brainstorming sessions and covered the walls of the room with photos. However, with the solution specification criteria in hand, the surprise choice the group came up with was Aerin Lauder, granddaughter of the founder.

Like her grandmother, Aerin was not only entrepreneurial and a working mother with a bent for luxury, but a person women could look at and say, "That's me." (A year after the CollabLab, Aerin's name or photo showed up in almost every issue of *Vogue*. She showed up on *Harper's* best-dressed list and *W* magazine called her a "fashion muse.") Along with the new brand image represented by Aerin Lauder, came ideas for new advertisements, new products like a perfume called "Intuition"—the essence of a woman—new counter displays, and new distribution channels such as boutiques that would never have been considered before.

PHASE 3. Do a Deep Dive—Build Out the Solution

The next step after people develop a conceptual model of the solution is to begin to take action by creating a rapid prototype. This means taking the group on a "deep dive," which means to *design, build, and test* a prototype in physical reality. Rapid prototyping is about acting when you don't have the answers, using whatever resources and materials are at hand. For example, the first PC mouse "track ball" came from a designer going to a local grocery store and buying a butter dish for $1.50. It seemed to the designer like an ideal container for placing your hand over and rolling a ball around in.

A good example of how rapid prototyping can apply to strategy, not just to products and services, comes from Jeff Bezos, the founder of Amazon.com. One day sitting in his office he read that the growth of products and services over the Internet for the next five years would be 2,500 percent. He quit his cushy job on Wall Street and told a moving company to pack up his things. He wasn't sure where he wanted to set up his office, so he told the movers to head west.

He called them one day later to tell them to drive to Seattle, where there were lots of high-tech workers. He scribbled the name of the company on the flight out, originally "Cadabra," as well as various items he could sell over the Internet—books, tapes, and electronic gadgets. Within three days, he designed a rapid prototype of a test website using a simple program he bought in a computer shop. He discovered by trial and error that books were the way to go and the company was off and running.

Rapid prototyping is a great way for a group to see whether they have truly built a shared understanding of a solution. For example, each person in a group may have a design for a beautiful car, but only when they start to build a scale model are they able to build a shared understanding of what beauty means, or determine whether the different parts of the car that each has worked on truly function as a whole. Finally, rapid prototypes can lead to accidental genius. Watson and Crick discovered the secrets of DNA, not in an ivory tower, but by playing around with spiral shaped metal sculptures.

In the CollabLab, this third phase usually involves asking the group to build a quick prototype in the form of a three-dimensional working model. We ask people to do this, whether the task is designing a new strategy, a new brand campaign, or a new product or service. Although the initial response to this is varied, it isn't long before the group takes up the task with enthusiasm. One of the things that moves matters along is that the CollabLab design team has usually raided the local hardware store, toy store, or newsstand and assembled some interesting items with which to get the group going on the 3D model.

For example, at Estee Lauder we provided scads of magazines and foam construction materials so the group could design camera-ready ads, build display counters, model distribution channels with wires. In the Conoco CollabLab, we provided TinkerToys® and Legos® and told the group to construct the gas station (the mini mall of the future) in two feet by three feet of space.

I am always struck by how people show up in a CollabLab session as they participate in this process of shared creation. They are brought back to the playful but creative days of their childhood where they made snowmen, built forts, created dolls and dollhouses. Instead of the bored expressions and glazed-over eyes you see in most *"set and get"* management trainings, people's eyes light up as they see the possibilities they have brainstormed come to life in three-dimensional form. At Estee Lauder, people were literally jumping out of their seats with enthusiasm as they designed a whole slew of prototypes. Soon these were appearing in magazines ads, in store displays, and in distribution channels with great results.

COACHING IN THE COLLABLAB

Some of the most important work of the coach in the CollabLab happens before people even come together, doing the research and development of the program, along with helping people to define the problem. In the CollabLab, the coach needs to focus on setting up the context of the day as well as the conversations. Then the coach needs to focus intently on moving the process along at a fairly rapid pace.

It is helpful that the coach have the mindset that building shared understanding best happens bit by bit. All too often, when people are given an assignment of coming up with a new strategy, process, or product, more often than not, they try to perfect a solution without soliciting enough feedback along the way or soliciting reviews incrementally. When others finally see the results, it could be either a joyous surprise or a depressing day. This is why in the CollabLab, we "*iterate, iterate, iterate!*"

Coach people not to come to conclusions too early and to build shared understanding in stages. For example, encourage people to create a rough-and-ready PowerPoint presentation of the new marketing campaign, show a rough sketch of the product, or a wire model of a new value chain, and then use these to right the course before it is too late.

Get into the mindset of coaching a quarterback who is facing a two-minute warning the moment people start a new project. For example, instead of coaching the group to throw a long ball, coach them to grind out a few yards, passing to the sidelines to stop the clock. Make sure the team is aligned in the huddle about the game plan. The idea is to keep the momentum, the energy, and the collaborative conversation going each step along the way.

The coach also provides tools as needed to move the process along. The following brainstorming guidelines capture the spirit and pace of the CollabLab.

BRAINSTORMING GUIDELINES

Post these in six-inch letters in the CollabLab room:

1. *Create a One-Sentence Problem Statement.* Create a problem statement that is well-honed. Edgy is better than fuzzy.
2. *Create Playful Rules.* Encourage wild ideas. Go for quantity. Be visual.
3. *Number Your Ideas.* "Let's try to get a hundred ideas." "Oh, I like idea Number 6."
4. *Build and Jump.* Build on ideas by developing them. Connect ideas so as to lead to new possibilities.
5. *Bring in Toys.* Go to a local toy store and find interesting toys or gadgets that can provide a spirit of play for the event as well as provide metaphors that stimulate creative thinking.
6. *The Space Remembers.* Create a "Knowledge Wall" for the best ideas. Connect and merge ideas as the session goes on.
7. *Do Some Energizers.* These can be group icebreakers or something physical like tossing a ball around the room to bring the energy level up.

HOW TO BE A SKILLED FACILITATOR OF COLLABORATIVE CONVERSATIONS EVERY DAY

The role the Masterful Coach plays in the context of a CollabLab is obviously different from what one would play in everyday business meetings. However, the CollabLab experience provides some useful guidelines for being a skilled facilitator on a day in, day out basis for collaborative conversations. To facilitate means "to make easy." The facilitator is not there to think for the group members or to tell them the answers, but to help them do their own thinking and discover their own answers.

Start with a High Level of Intention

What does it mean to be a skilled facilitator? How do you "be" in this role? First of all, it starts with having the sincere and honest intention for the group to be successful in reaching their goals. The art of facilitation is to support the group in reaching their goals faster by building shared understandings between the different members of the group that lead to being able to take coherent action. Skilled facilitators are increasingly being called on to help group members improve the way they think together, not just the way they talk to one another.

You may be absorbed in questions like, "How can I assist people to use the impasse in reaching their goals as an opportunity to go beyond paradigm paralysis and do some breakthrough thinking?" "How can I get the executive VP to see that his power is not only in speaking, but in listening so as to draw out the best ideas of others?" "How do I enable people to discuss the undiscussable?" There are often no easy or obvious answers, which can be unsettling.

You might try asking simple questions like, "What do you think?" to draw different members of the group out. Or you may directly intervene in people's thinking by pushing them to surface and question their business paradigms or the real causes of their defensive behavior. Another idea is to provide guiding ideas, methods, and tools that improve both people's cognitive skills and their interpersonal skills.

For example, one of the key roles of a facilitator is to help group members become more skilled at balancing advocacy and inquiry. Creating a community of inquiry requires helping group members learn how to ask a question or to say, "I don't know," rather than just give a pat answer. Instead of giving group members a recipe, like "positive thinking" or "better communication," creating this community is about helping people learn to take a reflective stance. Some questions to try: "How does positive thinking block rigorous thinking?" or "What makes it difficult for us to listen to one another?"

Contract: Create a Framework for Facilitation

Another key point in facilitating collaborative conversations is to contract with the group so as to have clear expectations. Contracting with the group involves clarifying the mission of the group, your role as a facilitator, and the nature of the intervention. This kind of contract is really a verbal agreement that states explicitly how the skilled facilitator and group are going to work together.

For example, there are two different kinds of facilitation. You might ask, "Is the group more interested in basic facilitation (goal-oriented) or developmental facilitation?" Basic facilitation involves helping a group to produce a desired outcome, to agree on its objectives, to make an important decision, and to iron out conflicts. Developmental facilitation involves helping the group learn to think and to interact better, as well as to achieve desired outcomes.

Developmental facilitation usually involves a "deep learning cycle" where group members inquire into the nature of group thought and behavior. It also involves creating "practice fields" where people experiment with new ideas, tools, and methods. Some of these might be "fluid framing," "dialogue," "ladder of inference," and so on. My experience has been that this kind of intervention involves working with a group from nine months to a year.

Establish the Governing Values

Once you are clear about the nature of the facilitation, the next step is to establish the governing values and ground rules. The facilitator can be more effective as a learning enzyme for the group if both the facilitator and the group are operating from the same governing values and ground rules.

At Masterful Coaching we introduce people in groups to a set of four governing values that provide a basis for improving the way they think and interact together.[5]

You might uphold the governing value of "valid information" by encouraging group members to share all relevant information. Or you may encourage people not to simply accept what others say at face value, but to test all opinions and assumptions by asking "How do you know that?" In this way, you become a role model for the group members and teach them to be co-facilitators of the conversation.

- *Sharing of valid information.* People need more than arbitrary opinions and assumptions on which to base a discussion. They need the speaker to provide valid information that can be supported with examples.

- *Free and informed choices.* This applies to agreeing to the objectives of the meeting, to the methods of inquiry, and to any changes in thinking and behavior.

- *Internal commitment to outcomes.* This means that each person feels personally responsible for the decisions that are made because they are intrinsically compelling or satisfying.

- *Learning is as sacred as results.* A meeting is not over until the group has learned something from it.

Establish the Ground Rules

In addition to establishing the governing values, introduce and ask the group to "play" by a set of ground rules for collaborative conversations. "I always explain to people that if they choose not to operate by the core values and ground rules," says Roger Schwarz, author of *The Skilled Facilitator,* "I will operate by them anyway, because I believe they work. If people have a problem with that, then I tell them maybe they've got the wrong guy for the job."

The following ground rules are especially useful for making effective decisions in situations where the group is trying to reach high-performance goals, introduce change, or deal with complex issues or problems.[6]

GROUND RULES FOR EFFECTIVE GROUPS

1. *Test all opinions, assumptions, and inferences.*
2. *Share all relevant information.*
3. *Use specific examples and agree on what important words mean.*
4. *Explain your reasoning and intent.*
5. *Focus on interests, not on positions.*
6. *Combine advocacy and inquiry.*
7. *Jointly design next steps and ways to test disagreements.*
8. *Discuss undiscussable issues.*
9. *Use a decision-making rule that generates the level of commitment needed.*

Used with permission of Roger M. Schwarz. From *The Skilled Facilitator* (San Francisco: Jossey-Bass, 2000).

Use the Diagnosis/Intervention Cycle

The intervention cycle has two phases: diagnosis and intervention (Diagram 7.1).[7] The diagnosis phase includes (1) observing behavior, (2) inferring meaning, and (3) deciding whether or not to intervene. It is important to avoid jumping to conclusions, making snap judgments, or projecting your own pet theories onto the group. In the intervention phase, carefully observe what's happening in the group, drawing inferences only from directly witnessable behavior. Think about what you want to say before intervening so as to promote learning versus defensive reaction. Keeping these things in mind will keep you out of trouble.

DIAGRAM 7.1 *The diagnosis/intervention cycle*

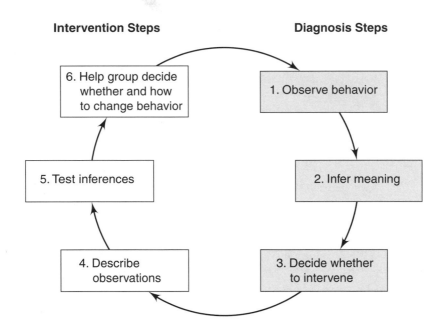

Used with permission of Roger M. Schwarz. From *The Skilled Facilitator* (San Francisco, CA: Jossey-Bass, 2002).

It is important to intervene to improve the way the group thinks and communicates when you see that (1) the group is rushing ahead to the next topic and it's obvious that there has not been enough shared understanding built on the last topic; (2) people are advocating a position but discouraging inquiry of the reasoning process by which they came to that position; (3) people are saying things and their meaning is not obvious, or what they are saying is confusing or not understood by other people in the group; (4) people are dancing around issues or making them undiscussable; or (5) the conversation is going too fast and there isn't time to question people's reasoning processes.

When you see these things, interrupt the conversation with one of the following:

- *"I think we need to slow the conversation down a bit here."*
- *"Let's do a deep dive on this topic."*
- *"What is the data on which you based that conclusion?"*
- *"When you said. . ., what did you mean?"*
- *"Is the group really addressing the issues that are on people's minds?"*

Encourage People to Balance Inquiry with Advocacy

I have seen executives struggle with various issues in attempting to engage their groups in a richer quality of dialogue. For example, forgetting about the importance of bringing people with divergent views and backgrounds to the table or being reluctant to disagree, which prevents the different views from clashing and thereby lighting creative spark. Yet by far the biggest single issue that executives struggle with is balancing advocacy and inquiry.

In normal business discussions, people tend to advocate their positions in order to win and discourage inquiry into them. For example, an executive may have fallen into the habit of saying, "I have decided this and I really don't want to discuss it." If he were attempting to balance advocacy and inquiry, he might begin by speaking this way, "Here is what I would tend to decide, and here are my reasons why. Now tell me how you see it differently." Or a member of a group might say, "Here's how I see the problem. My data is. . . . How do you see it differently?"

The same applies to listening. Normally, people listen through a stream of assessments: "That's nuts," "I fully agree," "That's wrong," or "I like that." The context in which people make these assessments is one of guarding their particular perspective or holding onto their opinions and assumptions. If our goal is to balance advocacy and inquiry, then we would listen by trying to understand what another person is saying and by having the courage to step into his or her frame of reference.

One of the reasons that people often resist collaborating is because they do not want to be influenced or to be changed by understanding what others have to say. The idea of suspending one's opinions and assumptions and stepping into someone else's frame of reference is scary. While this is understandable, this kind of mental rigidity, egocentric thinking, and resistance can lead to a group's demise.

Coach People to Use Action Language

One of the things that a coach can do to further collaborative conversation is to elicit powerful commitments from people, while at the same time creating a context wherein people are expected to honor their word as themselves. It is important that these promises and requests be explicit. Often when people listen, they think they have a promise when really what they have is an "I'll try." Or they think they made a specific request when actually it was vague and fuzzy. When coaching people, it's important to help them make a distinction between a promise and an "I'll try," between a request and a complaint, and between an offer to do something and an opinion on how things should be done. If you hold people accountable to making explicit promises, requests, and offers and to living as their word, you will not only forward action, but you will help people to learn and grow. Diagram 7.2 illustrates action language.

DIAGRAM 7.2 *Action language to build a shared understanding*

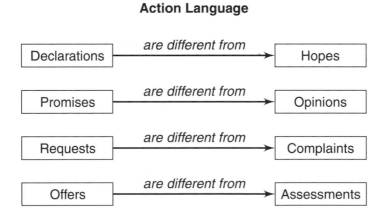

Action Language

Declarations	*are different from* →	Hopes
Promises	*are different from* →	Opinions
Requests	*are different from* →	Complaints
Offers	*are different from* →	Assessments

A COACH IS FIRST AND FOREMOST A TEACHER

It is also effective to provide the group a set of guiding ideas, tools, and methods that empower them to have a collaborative conversation. I have found the following helpful:

1. *Check In/Check Out.* At the beginning of each meeting, check in by asking each person to take a moment and say what's on his or her mind that could be distracting. Check out by asking people to say what they are left with from the meeting.

2. *Meeting Without an Agenda.* Occasionally have a meeting without an agenda to build a community feeling. Give people a chance to tell stories about who they are and what the project means to them.

3. *Use Self-Awareness as a Resource.* Ask yourself, "What am I trying to achieve by this conversation?" "What is on my mind?" "Am I willing to listen and to be influenced?"

4. *Balance Advocacy with Inquiry.* Question: "What led you to that view?" "What do you mean by that view?"

5. *Build Shared Understanding.* Ask: "When we say the word . . ., what are we really saying?"

6. *Explore Impasses.* Ask: "What do we agree on and disagree on? What does this impasse tell us about differences in basic assumptions?"

One last point: Giving feedback to the group rather than singling out an individual can often be more effective and cause less reaction. In any case, it is important to give feedback in a way that does not promote a favorite game called "kill the facilitator." Feedback can also be given offline to individuals whose behavior is having a negative impact on the group or to individuals whose influence or actions could actively help to move the group forward.

CHAPTER EIGHT

RECOGNIZING AND DISPERSING POSTURING AND DEFENSIVENESS

Tools for Empowering Individuals and Groups

It's like an attic in a one-hundred-year-old house that's never been cleaned, full of old baggage.
—IBM manager, on withheld communication in companies

Why do executives often preach teamwork but act in a dictatorial way without even being aware of it? Why do many managers come to the big meeting and advocate their views in order to win, yet are careful not to upset others? Why is it that every group seems to have a secret that everybody knows but nobody dares talk about—even though talking about it is essential to improving products, quality, or teamwork?

This strange, often bizarre, and frustrating behavior that happens in groups was expressed very well by a cartoon I saw in *The Economist* a number of years back. It showed a group of smiling, sophisticated executives sitting around a conference table discussing an important issue. Under the table were dozens of beasts of a demonic nature with hostile glares, sharp teeth, long nails, swords, and shields that would have made fitting gargoyles for any medieval castle.

While most managers intend to do a good job, they often invest a great deal of energy in what Harvard's Chris Argyris calls defensive routines.[1] This can be very debilitating for people. "I believe we suffer every day, in every single business meeting we go to," says Peter Senge. "Part of us is getting killed, is really getting torn apart. We can't talk about it, we can't even name it."[2] Yet, what can we do?

As one practitioner told me, "The despair that many managers feel about being unable to have an authentic communication where they discuss the undiscussable, talk about problems openly, and overcome the game playing that goes on in most groups is the same as the despair a peasant in a Third World country feels trying to overcome his poverty."

DEFENSIVE THINKING AND BEHAVIOR FOR AVOIDING THREAT AND EMBARRASSMENT

For many people, defensive reactions are almost second nature. As economist John Kenneth Galbraith says, "Faced with the alternatives between changing one's mind and proving it unnecessary, just about everybody gets busy on the proof." Chris Argyris defines a defensive routine as whatever an individual or group does to avoid situations that are embarrassing and threatening. Interestingly enough, many of the things people do to avoid embarrassment or threat do not eliminate the source of the embarrassment or threat. For example, people may be more concerned with "looking good" than with "being good"; they may protect versus correct their mistakes; they may collude with colleagues to avoid talking about hot issues; or they may not be able to admit that they don't know something.

The price people pay for this is enormous. Although they protect themselves from threat and pain, they are unable to be authentic, to learn, or to grow. The result is that they develop "skilled" incompetence, producing errors as a result of automatic behaviors that are carried out with skill and dexterity. People resist learning because it exposes their incompetence. Yet at the same time, they remain incompetent and are blinded to this because they are unaware of their defensive behaviors.

What Can a Masterful Coach Do?

One way the Masterful Coach can make a difference in breaking through the posturing and defensiveness that occurs in most organizations is to recognize and dispel it by bringing it to the light.

This means finding a way to help people talk about things that they generally make undiscussable because talking about them represents a threat or a potential embarrassment. For example, people may try to appear as though they are in agreement, even when they are not, to avoid a blowup.

Says Senge, "One key to unlocking real openness and honesty at work is to teach people how to give up being in agreement. We think being in agreement is so important. Who cares? You have to bring paradoxes, real conflicts, and dilemmas out into the open so collectively we can be more intelligent than we can as individuals."[3] As people begin to say what's really on their minds, they often hold up a mirror to themselves and others. This can result in people making a shift from posturing and defensiveness to authenticity, creativity, and learning.

Once people experience how good authentic conversations can be, they are often stunned. The German poet Goethe once said, "Conversation is the most sublime of human experiences." Many people would say there is no greater joy than to have a real conversation. The issue is how to create the opening or opportunity for this to happen, as well as to develop the skills so it can be done productively.

THE POWER OF DISCUSSING THE UNDISCUSSABLE

When Thomas Labrecque, chairman and CEO of Chase Manhattan Bank, summoned his top twenty-four company leaders to a three-day conference without an agenda, there was a great deal of anxiety about what was supposed to happen. Is he angry? Frustrated? What's this going to be about? What the participants found out was that they were being invited to what would later be called a "happening."

Labrecque, a thirty-year Chase veteran, knew what could happen when too many things in the organization become undiscussable. So before he solicited the views of the executive vice presidents about a mission statement, Labrecque started off by asking the participants a key question: "What are the issues we haven't addressed with one another?" He told them he didn't see the point of leaving the room until these issues were addressed.

Labrecque and an outside facilitator told the group members that the first thing they were going to do was to rate and then discuss their ways of working with one another. They would then break into groups and rate and discuss their own management skills. The members of each group would then critique their colleagues' assessments of themselves. It soon became clear that the group members profoundly distrusted one another.

Significant differences exploded among the different business-unit leaders, not only about how people perceived themselves, but over the direction the company should go and how it should get there. It was obvious that a raft of defensive routines had been built up over the years. Some executives had built up elaborate strategies for protecting their turf—including office spaces that were barricaded with electronic glass doors and that had three or four armed security guards.

According to one source, "I got a call on the first day of the program from my boss. I asked 'How's it going?' He said 'It's a bloodbath. We had better pack up now and get back to the office before all hell breaks loose.' He did call back, however, the next day to say that things had really turned around."

Another person said, "It's not that we don't like one another; it's that we don't like some of the things that the other people have done. Also, it's not just that we don't innately trust one another; it's that we never talked about things, saw things from other people's perspectives, or understood the reasons why people were doing the things that they did. Seeing just this was a real eyeopener."

According to Wright Elliot, one of the key people leading the organization change process, "The exercises that we did were not brain surgery. The intent was to improve our competitive position, to improve the way we think and work together, to communicate in a more personal and authentic way."[4]

Everyone I spoke to at Chase stressed that the whole process was very personal. One of the key successes of the program was to develop a customer ethic. It wasn't just a matter of the CEO standing up and waving the flag for customers; it was that the CEO took the opportunity to make sure that everyone, including himself, looked in the mirror and thought about the things they personally did that prevented a real customer focus from occurring. The idea that came out of this was to serve the customers first, even if that meant handing them over to another unit.

There were many issues that came up that were controversial. In most cases, after some initial hesitation, the company leaders began speaking to one another and tackling the issues at hand. Some of the issues that came up had to do with structures, executive compensation, and other measurements, especially in regard to who "owned" the customer. Instead of being handled by the product-line czars, customers were to be segmented according to discrete markets, with a senior executive in charge of each. In subsequent months, the executives successfully hammered out a new organization structure and compensation system. Less than half of their pay for performance was tied to what happens in the executives' own areas. "It's amazing how that changes your attitude," said one vice president. This would now ensure that executives would cooperate to make sure customers would be sold the products that suited them best.

According to one executive, "Those were the days that changed Chase." After the original meeting with the top group, 1,100 managers attended a similar session where they contributed to the crafting of the vision. The program was then rolled out to the other 35,000 people, in sessions led by the 1,100 crafters of the vision, to gain their participation and commitment to the vision. The next step was the development of leadership and team learning skills. How has it worked out for the bottom line? Chase still has a way to go to make its transformation and comeback complete, but return on earnings had jumped back up to 18.1 percent less than two years after they initiated the work, way ahead of most of the bank's competitors.

THE SOURCE OF DEFENSIVE ROUTINES

Certainly a committed leader and team can make a big difference in eliminating posturing and defensiveness, but this is only part of the equation. I know of many committed leaders and teams who wound up stuck in the same defensive thinking and game playing, despite their best attempts to avoid them. Let's take a deeper look at the source of defensive strategies.

According to Argyris, the defensive routines that people operate by in most groups are rooted in a "master program" or what he calls "Model I theory-in-use." The master program tells people to (1) pursue their own purpose; (2) stay in unilateral control of themselves and the situation; (3) maximize winning and avoid losing by advocating your position; (4) be invulnerable and suppress emotions; and (5) avoid the appearance of incompetence by covering up problems and bypassing errors.

The master program leads to face saving (for oneself and others), as well as persuading and convincing through force of argument or subtle pressure. Interestingly enough, this program can only be implemented when people become submissive, passive, and dependent. As this goes against human nature, defensive routines become a vicious circle. Here are some of the most frequently used defensive routines:

1. Avoiding, acting heavy handedly, or accommodating;

2. Suppressing dilemmas by discouraging testing of tranquilizing views and assumptions;

3. Advocating one's position in order to win, while not upsetting others;

4. Making those issues that represent a threat or a potential embarrassment undiscussable;

5. Using fancy footwork to pretend that problems are not that big or to deflect blame;

6. Covering up errors and then covering that up; and

7. Withdrawing and distancing oneself from problems in order to maintain high morale.

In many groups, people are aware that these defensive routines are going on but do not say anything about them because revealing them is potentially embarrassing or threatening. As one manager said, "It's like pretending that the emperor has clothes, even though everyone knows he's stark naked." Instead, people seek and extend support for their defensive routines in order not to be exposed. Yet, so that people do not have to feel like they are acting unethically, they often cover up the cover-up by saying things like "Think positively," "We don't want to have a blowup in the group," or "You have to be diplomatic." The result is a climate of resignation, escalating error, and an unmanageable organization.

EURO BANK: A SCENARIO OF DEFENSIVE ROUTINES

The following story stands in marked contrast to the preceding story about Tom Labrecque and Chase Manhattan Bank. The two banks are in the same industry, compete in many of the same businesses, and have similar business strategies. Yet, the leadership styles and commitment to transforming the organizations are at sharp variance. The story illustrates the power of the defensive routines that occur in most work groups.

Several years ago I worked as a consultant for a large bank that I will call "Euro Bank." The bank had been highly successful because of the vision and efforts of the previous chairman, but its core business had begun to decline and it needed to reinvent itself. The new chairman hoped to boost sagging profits by selling to core customers higher profit-margin products and services that were being sold by other parts of the bank. This strategy would require teamwork and cross-selling between the different departments. Yet, teamwork was not happening.

Bypassing and Covering Up Issues

I interviewed various people who worked at the bank. I discovered a critical underlying issue that was best summed up in the words of one executive vice president, who said, "The chairman preaches teamwork but absolutely abhors the process. He prefers to mandate things, as he has no patience with group discussion."

The chairman, Mr. Team, an ex-military officer, was very good at managing impressions and had a very affable personality. Yet he engaged in subtle forms of domination. He authored a vision statement, but there was not one free and open discussion about it to see if there was any commitment to it. At the same time, he tended to suppress the dilemmas around the complex issues facing the bank by making unilateral statements that left little room for anyone to rigorously question his thinking.

When executives brought up issues that were related to facing these dilemmas or to implementing real change, he would shout them down. He had inherited a successful operation and his basic position was "don't rock the boat." "We have to go global and that's all there is to it," he said to one member who asked about the huge sums of money lost on foreign operations. "It's not appropriate to bring that up here," he said to another who mentioned that the bank had some serious technology problems. "If you have something to say about it, send me a confidential report." One executive drew an apt metaphor about the chairman's tendency to bypass and cover up problems: "He's like a river running into a stone; he goes over it or around it, rarely dealing with it directly."

At first, the group members tried to resolve issues themselves at the chairman's office meetings, advocating their views on controversial topics, but being careful not to upset their colleagues. The chairman would privately mock group members for not speaking with more candor; "Pretty smiles and sharp teeth," he would say. Yet Mr. Team himself seemed to be averse to conflict and any time a heated discussion emerged in the group, he would start fiddling with his glasses, making calls to his boatyard, or telling the group to "work it out for yourselves."

Covering Up the Cover-Up

Mr. Team was frustrated with the group trying "to run every decision up the ladder" or making side deals with him instead of collaborating. Yet, he was unaware of how he was contributing to the problem by providing no real forum for dialogue and by making so many issues undiscussable. The members of the group were also largely unaware that they were contributing to the problem by allowing topics to be dropped. Said one manager, "If I speak up, I could get in trouble. If I just sit here, they will double my pay at the end of the year as usual."

Some of the issues that needed to be talked about were vital to implementing the chairman's strategy, such as the compensation issue. As one executive said, "Why should I sell the other guy's products? There's nothing in it for me." Soon the climate of fear, greed, and mistrust began to worsen as a result of shelving issues that were potentially embarrassing or threatening.

Changing the Form Versus Looking in the Mirror

People in the company began to question the chairman's competence and say that the chairman and his executives were a dysfunctional group. Curiously, when Mr. Team started to sense this, his response was to manage impressions. Instead of saying, "There is something about the way we think and work together as a group that doesn't work and I think we need to talk about it"—which would have provided a breath of fresh air—he made some threats to show he was strong and fired several weaker members, hoping the rest would shape up. "We've been having some good meetings lately," he later crowed. "People are positive and upbeat and there's lots of esprit de corps."

At the same time, the chairman began spending lots of time on the road on sales calls, withdrawing and distancing himself from problems, and seemed to have exceptionally good morale. One executive vice president said, "I can't understand it. We've been on the road with the chairman for a week and he has an empty briefcase. He brought no work to do."

I presented my findings to Mr. Team. I told him that while people wanted him to succeed, they saw a big discrepancy between what he preached and what he practiced. I gave him as many examples as possible. I also told him that his vision wasn't happening because people didn't own it and weren't being held accountable. Key strategic and operational issues were being made undiscussable, in part due to his behavior and in part due to the behavior of the group members. I then made some recommendations designed to transform the defensiveness into learning.

I told Mr. Team that the only way to deal with the controversial issues coming up in the group was to discuss them and that the only way to deal with defensive routines was to focus on them. I suggested that many members of the group wanted a forum for quality dialogue.

After Mr. Team had a chance to digest all this, he asked me to meet with him again. The chairman's response astonished me. He said, "Can you find me an organization solution?" I said, "You are looking for an engineering solution to a human problem." I explained that if he really wanted to help himself and the company, he had to be willing to hold up a mirror and look beyond changing the form. He had to be willing to ask the tough questions that would allow transformational learning to occur, both for himself and his group, for example: "Is my underlying assumption here to not rock the boat and, if so, what are the unintended results of that? What are the problems that I have with facing conflict in a public discussion? Why do we, as a group, cover up and bypass issues by making them undiscussable?" The chairman chose to ignore these suggestions.

As I watched over the next few years, I noticed that Euro Bank's stock price dropped dramatically, the bank's traditionally high return on earnings (ROE) sank below 18 percent for the first time in years, and serious operational problems began to emerge—a far cry from the outcomes experienced by Tom Labrecque and his group at Chase.

STRATEGIES FOR ELIMINATING DEFENSIVE ROUTINES

Curiously enough, every person in the Euro Bank story had a sincere intention to do a good job. Yet no one had the capacity to deal with the leadership, strategic, or operational issues they faced, especially as these sat on the table like a huge bowl of spaghetti intertwined with personal coping methods, relationships problems, and organizational defensive routines. For years I had been asking myself: "How do you sort out the spaghetti?" I talked with Chris Argyris and some of his former students, Bob Putnam, of Action Design Associates, and Roger Schwarz, author of *The Skilled Facilitator.*

According to Bob Putnam, there is a dilemma facing anyone who seeks to do this work. On the one hand, defensive routines are so pervasive that they are taken for granted. On the other hand, the very ways of thinking and acting that create defensive routines also prevent people from engaging productively in the learning activities that are necessary to change those ways of thinking and acting.[5]

Four Steps to Sustaining a Learning Process

Sustaining a learning process in the face of this dilemma requires at least four steps.[6]

1. Establish a compelling link between the current behavior of the group and the business results for which it is responsible. For example, the senior managers of a manufacturing company recognized that ineffective strategic decisions were due to rivalry among the leaders of different divisions. If members of the group do not see a compelling link to business issues, few are likely to commit themselves to the learning process. Thus, in most cases, it makes sense to begin with business issues that are causing difficulty and identify whether defensive routines are a key barrier to progress.

2. Help people see that, despite good intentions, they often produce unintended consequences due to lack of awareness. People are most aware of their own good intentions, of the poor results they seem to be getting, and of what other people are doing to contribute to these results. However, they are often unaware of other people's good intentions and of how their own actions contribute to poor results. This can lead to misunderstanding of motives or actions as well as to unintended consequences. The key is to help each party see how his or her actions contribute to results and how others are thinking in ways that, from their perspectives, make sense and have integrity.

3. Help people see that it is possible to learn to think and act in ways that reduce defensive routines and increase effectiveness in dealing with business issues. There are at least two major hurdles here. The first is to help people experience how discussing the undiscussable can be productive. The second is to help them gain confidence that they will be able to develop the ability to do this on their own.

4. Create a frame for intervening through the governing values and ground rules. As was mentioned in the discussion of shared understanding in Chapter Seven, it is important to establish governing values and ground rules before you begin to work with people. As Schwarz says, "This gives me a frame to work from and allows my facilitation skills to be effective. It also gives the participants a different frame to operate from than the 'master program.'" The frame emphasizes eliciting voluntary commitment from people versus exercising unilateral control and coercing others, being authentic in one's communication versus suppressing thoughts and feelings, and having a commitment to learning versus bypassing and covering up mistakes.

The governing values and ground rules are not as hard to learn as they might seem. They can be learned through practice in the process of applying them to business issues and problems. Once learned, they begin to displace the master program. (See Diagram 8.1.)

DIAGRAM 8.1 *Contrasting models for dealing with undiscussables*

Model I

- *I'm separate and pursue my own agenda*

- *Seek unilateral control of myself and others*

- *Maximize winning by advocating my position, yet not upsetting others*

- *Be invulnerable by suppressing feelings and covering up errors*

- *Manage impressions to be acknowledged and avoid looking incompetent*

Model II

- *I'm related and build shared vision*

- *Be committed to cause; inspire commitment in others*

- *Balance advocacy with inquiring into others' views*

- *Learn from mistakes and see how I contribute to my own problems*

- *Being good allows me to look good*

Based on the work of Chris Argyris.

At the same time, helping people break the grip of the old models can bring up emotions; thus it is important to contract with the group about how deeply you are going to go. The net effect of this kind of intervention is transforming posturing and defensiveness into learning.

Once these four steps are taken, you have created the readiness to work with the group. There are a variety of ways a facilitator can intervene with the group to move people beyond defensive behavior.

BOB PUTNAM ON FACILITATING DEFENSIVE ROUTINES

Three Levels of Intervention: Bypass, Name, and Engage

Putnam: Suppose you are at one of a series of meetings to review the strategic direction of a company. The head of one line of business argues, "Where we have a competitive advantage is in my line of business. That's where we should invest." The head of a different line of business says, "We may have an advantage there, but it's a dying business. We've got to invest in growth areas." Others are silent, but past experience gives you reason to believe that several of them may be thinking: "There go Bill and Charlie again. We're never going to get past their prejudices." You think this episode illustrates a defensive routine that reduces the group's effectiveness. You would like to help. What might you do?

If your objective is to help the group make progress in today's discussion of strategy, you might choose to *bypass the defensive routine.* That is, you might craft an intervention that improves the quality of the immediate discussion without naming or engaging the underlying defensive routine. For example, recognizing that Bill and Charlie are both advocating their positions but not inviting inquiry into them and have jumped to conclusions along the way, you might say, "When you say it's a dying business, what are the data you are selecting to reach that conclusion?" Later you might ask, "How do others read those data? Do you reach similar or different conclusions?"

If your objective is both to help today's discussion of strategy and also to lay the groundwork for altering the defensive routines that prevent the group from working effectively, you might *name the pattern without engaging it.* For example, you might say, "Bill and Charlie, I think that you are both advocating your views, but I'm not hearing any inquiry into the reasoning behind your views. When you say it's a dying business, what's the data you are selecting to reach that conclusion?"

If your objective is to alter the defensive routine, then it is necessary to *engage the defensive routine.* The price of engaging is that the conversation shifts away from strategy to how members of the group are interacting. You might say, "I hear each of you advocating your view and I don't hear any inquiry into the reasoning behind each view. I'm also thinking that each of you has made the same argument before; we didn't make progress then and I doubt we're making progress right now. Let me check—do others see the same, or do you differ?"

Depending on what other members of the group then say, you might follow up by asking Bill or Charlie, "When Charlie [or Bill] was making his case, what was it that you were thinking but not saying?" As the inquiry continues, it may be possible to identify a pattern. The group members will then be in a position to design corrective action so they no longer are stuck in the pattern. The conversation that is stimulated by engaging interventions also surfaces assumptions that had been undiscussable and makes it possible to test their validity. Done well, engaging defensive routines can help members of a group experience the possibility of genuine team learning.

The "Controlled Burn"

Putnam: Once in the early stages of working with a management group, we developed a metaphor that I think is useful for enabling people to discuss the undiscussable without causing a blowup. We were in the midst of discussing a policy issue when a senior member of the firm interrupted somebody else, who became quite upset. The person who had been interrupted said, "Wait a minute. I've got to stop and say that you keep doing that, and it makes me angry." This went on for a couple of minutes. Then someone across the table said, "That explosion seemed to come out of nowhere. It was like a finger snap turning into a firestorm. This little thing blew up."

I asked, "How can a finger snap turn into a firestorm? It happens when there is a lot of dry tinder. What occurs to me is that we should take a half-hour or so and do some *controlled burns.*" The idea of a controlled burn is to deal with an issue that might otherwise lead to an incendiary situation in a slow and controlled way. The objective is to do some work, gain some insight, and then go back to the agenda, not to change someone's personality or make everything all better.

In order to facilitate a controlled burn, I take an active role in asking people to look at the different sides of the issues. This involves asking individuals to give examples, checking to see if others recall the example differently, and inquiring into how people are thinking and feeling both at the time and as we now talk about it. We develop a shared understanding of the dilemmas each person experiences and how these tangles occur. Often members of the group start to understand one another better and identify what each might do differently in the future. Whether they will in fact be able to act differently gets to the next issue, that of longer-term learning.

Developing Learning Capacity: Performance and Practice Fields or Online and Offline Activities

Putnam: My partners and I believe it takes a year or so for a group to develop self-sustaining learning capacity. Of course, this varies depending on how diligently people practice and on the difficulty of the issues they face. I recommend a combination of online and offline learning activities. Online means while you are doing actual work at, say, a budget meeting or regular staff meetings. Offline means time set aside to reflect and practice. I find that it is vital to do both, and to have each activity inform the other.

For example, in one organization, the business task is developing strategy. Online sessions are designed to make progress on this task. Then offline sessions are scheduled where people can reflect on interactions that have been difficult, introduce concepts and skills, and practice using them. Then at the next online session, members try to use what they have learned in order to make better progress on the strategy task.

Metaphors, Tools, and Methods

One of the things that can be enormously helpful to a coach or facilitator in intervening in group defensive routines is to have a package of guiding ideas, tools, and methods. Bob Putnam uses three basic tools: the left-hand column, the ladder of inference, and advocacy and inquiry. These are generally introduced in an offline session or practice field and then put to use in online sessions or regular business meetings.

The Left-Hand Column Displays the Reasoning Process That People Use to Design Actions

Putnam: The left-hand column comes from a format that Chris Argyris developed. Participants write, in advance, a short case based on an episode that illustrates the kind of difficult situation that they would like to manage better. They divide a page or two in half, and in the right column they write what they and others actually said. In the left column, they write what they were thinking or feeling but did not say. The left-hand column shows what people treat as undiscussable and the right-hand column shows how they design behavior to deal with the undiscussable dilemmas. The cases are used both as data for participants to diagnose their own behavior and as practice fields for participants to apply new ways of thinking and acting. (See Diagram 8.2.)

DIAGRAM 8.2 *The left-hand column case*

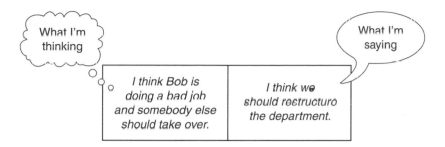

What I'm
thinking

What I'm
saying

| I think Bob is doing a bad job and somebody else should take over. | I think we should restructure the department. |

I encourage people to begin to say some of those things in their left-hand columns. It is important that people speak and listen with good intent so as not to damage relationships. As people say what is in their left-hand columns, it becomes possible to build a shared understanding (or interpretation) as well as for group members to redesign their actions to be more effective. It also becomes possible to recognize and disperse defensive routines that have been kept undiscussable until this point.

The Ladder of Inference

Putnam: The ladder of inference is a simple model of the steps in our reasoning as we make sense of what is happening in order to take action. (See Diagram 8.3.) The ladder of inference is placed on top of a pool of data

DIAGRAM 8.3 *The ladder of inference*

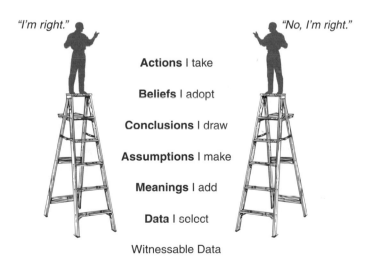

"I'm right."

"No, I'm right."

Actions I take

Beliefs I adopt

Conclusions I draw

Assumptions I make

Meanings I add

Data I select

Witnessable Data

Adapted from Chris Argyris and Don Schön.

consisting of everything that people say and do. Our reasoning processes begin with selecting what we will pay attention to and treat as important. That goes on the first rung of our ladder. For example, I might focus on Jack's coming late to a meeting. Then we move to the second rung of the ladder by interpreting or making meaning of what we have put on the first rung. I might think, "Jack doesn't treat this meeting as important enough to be on time." We might go through several interpretive steps. This is done almost instantaneously, without testing our assumptions. Then we draw a conclusion such as "Jack is not a team player." Finally, we take action based on our reasoning process. I might not invite Jack to be a member of the next group I form.

The first lesson of the ladder of inference is that people automatically jump high on the ladder. People are so skillful and quick in their reasoning processes that they do not notice intermediate steps in their thinking or whether they have forgotten to test their assumptions along the way. This is fine and necessary, but it gets people in trouble when they deal with others who have reached different conclusions based on different assumptions. What usually happens when people disagree is that they climb to the top of their respective ladders, hurl conclusions at one another, and explain the other's wrongheadedness by attributing nasty motives. This raises people's defenses.

Facilitating this interaction to bring defenses down involves helping people learn to notice that they have jumped high on the ladder and made attributions or evaluations that are not necessarily true. One way of facilitating here is to ask for examples on which people have based their inferences: "Joe, what was said or what happened that led you to believe that Charlie was blaming you?" "Joe, what did you mean by what you said?" Another approach is to teach people to use this and other tools themselves. One member in a group said when another member jumped to conclusions about a colleague, "Bill, you are so high on the ladder you need an extension."

Advocacy and Inquiry—A Tool for Productive Conversations

Putnam: Advocacy and inquiry are concepts for understanding how people interact. People can create better opportunities for learning from diverse points of view by combining advocacy and inquiry. However, just putting together a statement and a question is not sufficient. If I say, "That's a stupid idea. Do you want to wreck the deal?" I have both advocacy and inquiry, but I am not promoting learning. It is necessary to combine high-quality advocacy with high-quality inquiry. "What's your doubt about this deal?"

The ladder of inference is one of the keys to crafting high-quality advocacy and inquiry. People seek to advocate their views by communicating not only their conclusions, but also the data they select and the steps in their reasoning. People inquire not to sway others to their points of view, but to discover how others move up and down their own ladders of inference. And people encourage others to help them see gaps in their reasoning. (See Diagram 8.4.)

DIAGRAM 8.4 *Balancing advocacy with inquiry*

HIGH ADVOCACY/HIGH INQUIRY	LOW ADVOCACY/HIGH INQUIRY
• *Communicate: conclusions, data you select, steps in your reasoning* • *Inquire to discover steps and gaps in one another's reasoning*	• *Asking questions but not revealing your views* *"What costs do you have in mind?"*
HIGH ADVOCACY/LOW INQUIRY	LOW ADVOCACY/LOW INQUIRY
• *Advocating your view but not inquiring into others' views* *"What we've got to do is cut costs!"*	• *Silent withdrawal* • *Not revealing your views or questioning others' views*

ROGER SCHWARZ ON ELIMINATING DEFENSIVE ROUTINES

Roger Schwarz has some excellent ideas on facilitating groups, which he has accumulated both by study and practice. Roger named four things he does as a facilitator that produce results in helping people move beyond defensive behavior.[7]

1. Help people examine defensive thinking and behavior;
2. Ask questions that surface and test assumptions;
3. Help people see the unintended consequences of their behavior; and
4. Help people learn to change their assumptions and redesign their actions.

1. Help People Examine Defensive Thinking and Behavior

People often think and act defensively when they are in a high-stakes situation that is potentially threatening or embarrassing to themselves or to others.

When people start trying to save face, win the argument with unilateral statements, or answer the question: "How do I avoid losing?," it's a sure sign that "productive reasoning" has been replaced by "defensive reasoning."

Other signs of defensive reasoning are that people seem to be distorting reality in order to cover up mistakes, attributing negative motives to others, or drawing conclusions in an illogical way (logical to them, but not to others). This is all due to the fact that defensive thinking and behavior are usually based on very subjective opinions, untested assumptions, or soft data. The assumptions people are making may or may not be true, but people act as if they are true. The reason people do not check out their assumptions is that this often involves a high risk of embarrassment or threat.

For example, a boss in an architectural firm sends a mandate to a person who has not been demonstrating leadership to make some big changes. The person wonders whether the boss is asking him to do this because he wants him to make changes or because he wants him to mess up so that he can have a reason to fire him. Based on other people's speculations or his assessment of his boss's behavior over the years, the person makes an assumption that his boss just wants to "ease him out."

He does not test the assumption because asking his boss directly represents a potential threat or embarrassment. So let's say his assumption is inaccurate and he does what he thinks is reasonable and cautious, whereas it was the boss's intention for him to take more risks. By not carrying out the boss's request with vigor, he loses his boss's trust. By not checking out his assumption, he acts in a way that creates exactly the conditions that he is trying to avoid.

He may reason, "If I test my assumption by asking him, he might think that I'm incompetent. Or if I test it, he might know something I don't want him to know." We can see that defensive reasoning based on untested assumptions and soft data tends to become a self-fulfilling prophecy, as well as becoming self-sealing. It is self-fulfilling because it creates the consequences one is trying to avoid. It is self-sealing because one's reasoning prevents one from learning information that could prevent the self-fulfilling prophecy.

2. Ask Questions That Surface and Test Assumptions

One of the key roles a facilitator plays is to help people break the hold of defensive reasoning. You can do this by paying close attention to what people are saying and by asking questions designed to help people surface and test the assumptions underlying their statements and opinions. It's important to keep in mind that every opinion has an assumption behind it. "Hold on a minute, when you say 'X,' it sounds like you may be assuming 'Y.' Do you agree? If so, what led you to the view that. . . ?" Use your wisdom, intuition, and insight to develop a sense for the assumptions embedded in people's statements.

"I often work with the managers who report to elected officials and the managers are often given mandates by their bosses that they don't agree with," Schwartz says. "This presents them with a dilemma: 'Do I tell my direct reports that I disagree with my boss and risk being seen as unsupportive by my boss, or do I just go along in order to maintain a united front when I present the mandates to the supervisors at the next lower level?' In this case, the facilitator might point out that the dilemma is more complex than they imagined: The manager's direct reports are likely to see the same problems the manager saw with the decision. If the manager doesn't share his concerns or denies them, his direct reports may question his judgment."

Schwarz goes on to tell how one manager in this situation said that he decided not to question the elected official. He reasoned that by hiding disagreement in front of the supervisors, he would get their commitment. Schwarz said, "The question I might ask is 'What led you to conclude that? What, if any, assumptions are you making there?'"

3. Help People See the Unintended Consequences of Their Behavior

In many cases, people develop a theory of action assuming it will get results they want. In most cases, people are acting in a way that is rational based on whatever assumptions they have made. Yet as we have seen, when defensive reasoning is involved, people often do not check out the assumptions their theory is based on. Thus, they are often not aware of, and do not anticipate, how their actions are designed to produce unintended consequences. In most cases, the things people do to avoid embarrassment or threat do not eliminate the real cause of the embarrassment or threat.

For example, in the case above, the manager thinks he is doing the right thing to get commitment. Yet the supervisors may be thinking, "Wait a second. This man is either lying or doesn't see the problem and is incompetent." Then they say to themselves, "Do I raise the issues or play it safe?" The supervisors, as well, decide not to question the manager, assuming that it is better not to question the boss. In this case, neither the supervisors nor the manager can anticipate the unintended consequences of their actions because they are blinded by their defensive reasoning.

If you can help people see that their behavior might be getting them into trouble and producing unintended consequences, you can create the readiness to change. In the case of the boss, his defensive behavior and untested assumptions may produce what he doesn't want—the loss of the commitment of his reports. In the case of the supervisors, who would like to make a difference, they may lose any possible influence that they might have.

4. Help People Learn to Change Their Assumptions and Redesign Their Actions

As one of the values of effective facilitation is free and informed choice, it is not the facilitator's role to give people the answer or tell them what to do. Rather, it is the facilitator's role to help them decide whether they want to change, and if so, to help them. In most cases, helping test assumptions and interrupting defensive routines involves encouraging people to "discuss the undiscussable" or say what they are thinking but not saying. For example, a boss gives an employee a huge number of assignments to do in a short time. The employee can say "yes" or "no." If she says "no," she thinks her job is in jeopardy. If she says "yes," she thinks she could wind up looking incompetent.

Alternatively, you could discuss the undiscussable with your boss. For example, the employee in the above example might say, "You are my boss and I have some tough issues to raise with you, and frankly I'm scared as hell because I don't know how you'll react. If we take on all these jobs, I believe clients will suffer. If I just say no, then I think you might say that I'm not a team player. Do you agree with my assessment of the situation?" In most cases, it is important for the facilitator to remind people of the ground rule to jointly design ways to test disagreements and solutions.

Oftentimes, people do not say the things that they are hiding because they are afraid of the emotions and that people will strongly disagree. Paradoxically, two ground rules that help people express difficult thoughts as well as handle their emotions are (1) make statements and then invite questions, including disagreement, and (2) be specific. Use examples. By saying "I observed that you do. . . . Do you agree or see it differently?" you reduce the chance of drawing false conclusions that will anger others.

Another powerful tool that can help in preparing for a difficult conversation is to role play the conversation in advance. You can play the role of the boss and the coachee can play his or her own role. This enables the person to realize where his or her own thinking or behavior has been defensive and based on untested assumptions. You can also switch to the coachee's role at times to model effective behavior.

TOOLS CAN CREATE NEW POSSIBILITIES

Over the years, I have noticed that people appear to think they only have two possibilities: The possibility of the oppressive silence that comes from making things undiscussable or of speaking up and saying their thoughts and feelings and having them blow up in their faces. However, these ideas, tools, and methods show that people do have other possibilities and choices and that, as a coach, the more you work with people on these tools, the more they will see this and, at the same time, the more skillful they will become in exercising their possibilities and choices.

CHAPTER NINE

GO FOR RESULTS NOW!

Breakthrough Goals and Techniques

At the boundaries, life blossoms. —James Gleick, *Chaos*

From Archimedes to Plato, from Mozart to Madame Curie, from Edison to Einstein, and from Freud to Maslow, all the greatest artists, thinkers, and innovators in the world have had one thing in common: the ability to put to use the one durable resource they had—their minds. They had the ability to think more powerfully and more flexibly. The result was new possibilities and opportunities. For Einstein, it was $e = mc^2$. For Edison, it was the electric light and phonograph. For Freud, it was the subconscious. For Madame Curie, it was the x-ray. What does this have to do with creating new value, coaching, and outrageous goals? Lots!

We have talked a great deal about the importance of articulating an inspiring Impossible Future that people can engage in. Yet what is the process of moving from the notion of setting such an Impossible Future and actually pulling a group together and making something happen? This chapter provides the answer to that question in two parts. The first part involves articulating a one- to three-year company breakthrough goal that allows for and pulls for breakthrough thinking. The second part introduces the "breakthrough technique" for spearheading a larger breakthrough with a small group by going for a result now—something that can be achieved in weeks, not months.

If you don't demand something out of the ordinary, you won't get something out of the ordinary.

STRETCH GOALS, YEARNING, AND LEARNING

Company leaders, like GE's Jack Welch, Frank Shrontz of Boeing, L.D. DeSimone of 3M, and Dennis Gormley of Federal-Mogul realize that if you don't demand something out of the ordinary, you won't get something out of the ordinary. In fact, there is a lot of evidence developing that shows that setting ambitious goals provides people with the leverage to accomplish more. At GE, former chairman Jack Welch would say, "We used to nudge the peanut, moving along from 4.73 inventory turns to 4.91; now we want the big stretch like ten turns or fifteen turns."

Dennis Gormley, former CEO of Federal-Mogul Corporation, an auto parts manufacturer, used stretch goals to increase productivity and create value. He says, "Setting an impossible goal forces everybody to sit down, rethink everything, and break away from all the old traditions and habits. Goals that don't force that kind of exercise miss a tremendous opportunity."[1] To do this, Gormley set goals to slash lead times to days instead of months, to improve productivity by 30 percent, and to reduce scrap and rework by half—all to be accomplished in three years. (See Diagram 9.1.)

DIAGRAM 9.1 *The demands of stretch goals*

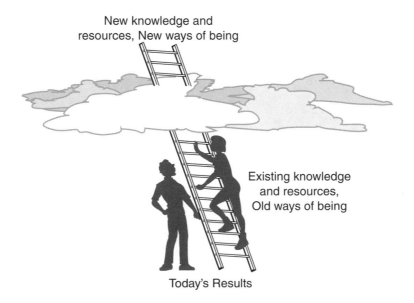

New knowledge and resources, New ways of being

Existing knowledge and resources, Old ways of being

Today's Results

3M traditionally had a goal of generating 25 percent of its revenue from products developed within the previous four years. This had led to products like Scotch® Tape and Post-it® Notes. In recent years though, the goal seemed to lose its magic. So CEO DeSimone increased the goal to 35 percent, encouraging managers to look for possible blockbuster products and rush them to market. He asked for breakthrough thinking and got it. A team developed a never-rust "scouring pad," made from recycled plastic bottles, to replace steel wool. 3M put up a plant and launched the product in one year, capturing a stunning 22 percent of the $100 million market.[2]

Judith Rosen, a consultant with CSC Index, notes, "Our data shows that one key difference between companies that win or lose at reengineering is that the winners aim high at the outset. High achievers hit the target; low achievers missed it by half. This was true for all goals—market share increases, reduction in cycle times, quality and productivity improvements."[3]

GUIDELINES FOR COACHING PEOPLE AND GROUPS TO PRODUCE A BREAKTHROUGH

GUIDELINE 1. Get Key Stakeholders Together; Talk About Stretch Goals and Why They Are Important

Stretch goals are seldom achieved through the organization chart but rather through a network of turned-on, talented people throughout the organization. Emphasize that people cannot really succeed in today's competitive environment by looking for ordinary or predictable results or by being run-of-the-mill in their approach. People can only succeed by looking for creative, entrepreneurial, breakthrough results. To validate this claim, use some examples from other groups or companies. For example, Toyota, CNN, British Airways, and Sony were all challengers who set stretch goals to become the leaders. (See Diagram 9.2.)

GUIDELINE 2. Perform a Team Audit of Future Opportunities and Today's Breakdowns

Coach people to develop a point of view about the future, as well as to recognize performance opportunities in today's processes. Some sample questions you might ask are: "What assumptions are the organization making about strategy or customer needs that are no longer valid?" "What breakdowns are showing up and in what functions of the organization?" "Do we have new products in the pipeline that will give us a future?" "What are our key customers saying about us or our competitors?" "What are marginal customers asking for that may represent a key to the future?"

DIAGRAM 9.2 *Setting stretch goals*

1. Get key stakeholders together; talk about stretch goals and why they are important.

2. Perform a team audit of today's breakdowns and opportunities.

3. Create one or two stretch goals.

4. Create a "case for action" that explains the importance of the goals and that builds motivation.

5. Explore how the goal is personally meaningful to individual players.

6. Emphasize that reaching the goal will require learning.

GUIDELINE 3. Declare an "Impossible Goal" for the Business and a Significant Leadership and Business Challenge for Each Key Leader

Whether you are coaching an individual, a group, or a business will determine what kind of stretch goals you set or aspirations you unleash. Start with an Impossible Future, like doubling your business, and ask each person on the executive team to create a significant leadership and business challenge on a one-to-three-year basis. Provide coaching on both the leadership and business issues that arise from that. Use these key questions as a guide in setting goals for people, and push back if you don't think they are truly a breakthrough.[4]

- *Are the goals based on a point of view of the future we have developed?*

- *Is the goal a significant business challenge?*

- *Does this significant business challenge make a difference?*

- *Pay people 80 percent of their variable compensation based on whether or not they reach this goal, 20 percent on the year-in, year-out stuff.*

GUIDELINE 4. Create a "Case for Action" That Tells Why the Goal Is Important and That Builds Commitment

People are often overwhelmed by a breakthrough goal that they don't have the answers to when starting out. Instead of reducing the goal or trying to answer the question of "how will we achieve it?" create a "case for action." Start by asking each person in the group to take a piece of paper and write one or two paragraphs on why reaching the goal is important to the company and to them. Revise this, then ask the group as a whole to write a one-page case for action. For example, "If we don't change, we will go out of business in eighteen months." Make sure people understand what is being requested of them. At some point, each person must choose to be either in or out. Give everyone the opportunity to stand up and declare his or her own commitment to the breakthrough.

GUIDELINE 5. Emphasize That Reaching the Goal Will Require Breakthrough Thinking

Achieving a breakthrough goal almost always requires breakthrough thinking—personal and organizational learning. Breakthrough thinking actually starts with making a non-negotiable commitment to the breakthrough goal. It involves suspending our opinions and assumptions about the one right way to solve a problem and then brainstorming alternative possibilities that create powerful new openings for action.

GUIDELINE 6. Coach People to Spearhead a Larger Breakthrough by Focusing on High-Leverage Places

Several years ago, I was doing a consulting project for Adidas. The company was slipping behind Reebok and Nike and didn't have the advertising dollars to compete. The company's marketing chief, Rob Strasse, an ex-Nike man, decided to spearhead a breakthrough by focusing actions in a small area. His theory was to create a new image for the company through a "mark" called "Adidas equipment." Then he asked the product development people to develop a small range of "equipment" shoes and textiles in the different sports categories. The last step was to focus all advertising dollars on the Adidas equipment line. The theory was that by making this part of the line successful, even though it only represented 15 percent, the rest of the company would be turned around. The project was incredibly successful and totally transformed the spirit of the organization.

GUIDELINE 7. Coach People in a Small Group to Get Going, Right Now, and Produce a Result

As we will see in the second part of this chapter, the best way to produce a breakthrough result is to recognize that you eat an elephant in small bites. Bring together a leader and a small team to create a razor sharp breakthrough goal that can be achieved in weeks, not months. The idea is to put aside elaborate planning and preparations and to get going, right now, immediately, and to produce a result.

TRIGGERING BREAKTHROUGH THINKING AT ENGELHARD CORPORATION

Ah, but a man's reach should exceed his grasp, or what's a heaven for?

—Robert Browning

In the following interview, Stephen Pook, a vice president of Engelhard Corporation in New Jersey, describes how Engelhard used the power of outrageous goals and breakthrough thinking to produce dramatic results. The change process started when the CEO and the senior management of this worldwide maker of specialty chemicals got together and came up with the stretch goal of reducing manufacturing costs 20 to 33 percent in twelve months.[5]

A Breakthrough Is Needed

Pook: As vice president in charge of information technology, I was chosen to lead an executive taskforce to spearhead the company-wide effort to reinvent the way we do business. We had a vision of being the premier catalyst company in the world. We had gone through the typical things that most companies have been going through for the last five to ten years. That is, all the restructuring, reorganization, exceptional quality, et cetera. And while they all provided some results, they only provided incremental results. And when added up, the results were insufficient to enable us to realize our long-term vision for significantly improved financial performance. For example, the restructuring effort mostly centered around a headcount reduction exercise, as opposed to really changing the way we do things. We knew that, on some level, what was needed was a breakthrough in the way we think and operate. Since the economy was growing slowly, we knew that the greatest opportunity to impact our business performance was on the cost side.

Set an Outrageous Goal, then Take a Stand and Make It Nonnegotiable

Pook: The first rule of producing a breakthrough is to set an outrageous goal. Our executive committee got together with the business-unit heads and identified an "outrageous goal and objective" for the company, which was to reduce our manufacturing cost at six key sites by 20 to 33 percent within twelve months.

The second rule is "don't change the first rule." People will say "Well, you know, it's going to take a little longer," or "We have all these things to do; can we settle for less?" Our COO Don LaTorre made sure everyone understood the goal was nonnegotiable. His answer was always, "No, I told you what the objectives are, and I expect you to deliver. I believe you can deliver it, and you will deliver it."

Create a Case for Action

Pook: We created a "case for action" that tells people why the breakthrough goal is important. Keep in mind that, in a process like this, you are asking people to think very differently than they have ever thought before. You are asking them to commit to things that they think are difficult or even impossible, and that is not an easy thing for anybody to do. If you don't have a strong case for action up front that people believe in and can really rally around, then you are never going to get them to go through things that make them uncomfortable. After our team came up with the case for action, each business-unit team came up with one, too, and each was different. One case for action was a page and a half long, but if you read between the lines, it boiled down to one line: "In five years, we will be out of business if we don't."

Introduce People to New Possibilities Through Breakthrough Thinking

Pook: We had to help people break out of their existing paradigms so that they could see new possibilities. For example, take the whole concept of reengineering. When we first went to the businesses and said, "We're going to teach you how to take 33 percent of your manufacturing costs out of your organization," they thought we were crazy. They said, "We've been through restructuring, we've been through reorganizations, an earnings-improvement program, and exceptional quality. We've already got everything out of the organization that's possible." The problem was that they didn't see any possibilities for reducing costs. So we asked people to take a "balloon ride" with us where they would start to see the organization from a process point of view rather than from the point of view of the functional silos. For the first time, they were able to see some possibilities that they didn't see before from the ground. The mindset of people began to shift from "There is no way that we can reduce costs any more or do these things any differently than we are doing them now" to "Wow, look at the possibilities" and "It's okay to change things so that we can really convert them into opportunities for reducing cost."

Generate an Approach

Pook: We created an enterprise map of each business unit, which gave us a picture of the key processes. We then looked at those key processes through various scenario exercises that helped us identify different issues and opportunities. For example, we looked at it from the customer's perspective, from a green-field perspective [starting from scratch], from the technology perspective. The intent of these exercises was to learn how we might reinvent these processes, reduce costs, and add value. We were able to identify a bunch of leverage points for improving each of these processes. There were those that were quick hits, those that were two- to six-month projects, and those that were true reengineering efforts—business transformation things. The important thing was that, as soon as we identified an opportunity, we told the team not to wait until we uncovered the rest of them, but to go ahead and implement some of those things.

Early Successes Generate Results and Momentum for a Breakthrough to Occur

Pook: Almost from the first meeting on, the team had an opportunity to implement ideas and suggestions as it came up with them. This helped to build the confidence level of the teams, both in the process and in themselves. The more we accomplished, the more this increased. We soon began to develop some real momentum, which drove the process forward. By twelve months, we were already running significantly above 20 percent cost reduction, and by eighteen months it was closer to 33 percent.

Outrageous Goals and Breakthrough Thinking Pay Off

Pook: There was a point where the taskforce started to feel: "This thing is going to happen." It was after the second workshop where we tried to quantify the possibilities without knowing how we were going to accomplish the goal. And the financial results of the quantification were one-and-one-half times what the objective was. At that point, we said, "Holy cow, we may be able to pull this off."

I'll tell you another story. In coaching one of the business-unit teams, what we found was that they kept coming back saying, "This is how much we've got." And we kept sending them back saying "But the objective is 33 percent." And every time they came back, they had an order of magnitude improvement for the business process in the way they were going to do it, but they were still short of the financial target. So we kept on sending them back and one day we had a conversation in the taskforce that went something like "Where do we stop?" because it seemed like they were coming back with better and better solutions in order of magnitude improvements and that there was no limit to their creativity and breakthrough thinking.

GOING FOR BREAKTHROUGH

We have to understand the world can only be grasped by action, not contemplation. The hand is more important than the eye, the cutting edge of the mind.
    —Jacob Bronowski

Outrageous goals, shared strategies, cutting through defensive routines in groups, many of the coaching strategies suggested in this book are designed to encourage more creative and productive conversations. The only way to utilize the insights gained from such conversations, however, is to take action. Yet, individuals, teams, and organizations often spend too much time discussing things or making elaborate plans and preparations and then do not take the action necessary to see the process through. To quote an old saying, "After all is said and done, a lot is said and not much is done." Here's how a Masterful Coach can get results.

Sidestep Elaborate Planning and Go for a Result Now

Experience shows that when people skip elaborate planning and preparations and go for an immediate result, they can produce breakthrough results that no one could have predicted or scheduled. You can see evidence of this when there is a challenge or crisis. Several years ago Motorola Chairman Bob Galvin became convinced that only by selling directly in the home marketplace of the top Japanese firms could Motorola learn how to compete on a better or equal basis. Then an opportunity arose. Motorola's communication sector was given the chance to supply Nippon Telephone and Telegraph with a particular pager.

The good news was that Motorola was one of the few companies outside Japan to be able to compete for the job. The bad news was that the time allowed for developing the product was less than two-thirds of what Motorola considered a normal product development cycle. Also, the quality requirements were so high, even for a company like Motorola that was already famous for its Six Sigma quality program, that the managers considered them impossible. The tight schedule precluded any search for new technology, elaborate planning and preparations, or specialized training. Success would depend on people learning to work together as a team and to leverage the knowledge that they had.

A team was formed that immediately began to look for innovations. The group decided to take a "zero defects" approach. In other words, any defects in the product were unacceptable. No repairs on faulty equipment would be permitted. Conventional wisdom and standard operating procedures were thrown out the window. The team used many innovative methods for success—and succeed they did. Here are some comments from team members: "The team was turned on by the challenge of doing something that was absolutely impossible to do." "Engineers were working one hundred hours a week and getting calls at three o'clock in the morning." "It was the most exciting time in my life."

When a pager was started down the line, a small green sticker was put on the chassis. The sticker remained unless a defect was discovered. The first time the hundredth consecutive pager reached the end with its green sticker on, the production line stopped and everyone cheered. How did they do it? The bottom line is that the team did not have a chance to do the usual. They didn't have any time to attend to strategy or the perfect organizational structure. Their success revealed that no matter how desperate the need for better technology, resources, or cooperation, people can get results with what they have. The question is how to make such miracles routine.

THE BREAKTHROUGH TECHNIQUE

Is there a coaching method for obtaining peak performance from your team? Is there a coaching technique for making sense out of ten-year strategic stretch goals or reengineering projects whose complexity is mind-boggling? Is there a way for people who feel overwhelmed by the discouraging complexity of their situations to experience a sense of significant accomplishment?

Most of us are skeptical of self-contained management philosophies, cure-alls, and quick fixes. Yet there is a technique that can be used to answer the questions posed above—it's "The Breakthrough Technique" developed by Robert Schaffer, author of *The Breakthrough Strategy*. The Breakthrough Technique is an approach that gives people a sense of accomplishment, that naturally leads to a feeling of collaboration between people of different views and perspectives, and makes everyone feel that they can make a difference, not in some far-off future—but today.

I interviewed Schaffer, who was kind enough to share his work with me. The following captures the essence of The Breakthrough Technique.[6]

Set Compelling, Urgent, Short-Term Goals

Many companies set big goals, make a plan, and lay out the steps—yet by the time they get started, they are often months behind in their goal. According to Schaffer, "It's good to set big, breakthrough goals, but companies often kid themselves about what it is they can accomplish. Furthermore, they get stuck in the planning and analysis phase and often don't achieve anything at all. Experience shows that achieving breakthrough projects through smaller goals or 'small steps' often proves not only to be more realistic but more powerful."

When Schaffer talks about a breakthrough project, he's talking about a short-term goal or a step where people can experience some success. For example, going to the moon involved solving certain engineering problems along the way. Each of these represented small successes in the scope of the project. Without those small successes, the rocket ship would never have gotten off the ground.

Schaffer said, "I am working with a financial institution that has set an ambitious goal of creating a 50 percent increase in its business over the previous year. That's pretty powerful and significant in terms of a target. Yet, what I have discovered is that everyone is milling around trying to figure out how to get the 50 percent. They set the goal in January and now we're into March, and they are not moving adequately toward it."

You can set a big, long-term goal and mandate that people achieve it, but unless you carve off short-term pieces, it often turns out to be just hot air.

According to Schaffer, "It's interesting that nobody said, 'Instead of getting paralyzed by the idea of increasing sales 50 percent, why don't we pick one line of business and try to increase sales 10 percent in the next four weeks?' The idea is that by producing some tangible results, the company will build momentum, as well as learn something that might create an opening for further progress."

Focus on What You Can Do Now

One of the most important aspects of this approach is to take advantage of the existing readiness for change. Instead of people saying, "That's not realistic" or "We tried that," you want people to say, "This is what we have all been waiting for." Just as important, if not more so, is to have people focus on what they can do with existing resources and authority. "Anyone can make a grand slam at bridge with thirteen spades," Schaffer says, "but how can you win playing with the cards you have?" That's the game of management.

Most groups say they would like to get better results, but they often preface their remarks with "But first. . . ." They go on to say that the boss has to change, they need a bigger budget, or the corporate culture has to be transformed. You have to have the confidence to say, "Yes, I can see how getting all of those things sorted out might lead to better results, but possibly there are some things that you can do on your own."

Schaffer tells of a good coaching method for these situations. Tell group members to make two lists. On the right side of the paper, have them write down all of the things that are needed from the boss or the ways that the culture or situation must first change to help produce better performance. On the left side, have them write down all of the things that can be done right now. These lists help people see that to succeed on the right side, they have the difficult task of persuading others to change the culture. You need to say to people: "On the left side, it is *you* who can make it happen. If you identify those things and start on them, no one can prevent you from making progress." It doesn't matter if it's not a perfect solution. When people start accomplishing things, top management starts to get on board and the culture starts to loosen up.

The next step is to suggest that people select something to get started on. Which one of the things that the individual or team has identified would they most like to try? Where could they make the most progress with the least amount of effort? This is not just to get people moving but to have them break out of the "I can't" mindset and into the "I can" mindset.

Think in Terms of Weeks, Not Months

After this kind of dialogue, you might ask the manager and team to select a concrete first-step goal that could be achieved in a matter of weeks rather than months. The very act of carving off something that they can commit to, where success is near and clear and where there are no "outs," creates excitement. Team members will look at one another like they are about to invest themselves in something that they know will require initiative and risk.

An early success will build momentum, creating additional readiness for change. People will then feel ready to set new, more challenging breakthrough goals. To encourage people to greater heights, you might well say, "You know, that product improvement is something our customers will appreciate; it gives me an idea of how we can do the same thing across the whole product range."

Build in a Sense of Urgency and Excitement

The Breakthrough Technique is based on designing each project for success by building in what Schaffer calls "zest factors." These automatically elicit the fun and excitement of high-performance teams.

Zest Factors
- *A sense of challenge and risk*
- *Urgency*
- *Near and clear success*
- *Collaboration*
- *Cutting through bureaucracy*
- *Fun and excitement*

Making Teamwork Work

"What about teamwork?" asked one manager who tried this approach. "You can talk about teamwork all day long, but people will not really understand what you are talking about until they actually start to accomplish something." The fact is that teams are a vehicle for getting something done. They develop by facing a real challenge, by taking disciplined action, and by struggling to produce results. We saw this in the Apollo project to put a man on the moon. We see this as any sports team makes a run for the championship. To generate excitement and fun, some companies turn Schaffer's notion of a breakthrough project into a worldwide competition.

At Motorola, teams with names like *Flexperts, Mission, The Ronamakers,* and *Cycle to Success* compete each year. These teams become examples of excellence that help inspire the rest of the company. For example, the *Flexperts* group of manufacturing and process engineers dramatically improved a changeover bottleneck in a pager assembly line. They reduced conversion time from eight hours to only one-half hour in only a few weeks while greatly improving quality. The *Cycle to Success* team, made up of administrative people, reduced the time to process an invoice by 125 percent and saved the company $750,000 in processing and materials costs. On a human scale, the results are impressive too. Teams from Motorola worldwide who were doing breakthrough projects competed to see who could achieve the most outstanding results and learning. One team member who went to the Motorola world finals competition said, "This was the most profound experience of any in my career, and the first time in my life that I have felt truly recognized."

Do Just-in-Time Training

One of the most important roles the coach has to play in reaching stretch goals or in helping people reach aspirations is to encourage a basic attitude of learning.

The same approach goes for elaborate training efforts and other preparations. Says Schaffer, "Training needs to be presented on a just-in-time basis to help people take the next step in the project, not by sending people off to abstract training programs in quality or empowerment that don't lead to concrete results." While writing this, we heard of a Fortune 100 company TQM manager who worked for eleven months on an elaborate plan for introducing the company's total quality program. According to the plan, there would be no visible results for over two and one-half years. It would take that long just to get everyone trained!

LAUNCHING THE BREAKTHROUGH TECHNIQUE

So how do you get started with The Breakthrough Technique in an organization? Following is a model that coaches can use in almost any situation. The model was developed by Charlie Baum, a masterful facilitator and a former colleague of Schaffer's. It grew out of work done with companies like Motorola, Dun & Bradstreet, and others, where it was applied to furthering the success of those companies' quality and customer programs.

Preliminaries

Launching The Breakthrough Technique in a group or organization requires some preliminary steps. First you must persuade someone in senior management or line management to use the approach. Once there is buy-in and an understanding of how the process works, the next step might be to review your group's overall strategy and then to ask the different department heads to identify performance opportunities in their areas. These become the places where people can sponsor a team to work on a specific breakthrough project. Start with designing a pilot project for success and then use small, incremental steps to build on that success. Baum says that "If you are tight on the following four points, you can be loose on everything else."[7] (See Diagram 9.3.)

DIAGRAM 9.3 *Introducing breakthrough projects*

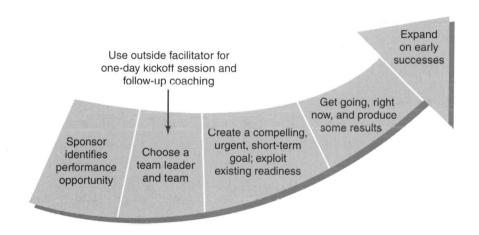

STEP 1. Find a Sponsor Who Identifies a Performance Opportunity

Once the leader defines a performance opportunity—and has made sure it's in an area that is measurable, like cutting product development time, reducing the number of product defects, or increasing sales revenues—it's important to find a local sponsor.

```
The Sponsor's Role

•  Identifies what performance is today

•  Takes a stand for the opportunity

•  Brings the team together

•  Presents the opportunity to a team to see whether they want to go
   for it

•  Gives the team the confidence to move across traditional functional
   boundaries to do the job

•  Reviews the team's short-term goals and work plan and removes
   obstacles
```

STEP 2. Choose a Team Leader and Team

It's important to choose a team leader with a proven record of achievement as well as good people skills. Team members are selected based on their knowledge and capabilities, not on their personalities or status. Invite everyone to attend a *breakthrough briefing session* where you generate enthusiasm about the project and invite them to set a specific goal. Make use of facts that show where the company's performance is today. For example, "The competition has a defect level of 3.4 per million on consumer electronic products. Ours is 3 per hundred thousand."

```
Team Leader and Member Qualities

•  Have a proven performance record

•  Know how to get along with people

•  Treat everyone on the team as a colleague

•  Have demonstrated necessary and relevant knowledge and capabilities
```

STEP 3. Design a Breakthrough Project by Creating an Urgent, Short-Term Goal

The next step involves setting a goal that is clear-cut and attainable, as well as one that represents a significant step up in performance. This tends to quicken the pace and generates a sense of teamwork. It's also important that the goal be based on existing resources, authority, and readiness for change. The response from others should be "This is what we have all been waiting for," not "That's not realistic."

> **Goal Qualities**
>
> - *Razor-sharp and measurable*
> - *Accomplished in two to twelve weeks*
> - *Have clear conditions of success—who, what, by when*

STEP 4. Bring in an Outside Facilitator for the One-Day Kickoff Session and Follow-Up

To help the team to design a breakthrough project, it's a good idea to organize a one-day kickoff session. Use an outside facilitator to work with the team on this day to set the breakthrough goal. This needs to be in keeping with the shared strategy of the organization. For instance, you might focus on the design of new products or improving work processes that have direct customer impact. The breakthrough project can be a discrete project or part of a larger project. You might decide to build a particular component of a new high-definition television in the next six weeks.

During this day, the facilitator also helps the team create a written work plan. The facilitator meets with the team on the second, fifth, and eighth weeks of the project to see whether the project is on track. The projects are usually completed by the eighth week. At that point, the facilitator meets with the team to harvest the insights that have been gained from the project and to see how these insights could be applied to expanding the scope of the project or to institutionalizing the success that has been achieved.

> **The Facilitator's Responsibilities**
>
> - *Makes sure goals are razor-sharp*
> - *Assists in creating the work plan*
> - *Ensures that work plan includes diverse views and perspectives*
> - *Monitors progress at weeks two and five*
> - *Harvests opportunities with team at week eight*

ACTION LEARNING

One of the big pluses of the approach is that achieving the breakthrough goals often results in people learning how to think and act differently as they take action. The combination of thinking about solutions and taking experimental action has a multiplier effect on learning as progress toward the target is made.

One of the most important steps in the process is to take time out to capture the insights that are gained along the way. This is one of the purposes of the follow-up sessions with the facilitator. If you experiment with this approach a few times, you will discover that breakthrough expansion routes are naturally clarified as the goal is reached, management development happens by management achievement, and the organization naturally expands its capacity to create the desired future.

The breakthrough strategy is also easily applied to larger reengineering projects or where a stretch goal has been set. Again the advantage is that people create momentum and new openings for action by building on early successes. (See Diagram 9.4 for how the breakthrough projects fit into reengineering projects.)

DIAGRAM 9.4 *Breakthrough projects within reengineering*

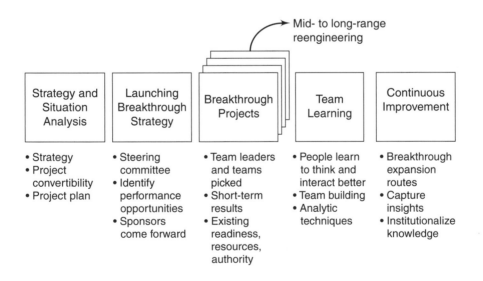

THE BREAKTHROUGH TECHNIQUE AT DUN & BRADSTREET

To find out how breakthrough projects work in the real world, I spoke with three people involved with breakthrough projects at Dun & Bradstreet (D&B): Mike Berkin, Charlie Baum, and Sharon Shelton. Berkin, a senior vice president of performance quality at Dun & Bradstreet Information Services, has set up hundreds of breakthrough projects. Baum acts as an outside facilitator. Shelton was the team leader for a project called Operation Clean Slate at D&B's Greensboro, North Carolina, facilities. She is now an assistant to the president of D&B and has acted as a facilitator for many breakthrough projects.[8]

Finding Out What Worked and What Did Not Work in Quality Programs

Berkin: When we started in 1991, my role was to take us from the design stage into action. From a study we had conducted over a ten-month period of time, we found that seven out of ten TQM efforts fail for various reasons—lack of senior management commitment, lack of business performance gains, over-investment in training at the expense of measurable results, and so forth.

Thus, we designed our Performance Quality Program based on five key characteristics: (1) business performance gains based on measurable goals; (2) early successes—getting something meaningful done in a matter of weeks; (3) fast team formation; (4) just-in-time training—giving people just the right kind and amount of training needed to take advantage of a specific opportunity; and (5) a nontraditional launch. For example, we knew that if we launched quality in the typical fashion with a big leadership kickoff and lots of education, there would be many cynics in the company who would say something like "This, too, shall pass." So instead, we decided to launch some breakthrough projects and, after a while, people started hearing informally about these projects, got excited, and wanted to hear more about them.

An Example of a Successful Breakthrough Project

Berkin: One of the most successful breakthrough projects was called Business Scope. It had to do with our business analysts selling products to businesses about which we were gathering information for our credit reports. The idea bubbled up from the Pittsburgh office, and a team was immediately formed. The team soon realized that they had to build a business plan. So we brought some people in from marketing who showed them how to come up with a product design, a forecast, and pricing. Well, the team defined the market, defined the product, and figured out the pricing and forecasts. In a matter of weeks, the product was being offered—first in Pittsburgh, then nationally. Since it was launched, it has contributed over $8 million in revenue to our business.

Finding Performance Opportunities

Baum: In another instance, Doug Nay and Tal Phillips, two street-smart managers from the New York-area office, were responsible for collecting information for credit reports on companies. They discovered that too many customers had been calling for credit reports on companies not in the D&B file and then disappearing without buying anything. It was taking seven days to create new reports on companies not in the D&B file, but the customers needed them much sooner. Doug and Tal got on the phone and asked the manager of the Greensboro office if he would help sponsor a team to dramatically reduce turnaround time. The manager at the time, John Hubben, said, "Okay. I've been working on a plan." Doug and Tal said, "You don't know what we mean. We want this to be a bottom-up project, with the people on the front line setting the goals and coming up with the solutions."

A Team Leader and a Team Set a Breakthrough Goal

Baum: Doug and Tal flew down to Greensboro, and Sharon Shelton was chosen as a team leader. Sharon is an exceptionally bright person, but at the time didn't feel like she was being creatively challenged. In fact, she was getting worn down by having to fight day-to-day battles.

A team was then selected from all of the functions that would be necessary to meet the goal. I spent one day with the team helping them to carve off a short-term, measurable objective and to create a written work plan. They were enthusiastic participants as we went through the process of brainstorming and problem solving. They knew that that evening they would have to present their goal and plan to Doug and Tal and were excited about it.

The Team Jumps into Action

Shelton: Once we defined our goal, we immediately began creating a work plan. Our freewheeling idea-generation session lasted until late in the afternoon. By the end of the session, the conference room walls had been covered with a blizzard of suggestions for eliminating waste or unnecessary steps. We developed an action plan by grouping the best ideas into categories that we called "action cells." Individual team members assumed responsibility for the cells, and we were ready to roll. It wasn't long before results were realized.

Baum: I got a call later from John Hubben, the manager of the group, when I was in New York. He said, "It seems like the team is running the place now. All I seem to be doing is ordering lunch. In fact, I just walked into the meeting and asked if I could help, and they asked me if I could get some sandwiches brought in." "Well, John," I said, "You'd better make sure that the sandwiches are good." He laughed. At that moment, John had begun to make the shift from a top-down middle manager to a team cheerleader.

Shelton: We soon realized that the reason it was taking us seven days to process the reports was because we were operating under an old paradigm. A big part of the problem was that we just had too many customer requests waiting at various stops in the process. We started decreasing the inventory, as well as making other paradigm changes in rules and procedures. In a matter of weeks, we were able to get the processing time down to three days. We developed contingency plans for fluctuating inventories so that we could continue to serve customers within three days.

Not Just Breakthrough Results, but Breakthroughs for People

Shelton: After participating in this project, I have a very different attitude about myself. I think this has something to do with the fact that we not only accomplished our goal, but we shared our insights with other offices across the country who, in turn, reduced turnaround time to three days or less. I also became a facilitator for other breakthrough projects. The biggest difference for me is that I believe I, as an individual associate, can make a significant impact on a large corporation. This impact is felt in day-to-day activities and outcomes, the corporate culture, and the bottom line. Instead of hearing people saying things like "Why doesn't somebody do something?" and "What's the matter with management?" you now hear people saying "Let's change this," even if it's a whole work process and it's always been done that way!

D&B Starts Small to Win Big

Berkin: We have initiated over one thousand breakthroughs like this since we started our performance quality improvement effort. This has had a significant financial impact, with approximately $19 million in annualized cost savings and $34 million annually in additional revenue.

PART III

THE SECRETS OF MASTERFUL COACHES

This section of the book provides Masterful Coaching candidates with the guiding ideas, methods, and tools for dealing with business situations that might otherwise confound them. For example, how do you get powerful leaders with very strong egos who "know they are right" to recognize that they are dangerously wrong? How do you motivate people who are experts at looking good while coasting in their jobs to play a bigger game with passion and determination?

Each of the chapters in this part contains a secret of Masterful Coaching that has a wide variety of practical applications.

Chapter Ten, "To Cause People's Success, Coach Them to Understand the Unwritten Rules of the Game," starts with the idea that coaching often involves working with managers to reach their personal goals and aspirations; for example, to become CEO or vice president, go ahead on a pet project, or receive a big raise or bonus stock options. One of the issues that often gets in the way is that people do not know the "unwritten rules of the game" as determined by the boss's corporate politics or "changing company norms." There are three dynamic principles to understand. This chapter will help you discover the motivators, enablers, and triggers at work.

Chapter Eleven, "To Provide Meaningful Feedback, Rip the Blinders Off So People See Themselves as Others See Them" points out that one of the coaching issues most managers speak about is that they go through their entire careers with little or no feedback. The real issue in giving feedback is not the sandwich technique—say something positive, say something negative, and say something positive again—but having the courage and commitment to discuss the undiscussable.

Chapter Twelve, "To Teach New Skills and Capabilities, Coach Others to Study and Practice," emphasizes the fact that, while today there are a great many tools for assessing where managers need new skills and attitudes, there are few reliable means for enabling managers to develop these. This chapter is based on the premise that new skills and attitudes are developed, not through the classroom, but rather through experiences.

Chapter Thirteen, "To Get People to Bring Their Whole Selves to Work, Give Them an Opportunity to Make a Difference," will show what some companies have discovered—that giving employees an opportunity to eliminate the artificial boundary between the things they care about at the office and the things they care about as human beings can create a context where people bring their whole selves to work. This starts with providing employees the windows of opportunity to not only impact the bottom line but to also make a difference in the world. The chapter will show that this is not something that is just relegated to the leadership of a company, but that managers at all levels can create a context that inspires and empowers people to add value.

CHAPTER TEN

TO CAUSE PEOPLE'S SUCCESS

Coach Them to Understand the Unwritten Rules of the Game

Don't fight forces, use them. —Fuller Sheller

I see my role as causing my clients' success. One of the first things I do to achieve this is to work with them to articulate their personal and organizational aspirations and a concrete action plan to achieve them. I also take every opportunity I can to advocate for my coachee with the intent of creating a positive listening for them (a listening for greatness) in their environment and to transform any negative listening in the organization based on gossip, rumor, or a rap sheet. It doesn't take very much to start a positive conversation about someone, just as it doesn't take very much to start a negative conversation.

The next thing I do to cause people's success is to encourage them to look at their goals and expectations in terms of the unwritten rules of the game they are playing in. An (un)written rule is an (un)stated expectation that a person behave in a certain way in a given situation. For example, "Stop on the red and go on the green." I find that most people will follow the rules as long as they know what they are because it supports their well-being. Yet I am often amazed by the enormous discrepancy between people's perceptions of what the goals, expectations, and unwritten rules for what they have to do to succeed are and their bosses' perception of the same.

THE POWER OF RULES IN OUR LIVES

First, it is important to understand the power of rules in our lives.

1. Whatever the game, the rules establish what the boundaries of the field are and tell us how to be successful within those boundaries.

2. People follow rules when: (a) they are clear about what the rules are; (b) the rules support their well-being; and (c) there is a consequence to not following them.

3. There is often a discrepancy between the formal policies or written rules of the organization and the *unwritten* rules leaders create.

4. The written and unwritten rules determine people's behavior within a social system or organization.

5. Leaders are often unaware of the unwritten rules they put in place; followers are also often unaware of what the unwritten rules are.

6. A leader cannot advance his or her career or bring about significant change without mastering the unwritten rules.

7. Mastery starts with understanding what the unwritten rules are. Ultimately mastery involves changing the game and creating new rules.

People's Winning Strategies Can Prevent Them from Understanding the Unwritten Rules

One leader I coached who did not understand the unwritten rules was a very bright, competitive, up-and-coming marketing manager named David Chamberlain. David was not only brilliant at coming up with new marketing ideas, but he was also a terrific nuts-and-bolts manager. Interestingly enough, on certain levels David had figured out the unwritten rules of the game and was doing quite well. He worked for a boss named Bill Orlowe, who had a lot of bravado and a lot of ego to match.

The unwritten rule in the marketing area was: "Give the boss lots of space at meetings to express his personality, and don't take up too much space by expressing yours." There were several other unwritten rules that went along with this: "Challenge the boss in a public meetings at your peril" and "If you come up with a great new marketing scheme that you want to have adopted, make the boss think it was his idea."

Chamberlain, whom I would describe as a man of great personal power in an understated way, was very ambitious and achievement-oriented. Soon after taking over his job, he figured out the unwritten rules for succeeding with his boss and developed a whole Winning Strategy around this. He learned how to come with ideas, create a better-running marketing department, and get things done by not making very much noise and keeping his head down. He later confided, "I adopted a 'yes, sir,' highly capable, humble, and deferential act."

The problem was that Orlowe tended to take credit for all of Chamberlain's ideas. The result was that Chamberlain was not really getting that much notice in the corporation. After a year or two of this, Chamberlain was very frustrated and he came to me for help. By observing him in corporate meetings outside of his own department, especially when the CEO and executive VPs were in attendance, I discovered what Chamberlain was doing to compound his own problems.

At these meeting, Chamberlain tended to act the same way he had learned to act in relationship to his boss. As a result, he was not being seen for all his extraordinary leadership potential or as a candidate for promotion. One senior leader in fact told me, "David is very bright; he just doesn't show up as a leader." Another said that, at big meetings, Chamberlain barely gave his opinion when asked unless in an obscure, ironic way.

I made Chamberlain aware of this through some very strong feedback and I could see the scales fall from his eyes. To advance his career, I told him, he had to first recognize "the rule of rules." I said, "You have failed to understand that there is a larger game at the corporate level than the game you are playing, and that there is another set of unwritten rules that you have to come to understand." I continued, "You have developed a skew of attitudes and behaviors that don't support you. You are unaware of these behaviors and you are unaware that you are unaware. Part of my job is to make you aware of these so you can transform them." I coached him, "The first unwritten rule is that, if you want to advance, you have to make an impression on the CEO and the EVPs. To do that, you have to show up as a leader."

The corporate game of advancement is played on multiple chess-boards and people have to master the unwritten rules of each.

I approached this problem as a coach on four different levels. First, I strongly advocated for Chamberlain with highers up in the corporation: "He is one of the best and the brightest." Second, I had a conversation with

Chamberlain's boss about "being a contribution" rather than "being a competitor" and creating space for others like David to shine.

The third thing I did involved getting Chamberlain himself to see that his Winning Strategy was a defensive routine that had made him succeed in his current job, but would prevent him from going further. Fourth, as Chamberlain has been running this racket for years, it was actually difficult for him to express himself with passion, commitment, and zeal. So I began working with him for an entire year on a breakthrough in self-expression. To make a long story short, David received three promotions within eighteen months of the time this coaching engagement started.

Leaders Often Derail when They Fail to Recognize That the Unwritten Rules of the Game Have Changed

The leaders of today's business organizations are likely to be striving to achieve ambitious aspirations, as well as to bring about a radical change in their corporate cultures. As a result, the written and unwritten rules for what makes a good leader in any organization are likely to be in a state of change. In reality, what happens is that the context-setting CEO often sends inconsistent messages that confuse the organization. Another issue is that senior leaders who have been around a long time often are slow to pick up on the fact that the unwritten rules have changed.

For example, I once coached a charismatic, new CEO who came into a company and declared a new era where leaders were expected to act less like *stewards* who polished up grandma's china and more like *entrepreneurs* who fostered a dynamic growth-oriented business. One regional manager named John Hawks thrived under the previous regime where the unwritten rule was to be a great "fix-it" manager. Hawks was confused, "The CEO talks 'growth,' but he calls every month to talk about earnings."

The CEO visited Hawks' region and became extremely frustrated with him when he found out how little Hawks had done to "get with the program" and asked me to facilitate matters. The first thing I did was to make it very clear to the CEO that he had to create much clearer expectations of people.

I told the CEO, "Your formal policy is that leaders need to shift from mere stewardship to entrepreneurship. You want them to be growth-oriented, but you have unknowingly put in place an unwritten rule that tells people, 'You get paid only for earnings.' You need to close the gap between the written and unwritten rules by sending out a consistent message of 'profitable growth.' You have to realize that, given the message you have been sending, what people are doing is the logical way for them to behave."

People are willing to play by the rules as long as they are clear what the rules are.

I told him, "People are willing to follow the rules as long as they know what they are." I also stressed that, "Being direct is better than polite hints." I suggested that he make his expectations crystal clear with Hawks, then give him a deadline (four to six months) to make a dramatic change in his approach. I have found that giving people a deadline helps them to accept reality (especially with remedial cases).

Then I sat down with John Hawks and had a "come to Jesus meeting." I said it didn't matter whether he agreed with the changes in the unwritten rules. He had to play by the rules if he wanted to keep his job. This was the cold splash of water he needed. Along with the changes made by his boss, it wasn't long before he made some dramatic changes and got some very impressive results.

To Realize an "Impossible Future" and Overcome Resistance to Change, Alter the Unwritten Rules

Why do so few chief executives succeed at making their vision statements come alive, even when people agree with them intellectually and emotionally? Why are so many employees frustrated, skeptical, and even cynical about their own ability to make something happen? What is the source of resistance to change?

Understanding how the unwritten rules apply is essential for anyone coaching an individual or group to create high performance or to introduce real change. Peter Scott-Morgan, of Arthur D. Little, points out that the way to create an opening for real change is to close the gap between the formal policies and the unwritten rules.[1] To do this, a coach must understand that most people have a good reason for following the unwritten rules.

Seen this way, it becomes possible to understand people's behavior and to deal with the real impediment to change rather than to reduce the vision, abandon the project, or feel frustrated and hurl accusations at people. The idea is to take the unwritten rules into account so that you can either use the forces that they generate or consciously and intentionally attempt to change them. If you simply ignore them, you will wind up bumping into obstacles you didn't know were there.

How Ford's Impossible Future Was Scuttled by Unwritten Rules

In 1990, Ford Motor Company started a breakthrough project to create the next generation Lincoln Continental in half the usual time, while at the same time practicing new "learning disciplines" such as group dialogue and reflection and inquiry. What happened? The project team broke, by a wide margin, nearly every speed record for product development at Ford. Quality defects in the Lincoln prototype were 20 percent lower than usual for a new car. Also, as a result of the atmosphere of learning that took place, the team was able to return some $65 million of budget money that had been allocated for fixing engineering glitches. By all objective standards, the project was a huge success.

However, the manager of the project, Fred Simon, was passed over for promotion and given early retirement. The reason, although nobody said it outwardly, was that the learning organization environment that was created broke the unwritten rules of the Ford organization, where it wasn't okay to talk about problems or acknowledge mistakes. However, in Simon's group, a norm was created where problems were openly talked about. The idea was to get all of the problems on the table and resolve them quickly, rather than wait for the otherwise inevitable crisis to emerge.

When upper management found out that three hundred engineers were talking about problems, not only to the people in the project, but to other people and departments in the organization, they went into a state of high anxiety. When building a new model, a process that usually takes at least three or four years, automakers typically expect 150 or so engineering problems to be outstanding early in the design stage. Simon found, as people began to talk about the problems, that they had over five hundred. One of his colleagues went to top management, who wanted to know how the Lincoln was going and said, "If green is go, yellow caution, and red danger, Simon's project is purple."

Even though Simon felt he was on the right track, and regardless of the project's outstanding results, Simon's approach went against the organization's culture and norms. Had he taken into account the unwritten rules of the game, he might have made some adjustments and been promoted to the next level, rather than forced into early retirement.[2]

As the people at Ford found out, the discrepancy between the formal policies, the company- or team-stated objectives, and the unwritten rules presents very serious consequences. The leaders of the project would have turned out a lot better if they had taken the unwritten rules into account and figured out how to either go with the forces that the rules created or consciously and intentionally altered them.

A COACHING METHOD FOR UNCOVERING AND REALIGNING THE UNWRITTEN RULES

The chances of realizing an Impossible Future are much higher if people take the unwritten rules of the game into account. If this is not done, people will never escape the forces of history. It consists of a coaching process called an "Unwritten Rules Assessment," which is done in a few weeks. The assessment results are then presented to leaders and employees with the intention of recognizing and realigning the unwritten rules with stated goals and expectations.

To do the unwritten rules assessment, I would suggest interviewing twenty to thirty people in different levels and areas of the company. As a rule of thumb, it's a good idea to ask a few questions, then be quiet and let people do 90 percent of the talking. This can be done in formal meetings in someone's office, in informal settings like the company cafeteria, or in some cases small group gatherings.

STEP 1. Talk About the Impossible Future and the Unwritten Rules That Could Impact It

Once an Impossible Future has been articulated, it is important to talk to people about the unwritten rules and their influence on human behavior.

First, to set the stage, talk about the Impossible Future, big game, and stretch goals that have been set. Discuss some new attitudes and behaviors that will be required in reaching the goal, for example, authentic communication, taking risks, or experimental action. Then ask people to consider the prevailing management culture and list some of the unwritten rules. Finally, ask them to look for the "disconnects" between the prevailing culture and unwritten rules and the new approach.

Next engage the individuals in a conversation about what their personal motivations are in the company. You are not looking for answers like, "I'd like to see a 20 percent increase in growth and earnings" or "We want our quality program to succeed," but answers more like, "I would like a budget for a pet project" or "I'd like a promotion or raise in pay." Then ask people: "Who could enable you to achieve that [the boss]?" and "What would you do to trigger that person in giving it to you?" These then are the unwritten rules of behavior for getting what they want. Ask people if they see any disconnects between the Impossible Future, big game, formal policies, and the unwritten rules.

STEP 2. Talk to Stakeholders About the Business Initiatives That Matter to Them

It is important to have an informal talk with key stakeholders where you can get their candid opinions about the Impossible Future, big game, and stretch goals. This will tell you a lot about what issues really matter to people, as well as why someone is behaving in a certain way.

For example, you might say, "You are trying to implement an Impossible Future that includes a business concept incubator, a Six Sigma program, and a new performance management system based on an ABCD model for key leaders. Could you tell us how you feel about this, as well as how this impacts your area?" Here you are not trying to get people to talk about formal policies or unwritten rules, but about the business issues they feel are important to them.

As they talk, listen for any disconnects between the business initiatives they care about and the behavior that is showing up in the organization. These might be comments like: "Leaders in this company do not really encourage innovative ideas," "There are turf battles that will prevent Six Sigma quality from being successful," or "People in this company don't have enough edge to make the tough calls about people."

It is important to understand that these are just the symptoms. Most people in the company could write these down on the back of an envelope in ten minutes. At this point, instead of stopping, you need to ask: "Why is it that these seem to be sensible ways to behave in the company?" You have to understand the logic behind the unwritten rules.

STEP 3. Cluster Comments Under Three Major Headings

Peter Scott-Morgan suggests organizing the comments into three categories: motivators, enablers, and triggers.[3]

Motivators

The first category is the motivators, which answer the question: "What is important to this person or group?" It is important to distinguish the difference between the things that people are supposed to be motivated by and what they are actually motivated by. For example, people are supposed to be motivated by making the organization successful or by making the company's vision of game changing ideas, Six Sigma, and so forth a reality, when in fact, they may be motivated by making themselves successful or by gaining more power and influence, getting a promotion or a raise in pay, or making a difference.

Enablers

The second category is the enablers. To find out who the enabler is, ask, "Who can help this person or group get what is important to them?" It is important to distinguish between who the enabler is supposed to be and who the enabler really is. If you want a big promotion, the person who can give you that may be a level or two above your boss. If you want acceptance from other people on the team, the person who can give you that may be the person whose approval matters most to you. Or if you are looking for a raise in pay, the person who can give you that may be your boss.

Triggers

Triggers answer the question: "What are the conditions that will trigger the enabler to grant a reward or impose a penalty?" Now that you have determined what is important to people and who is important to them, you need to determine how the triggers work. For example, let's say Bill wants a chance to lead a big project and the person who can give him that chance is his boss, Jim. If we also say that Jim likes people who think for themselves and can manage others, then that is the trigger, and the sensible way for Bill to behave becomes obvious.

Questions That Help to Distinguish Unwritten Rules

- *What are the people I am coaching trying to achieve?*
- *What do they think and feel about the project?*
- *What are the motivators? Who are the enablers? What are the triggers?*

STEP 4. Create a Forum for People to Become Aware of the Gaps Between the Impossible Future and Unwritten Rules

It might be a good idea at this point to bring leaders and employees together to discuss the gaps you have found between the Impossible Future and the unwritten rules that influence behavior, as well as how to close them. Show people by way of examples what, given the unwritten rules of the game, is the sensible way for people to behave in the company. Build a chain of logic. Also use diagrams to map the unwritten rules. Diagram 10.1 illustrates an example of this.

DIAGRAM 10.1 *Making the unwritten rules work*

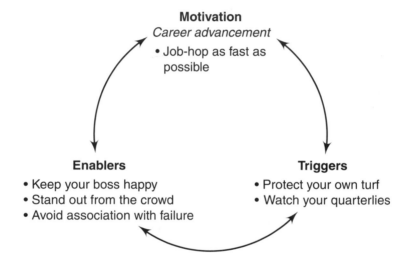

For example, the formal policy around the XYZ Corporation may say that leaders "Be generative," "Be innovative," and "Take the initiative," but the unwritten rules for years have been "Look good for the boss," "Watch your quarterlies," and "Don't take risks." As a result, the sensible way to behave in the company may be to "Talk big about innovation, but not do it."

The unwritten rules don't exist alone, but in patterns that often lead to absurd behavior. For example, another formal policy might be "Pursue your passion by spending 20 percent of the time you are on the job doing something weird, wacky, and innovative," yet there is an unwritten rule that says, "You must always say yes to requests by others." As a result, the logical way to behave is to look good by getting involved in lots of meetings and projects. You make a gesture toward spending 20 percent on your passion, but it doesn't amount to much.

After seeing the gap between the unwritten rules of the game, the formal policies, and the stretch goals of the Impossible Future, it is important that leaders (the articulators of the Impossible Future) take a stand to close the gap. As Peter Scott-Morgan says, "Just having knowledge of the unwritten rules means that you can come up with a pragmatic win/win design that treads on as few toes as possible."

STEP 5. Change the Rules or Go with the Flow

Depending on your level in the organization, there are different things you can do about the discrepancy between goals and the unwritten rules.

When You Are in Charge, Do What Is Necessary to Alter the Rules

If you are coaching those who have control over all or part of a company, you can suggest to them that they change policies and procedures and encourage new behaviors in their areas. Say, for example, that the person you are coaching is trying to encourage teamwork across functions and the unwritten rule is not to speak candidly for fear of embarrassing someone. You might coach them to tell people, "In the future, you will be evaluated as a leader by your openness and candor in discussing the undiscussable." Or you might suggest they address the compensation system that makes people think, "I get evaluated on my individual performance and get nothing out of collaborating." Or you could coach them to throw out provocative questions at meetings, such as, "What are the issues we have not addressed with each other?"

When You're Not in Charge, Find a Sponsor

Let's say, in the process of talking with people, you find out that the previous CEO fostered an unwritten rule to "collaborate with people from other areas, but not too much." Now, if you are coaching someone who is accountable for a key project that involves gaining cooperation from people he or she has no control over, and those people are resisting because of unwritten rules, what do you do?

This is when you coach people to find sponsors who are higher up in the organization who can change procedures and policies and encourage new behavior. Coach people that the way to persuade the sponsor to support them is *not* to hurl accusations at other groups, but to start by saying that people in the project are not getting enough information, citing two or three examples. Then they can explain to the sponsor that people's behavior is perfectly logical given the unwritten rules that have been created by formal policy or encouraged by management behavior. Once the sponsor sees the logic of this, he or she will find a way to intervene, and the problem will be a step closer to being solved.

When There Is No Committed Sponsor, Go with the Flow

If you are coaching people in a situation in which they are unable to find a sponsor and begin to alter the unwritten rules, you can still coach people to use their understanding of the unwritten rules to come up with solutions. Instead of thinking in terms of fighting the forces that the unwritten rules generate, coach people to think in terms of harnessing them. Ask, "How can you get what you want by giving others what they want?"

IN CONCLUSION

Understanding how the unwritten rules apply is essential for anyone coaching an individual or group to reach high performance or to introduce change. The key is to find out how you can use the forces generated by the unwritten rules to get where you are going. If you try to avoid them, you may wind up bumping into barriers you didn't know were there.

CHAPTER ELEVEN

TO PROVIDE MEANINGFUL FEEDBACK

Rip the Blinders Off So People See Themselves As Others See Them

A Masterful Coach is someone who can walk into a situation and see things that others do not see, giving people penetrating insight into the situation.

When I talk to managers about declaring an Impossible Future, some look at me as if to say, "This is madness." Perhaps it is, but rest assured there is method in my madness. In one sense, inspiring leaders to declare an Impossible Future is about taking their business to the next level. In another sense, it is merely a ploy for talking about what I really stand for—personal and organizational transformation.

I start the conversation like this, "Look, realizing an Impossible Future may require you to declare some new possibilities for yourself as a leader, as well as give up old patterns." Then I add something like this: "I am not saying that you are not a good leader already in terms of the kinds of the game you are currently playing or that you have to change. I am just saying that, once you put a stake in the ground for the Impossible Future, it's a whole new game and you may need to transform who you are as a leader. Let's get some 360-degree feedback and find out just how."

AN ALCHEMICAL CHAMBER OF PERSONAL AND ORGANIZATIONAL TRANSFORMATION

It is amazing to me how even the most brilliant executives, full of self-confidence from repeated success, who have never fundamentally questioned their leadership style for any reason, blithely accept the train of logic that says in order to achieve an Impossible Future they must transform who they are as leaders. In so doing, they have unknowingly stepped into an alchemical chamber of personal and organizational transformation. What happens in this alchemical chamber is well-described by Kurt Lewin as *unfreeze, transform, refreeze.*[1]

Throw the desired leadership attributes in the wastebasket, along with the hallowed 360-degree forms.

The first phase of the transformation model involves interacting with the leaders in a way that *unfreezes* their noble certainty in their leadership and management style. The secret here is ripping the blinders off so that people see themselves as others see them. For example, "You want to become CEO, so you drive your organization to get results. The chairman knows you can get results, but questions whether you can positively motivate your organization." The goal is to provide feedback with enough impact that people drop their "I've got it all together act," become vulnerable, and begin to hold themselves in question. This makes them transformation-ready.

The second phase is to be able to *transform* who people are. It is the context (background) that produces people's way of being and the behavior that is described by 360-degree and other feedback. The secret to this phase of the transformation process is to intervene in the context that is getting the person in trouble. This involves three steps: (1) Pondering all the feedback you have received about the person; (2) distinguishing the context that shapes their being and actions in language; and (3) distinguishing a new context, for example, being a generative leader versus a controlling manager, being a collaborator versus a lone ranger, being action-oriented versus an analyst.

The third phase of the transformation process—*refreeze*—requires leaders to integrate the new context that you have provided them so that it becomes an experience, not just an intellectual exercise. For example, if you have coached someone that she needs to show up as a generative leader rather than a cost-cutting control freak, and she is switched on by the idea, the next step might be to ask her to stand in a commitment to being a generative leader and begin to imagine how she is going to be different, think differently, and act differently in the future. It might also involve study and practice. (Learning new skills and capabilities will be discussed in the next chapter.)

A METHOD FOR UNFREEZING, TRANSFORMING, AND REFREEZING PEOPLE'S LEADERSHIP STYLE

I can think of no more effective tool for initiating this three-phase leadership transformation process than the 360-degree feedback that is done according to Masterful Coaching—The Method™. It is particularly important to the unfreezing of people's leadership style to provide feedback that both builds on strength and demolishes certainty. Yet at the same time, the feedback process also focuses on the context that the person is coming from that is leading to unproductive behavior, as well as identifying new skills and capabilities to be developed.

Interview people about the leader's strengths and gaps on a 360-degree basis, drawing out in-depth insights.

What then is the secret of Masterful Coaches when it comes to providing meaningful feedback? Let me answer that question by sharing my experience of coaching others in the Masterful Coaching organization. The Method™ begins with throwing such things as lists of desired leadership attributes and 360-degree interview forms in the wastebasket. Instead, we ask coaches to interview at least ten people on a 360-degree basis on the person's possibilities, strengths, gaps, blind spots, derailers, next developmental steps, and so forth. At this point, our coaches usually visit with me in preparation of their 360-degree feedback session with the client.

The first question I ask is something like, "You have all this wonderful feedback about this person. Now, let me ask you a question: 'What are you going to say to this person that will have a life-altering impact?'" It is quite often the case that people don't have an answer. What they have instead is a thick pile of papers with a lot of information that describes the person's attitudes and behaviors.

In most cases, people will then begin to summarize the information they have gathered in terms of a few patterns that have emerged: "Joe is command-

and–control oriented, doesn't listen, doesn't trust people" and so forth. I say, "That's interesting, but in reality, all this behavior is a symptom. I am interested in root causes. Imagine yourself sitting down with Joe and giving him all the feedback you have gathered. Then ask yourself, this question: 'What can I say to Joe that goes beyond making a report? What can I say that will actually make a difference?'"

Let me give you an example.

One of our coaches, David Korkosz, was coaching a leader at a high-tech company whom we will call Bill Farley. The 360-degree feedback on Farley revealed that he was a very smart guy with a big brain, a big bravado, and even bigger ego. He was in many ways a very personable guy, with sharp political instincts who had a tendency to kiss up to the boss and kick down at the troops.

He tended to take up most of the space pontificating at meetings with his direct reports, claiming most good ideas as his own, and making sarcastic remarks if people disagreed with him. He was very good at selecting talented people and delegating to them. He spent a good deal of the day doing things like reading *The Wall Street Journal,* having lunch, and going to meetings with higher-ups to report on his department's efforts. Korkosz was preparing to have his feedback session with Farley and was really wondering what he could say beyond laying on all the feedback he had gathered that would make a difference.

He then picked up a copy of music conductor Ben Zander's book, *The Art of Possibility,* in the airport bookstore on the way to the coaching session. Zander had written quite poetically about the story of his life, most of which he had spent trying to be successful, usually by competing with others in his environment. Zander had a great teacher who at one point led him to make a distinction between being a successful competitor and being a contribution. The result was that Zander turned his life around 180 degrees. He became a great teacher, who was concerned with liberating the greatness in others, rather than trying to establish his own greatness.

David was very moved by what he had read in Zander's book and decided to begin his 360 session by reading from it. He told Farley, "I want to read you something to set the stage for our talk today," and then read some very moving passages about the difference between being successful and being a contribution. Bill Farley was visibly inspired by what he was hearing; Korkosz now had his full attention.

"Bill," he said, "I can see that you are moved by the possibility of being a contribution and that is powerful, but I also want to tell you that today you are not showing up as a contribution, not at all." David continued, "Now I would like to give you the 360-degree feedback from your boss, direct reports, and even your wife." Korkosz read the feedback he had gathered word for word, without adding anything to it by way of inference or taking anything away. There were several occasions during this time when Farley's eyes welled up in tears.

Bill Farley had stepped fully into the alchemical chamber of transformation and had undergone the unfreezing of his leadership style, as well as initiated its transformation. "I am already a successful person on many levels," he acknowledged. "I don't need to go around anymore trying to be successful by competing with others. I am declaring my commitment to be a contribution." He also committed himself to showing up differently, particularly with his direct reports: "I am going to stop taking up all the space trying to show I'm great and create much more space for others around me to be great."

David Korkosz knew at this moment that Bill Farley had transformed the context that shaped his ground of being from "competition" to "contribution." The question he asked himself next was: "What kind of coaching program could we design that would support Farley in integrating and sustaining this transformation?" or to do what Lewin called "refreezing."

These musing led to designing a personal breakthrough project for the next year with special emphasis on how Farley was going to show up around his direct reports. At the same time, Korkosz recognized that he would not be there to observe how Farley was showing up on a day-to-day basis. This kind of coaching would be necessary, both for acting as a cheerleader when Farley succeeded and also for calling him on his act when he allowed himself to backslide into the old Winning Strategies, attitudes, and behaviors.

According to Korkosz, "I knew there was something missing in terms of a means of getting day-to-day feedback on how Bill was showing up." Korkosz came up with a brilliant idea—just what was missing that would make a difference. He decided to appoint two to three people around Bill as his "official deputy coaches," who could give Bill feedback on an ongoing basis. It worked marvelously.

A COACH IS A GROUNDED OBSERVER: GUIDING IDEAS FOR GIVING FEEDBACK

You see, but you do not observe. —Sir Arthur Conan Doyle

It is important for a Masterful Coach to not only provide 360-degree feedback at the beginning of an engagement, but also on a regular basis. The feedback process follows an intervention cycle of (1) making observations, (2) making assessments/diagnoses, and (3) deciding when and how to intervene. A good principle to follow is to speak with good intent. At the same time, talk straight without avoiding or sugar coating your message. First take a moment to focus on the person before speaking. When you give feedback, speak slowly. This gives you time to integrate your intuition and intellect in saying things in a way that will make a difference. Diagram 11.1 shows this cycle.

Declare Your Commitment to the Person at the Outset

This is so the person sees the feedback as an opportunity not a threat. I always begin a feedback session by declaring my commitment to the person and how much I believe in him or her. For example, "I am totally committed to you being a powerful leader in this company who makes a big difference. Further, I totally believe in all that you are as a leader today and all that you can be. There are just one or two small things that are missing from your leadership approach I would like to talk to you about. If you could make some progress in these areas, there would be absolutely nothing to stop you." In general, the things to give a person feedback on are (1) future potential, (2) general and specific performance, (3) attitude and behavior, and (4) patterns of self-deception.

DIAGRAM 11.1 *The observation and intervention cycle*

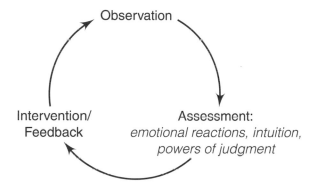

Present Personal Goals and Aspirations to Create Pull for the Feedback

As I have said many times in this book, supporting people in articulating personal (organizational) aspirations they can passionately engage in not only serves the purpose of stretching people, but also creates the *pull* for feedback and learning. This is far more powerful than the *push* approach based on listing company leadership attributes and identifying and filling gaps. A way to begin is to say, "In order to create the powerful new future that you want, you need to be open to feedback and learning. Are you in a place where you would consider some honest feedback a gift?" Sometimes introducing anxiety is necessary to get people's attention: "I know that you want to make a difference on the team. Here is what I see you doing that is getting in the way and that could derail the team."

Make Assessments Based on Observable Behavior

A big part of the role of a coach is to observe people's behavior and make assessments that become the basis of coaching comments. It is an important part of the integrity of the whole coaching process that the coach make assessments, not just based on subjective experience, but also on witnessable data. The coachee will also be more likely to embrace the feedback if you can back it up with specific examples. Instead of saying, "You have great potential as a leader" and leaving it at that, give examples of three things that indicate that great potential. The same applies to giving critical feedback. Instead of saying, "You tend to dominate your direct reports and shut them down at team meetings," share your observations of where and when the behavior occurred. Ask people to confirm your assessments. Perhaps they have different assessments, with different examples.

Connect How People Are Showing Up to Unintended Results

One of the messages I often give leaders and groups is that the problems that they are facing are usually directly related to their thinking and behavior, rather than something in the organization. Typical feedback to a leader might be, "I know you have a sincere and honest intention to realize the vision. However, it isn't being realized and there may be a few ways that you are contributing to this. My sense is that there is something in your thinking or behavior that is getting in the way." I then illustrate this with some examples. This is a chance to bring triple loop learning into the 360-degree feedback process: "How do you think you need to be different, think differently, or act differently?"

Develop Transformational Metaphors That Transform Who People Are

Rick Hamm, president of Conoco Refining and Marketing Europe, was a wonderful southern gentleman—a steward of the company's legacy, but not that entrepreneurial.[2] After he took the Masterful Coaching workshop, I worked with him to develop a vision of dramatically growing his business (doubling its value). He went forth with the vision across Europe and began to really inspire his minions. Yet my observation after a few months was that his Winning Strategy was keeping him from bringing it to pass.

One day I had a conversation with him that went like this: "Rick, you are starting to show up for me like a gentleman farmer, lord of the manor type, who like a good steward peruses his vast estate with his dogs, treating workers with indulgent kindness, and giving the occasional instruction that a fence or two be mended." A few of his direct reports had told me that he never made a powerful request or demand of them. Rick's response was that he liked the values of being a gentleman farmer. In fact he told me something to the effect of: "I like to talk the part, dress the part, act the part."

"It's fine," I said, "to have the values of a gentleman farmer—like good stewardship, integrity, and fairness, but you are never going to reach your goals if you keep operating at an agrarian pace and don't set higher expectations of people."

I knew I had hit a bull's eye when he immediately started talking about the importance of having more "impact" and reaching a much higher level of "velocity." He then came up with a contrasting metaphor on his own: "I want to be much more like the Scarlet Pimpernel, an English nobleman during the days of the French Revolution who, although a gentleman, would go into situations quickly, have an enormous impact, and then leave, go in, have an impact then leave, and so on."

Announce to People: "Now I Am Going to Be Provocative"

A Masterful Coach deliberately makes provocative statements to jar people from their everyday view of the world and to get them to see things differently. For example, most people have had the experience of going to a big meeting intending to take a stand for real change, but then caving in to gain approval from someone else in the group. In a case like this, I might give feedback to empower the person to take a stand: "And now I am going to be provocative. If you compromise half of what you want today and half again tomorrow, you will have nothing left of what you believe in by next week." By announcing that you are going to be provocative, people get the message, but tend not to take it personally or resent you for it.

Penetrate Illusions, Reveal Patterns of Self-Deception

Many people are not aware of their own possibilities and potentials and unknowingly make themselves small. I once did a coaching program for a German company, Adidas, whose sourcing office was in Hong Kong. The seminar included expatriate managers ("expats") and local Hong Kong Chinese. I noticed that the locals frequently referred to themselves as "just small potatoes." I told them, "Even a small potato can make a difference." I also told them that their "small potato act" was a way to avoid having to take responsibility. The group resisted the feedback at first, but it later led to a groundbreaking discussion with the expat managers, who had reinforced the locals' small potato self-image while blaming them at the same time.

Focus on What's Missing, Not on What's Wrong

Almost anyone can walk up to any person or group and say what's wrong or who is at fault. The most difficult thing is to give feedback in a way that will impact people's ability to perform in the future. Figuring out what's missing usually involves observing breakdowns, separating causes from effects, and then pondering for a while until a creative idea comes to mind. Pat Riley, while coach of the Los Angeles Lakers, was in a championship playoff game with the Boston Celtics. His players felt intimidated by the legendary Celtics' general manager, Red Auerbach, who was famous for tricks such as turning off the air conditioning in the visiting team's locker room, as well as by the fact that they were in a strange and hostile town. Riley knew his team could win if he could make them feel at home. He came up with a brilliant idea; he went out to a store and bought every member of the team huge, plush, pastel towels. He reasoned that you only get pastel towels at home. The Lakers swept the series and won the championship.[3]

Praise People for Who They Are, Not Just for Their Accomplishments

You can have the biggest impact with people by acknowledging them for who they are and their unique qualities of excellence. The clues to who people are, however, are often revealed in the things that people do. To acknowledge someone, a coach might say, "I want to acknowledge you, not only for the work you put into that great presentation, but also for your personal commitment to excellence. Here are some specific examples. . . ."

USING ACTION MAPS TO PROVIDE MEANINGFUL FEEDBACK IN GROUPS

There is also a method for providing feedback for groups. Here we are focusing especially on how people think and interact in a small-group setting. A coach is highly useful in situations where group dynamics take over because in these situations a group rarely has the ability to observe itself. Observing groups tends to be much more complicated than observing individuals. All too often, people who seem bright, intelligent, and committed to learning as individuals wind up in a group whose collective intelligence seems less than that of the individual and where defensive routines and anti-learning patterns take over. The results can be frustrating, strange, and even bizarre.

The six-step methodology presented in Diagram 11.2 and discussed below will help you to provide meaningful feedback to groups.

DIAGRAM 11.2 *Six steps for providing feedback*

---

1. Interview and observe key players.

2. Pay attention to the nature of people's responses to individual and collective illusions.

3. Design the group feedback using an action map.

4. Provide feedback to the leader.

5. Provide feedback to the group.

6. Have a dialogue with the group on what will make a difference.

STEP 1. Interview and Observe Key Players

When coaching a group it is necessary to get a sense of the big picture, as well as the small. One way to do this, whether you are group leader or outside coach, is to interview and observe the key players, asking them for their views about what is happening in the group. Doing the interviews tells you a lot about the underlying patterns that define the group situation and allows you to make observations about the individuals. Some useful questions for the people in the group are as follows:

- *Do the group members have a shared vision of what they are creating together? What is your personal vision for the group or organization?*

- *What type of team, organization, or community do you want to develop?*

- *How would you describe how the group members think and interact when they meet? What, if any, breakdowns do you see?*

- *What are people's relationships like outside of meetings? What do they talk about in the hallways? What's working and not working?*

STEP 2. Pay Attention to the Nature of People's Responses to Individual and Collective Illusions

As you listen to people give their opinions, you can gain a lot of insight about the underlying beliefs and assumptions that govern their behavior. As you listen, ask questions that determine the governing values that the group preaches and that help you find out where behavior is inconsistent with these values. Inquire with openness and candor about counterproductive behavior:

- *What are three norms that people in your group would say are important? (For example, being authentic, balancing advocacy and inquiry, being action oriented.)*

- *What inconsistencies do you see between what people say and what they do? How is this a matter of group dynamics? How is it a matter of individual behavior?*

- *Where do you see behavior going on that is counterproductive?*

STEP 3. Design the Group Feedback Using an Action Map

The ways people think and interact in groups represent a complex phenomenon that presents many puzzles and problems. Now that you have done the interviews, it is important to analyze and organize the findings in a way that reveals powerful insights. One powerful vehicle I have found for providing meaningful group feedback is called an "action map." It consists of five categories: (1) context or background; (2) the managerial frames that are the basis of decisions and actions; (3) dilemmas and puzzles; (4) action strategies; and (5) unintended results. Diagram 11.3 shows an example of an action map.

The tendency is to oversimplify what is happening in a group with a pet theory such as: "There is no shared vision," "We're too pie-in-the-sky," "The group is a plane without a pilot," or "Everyone has crawled into their bunkers." In many cases, these comments are based on untested assumptions.

In using action maps to give feedback to groups, you have to adapt the presentation according to your situation. Are you an insider or outsider? If you are an outside coach, as I am, you might want to present your findings to the leader of the group first.

STEP 4. Provide Feedback to the Leader

Start by giving feedback to the leader about his or her behavior and the impact that it is having on the group. The key is to help the leader see that, despite a sincere and honest intention to do a good job, he or she might be contributing to the problems of the group. Show with specific examples where the leader's attitudes or behaviors are leading to unintended results. Getting the commitment of the leader to change creates the space for others to commit to change.

DIAGRAM 11.3 *Sample action map*

Context/Background			
• Increased market pressure	• Company not integrated, run like small businesses	• Main customer becoming competitor	• Loss of money for past three years

Frames		
Demands	*Constraints*	*Mental Models*
• A marketing breakthrough • Design and engineering excellence • Collaboration—functional structure	• One year to do it or be sold to bigger company • Separate product divisions • Increasingly complex problems in market	• Engineering, manufacturing mentality • Entrepreneur vs. team • Local vs. global

Dilemmas or Puzzles		
No Obvious Solutions	*Polarized Views*	*Embarrassing/Threatening Situations*
• How do we expand manufacturing? • How do we break into new markets?	• We should use a team approach to increase sales. • We should keep separate product divisions and not hurt business.	• If I confront division heads, they will blow up; if I don't, we can't solve problems. • If I become a team player, I will lose control of my area; if I don't, I might lose my job.

Action Strategies			
• Cover up and bypass hot issues • Make unilateral decisions	• Keep thinking private; no public inquiry into dilemmas • Don't rock the boat	• Make results look good, even if they're not • Camouflage mistakes	• Make attributions; do not test them • Secretly collaborate against leader

The First Order of Breakdown		
• People feel bewildered, frustrated, and in the wrong place	• People assume others had nasty motives	• Crazy behavior from pressure of dilemmas

The Second Order of Breakdown		
• Issues made undiscussable; no shared understanding	• Group becomes dysfunctional; adopts self-protecting and anti-learning attitude	• No questioning of self-sealing logic or assumptions, no new possibilities

The Third Order of Breakdown			
• Organization unmanageable due to camouflaged operational issues	• A piecemeal, fragmented approach to new product development and marketing	• Key opportunities missed; lose time in turnaround	• Crises and over-dependence on the leader

STEP 5. Provide Feedback to the Group

After presenting the feedback to the leader, present the feedback to the group. Start by advising the group that some of the information might be potentially embarrassing or threatening and requesting that they adopt an attitude of learning rather than automatically reacting and becoming defensive. Then go through the action map, illustrating it with as many examples as possible. Be especially emphatic where the group is making things undiscussable, as well as where they are showing bypass and camouflage tactics. After the presentation, ask people: "Where do you agree and where do you disagree with what I have said?"

STEP 6. Have a Dialogue with the Group on What Will Make a Difference

After looking at the feedback, have an open dialogue with the group focused on what is missing and what can be provided that will make a difference. The following recommendations are possible examples of what is missing that would make a difference:

- *A session to clarify that the vision is based on a strong business case as well as what matters to people.*

- *Seeing impasses as opportunities for breakthrough thinking, which requires rigorous inquiry and dialogue to both come up with solutions and to build a shared approach.*

- *Doing more work in overcoming defensive routines, starting with all the things made undiscussable, for example, using a left-hand column exercise to help people speak with more openness and candor. (See Chapter Eight for more on the left-hand column exercise.)*

IN CONCLUSION

The most intolerable state is the absence of acknowledgment.

—William James

Giving high-quality feedback has more to do with caring enough about people to tell it like it is than it has with having a particular skill or technique. On the one hand, it involves having the generosity of spirit to acknowledge people for who they are and what they are capable of. In my experience, people are starved for praise—not just praise of their accomplishments but for who they are as human beings. On the other hand, generosity of spirit includes being willing to have the tough conversations with people. Remember to praise publicly and criticize privately and, most of all, to do it with heart.

CHAPTER TWELVE

TO TEACH NEW SKILLS
AND CAPABILITIES

Coach Others to Study and Practice

Knowing "what" is different than knowing "how."
—William Isaacs

One of my fundamental premises is that a Masterful Coach is first and foremost a teacher. Being a great teacher not only means inspiring people to take a stand for an extraordinary future, but expanding their capacity to achieve it. I see coaching as the most powerful vehicle available for teaching people to develop new skills and capabilities, much more so than the typical three-day training program. The model that I use is goal-oriented and situation-specific. It is very similar to a ski or golf lesson where people learn by doing—teach a little, practice a little, provide feedback and learning (repeat) until the new skill is ready at hand.

Teaching new skills and capabilities is a matter of study and practice.

What is the source of skill? If you look at the people you know who are masterful at something, and look behind what's easy to see, you start to observe that a high level of skill development is a complex phenomenon. First of all, mastery at anything is often much more a way of being, something that a person seems to embody, than a set of tips and techniques. I once saw a tee-shirt in Tortola, British Virgin Islands, that expressed this very well: "It is who I am; it is not attitudes and behaviors." Developing a new way of being starts with taking a stand for a vision and asking: "Who do I need to be in the matter?" and "What do I need to give up?"

Having said that, people who are highly skillful at a particular domain usually operate from a balance of theory and practice. Every great golf or ski teacher, for example, has a theory of "the perfect golf swing" or "the perfect turn." This theory is not something abstract, but becomes a mental map for being able to take effective action. Teaching any business skill, such as effective communication, is a matter of providing a solid set of guiding ideas (synonymous with theory), as well as teaching people to master the fundamentals of the skill–learning by doing. For example, two fundamentals of effective communication are "committed speaking" and "committed listening."

FIVE ESSENTIAL SKILLS THAT OFTEN SHOW UP AS MISSING

Part of the coach's role is to observe people as they make committed attempts to perform and see which skills and capabilities are missing. This then becomes the basis of creating a personalized coaching and training program. Here we will focus on five key skills that all leaders need to have in order to take their organizations to the next level and that often show up as missing:

1. Extraordinary leadership;
2. Creating a shared vision or context (the social architecture for your organization);
3. Team dialogue and conflict resolution;
4. Reflecting on mental models; and
5. Systemic thinking.

SKILL ONE. Extraordinary Leadership

Extraordinary Leadership Is Missing When
- *There is a lack of excitement about the future;*
- *People vacillate about a situation rather than take a stand; and/or*
- *People are not taking risks or initiative.*

What is leadership? Leadership involves shaping an organization's vision and values so as to bring out the best in people and to generate a conversation for action that makes something happen and that results in things being different. It is a sad fact of life that, in most organizations, leadership often shows up as missing. If we can acknowledge that leadership is missing in a way that people see it as an opportunity rather than a threat, it is the first step toward calling forth the leadership that is needed and wanted.

This often begins with having a "come to Jesus" meeting with a manager: "You are not showing up as a leader and making the difference that others expect you to make. You are showing up at the most on the high end of being a manager. This means you occasionally show up as a leader, but not at all on a consistent basis."

Leadership arises when people discover themselves as the stand that they take and begin to think, talk, and act from their stand. The first step then in teaching someone to be a leader involves inspiring him or her to take a stand. Here are three of my favorite questions:

- *What is the future you want to create for yourself and the people you care about in this company?*

- *What is it that you want to achieve, if only it were possible?*

- *What do you want to create so much that you would be willing to reinvent your entire self?*

SKILL TWO. Building a Shared Vision (Context)

Building a Shared Vision (Context) Is Missing When
- *Managers do not have a point of view about the future;*
- *People spend their time trying to fix, help, or solve today's problems; and/or*
- *It is difficult to coordinate mundane activities between different areas.*

Building a shared vision involves people in a group asking: "What do we want to create together?" Answering this question requires constructing a shared mental model of the desired future and how it will be realized. *What is shared vision?* As mentioned earlier, ordinary leaders create a vision statement on the wall somewhere. Extraordinary leaders create a context that becomes the vision, climate, spirit of the company. When I am speaking of the *context,* I am speaking of the social architecture of the organization.

Context includes such things as these:

- *A vision of where you are going, for example, "To be number one or two in our industry";*
- *Your teachable point of view that will foster the necessary mindset to realize the vision; and*
- *Two or three powerful initiatives, such as: Masterful Coaching for all key leaders, a shift from products to services, Six Sigma quality, a business concept incubator.*

This is an opportunity to create a new future that gives people in the organization the chance to be a part of something larger than themselves, as well as to experience being the authors of their own destiny. Unless the vision is shared and means something to the individuals, however, it will never be implemented.

SKILL THREE. Team Dialogue and Conflict Resolution

Team Dialogue and Conflict Resolution Are Missing When
- *The team is faced with an Impossible Future that is beyond what they already think and know;*
- *The individuals in the group are faced with dilemmas for which there are no easy or obvious answer; and/or*
- *The organizational defensive routines impede the way people think and interact together.*

To be sure, when an organization sets a stretch goal, it places itself in a situation where there are complex problems, dilemmas, and puzzles—and there are no simple or obvious solutions. One of the first steps to take is to create a community of inquiry in the group to help people ponder the dilemmas they are facing. This involves taking the time to really think deeply about the problems they are facing, rather than just jumping to conclusions. (See Chapter Seven for some guidelines for building a shared approach through collaborative conversations and group dialogue.)

One of the first things to do in meetings with the inquiry group is to frame the problem. This will determine the kind of solution to look for. The question to ask people is: "Will the solution to the problem give you results you would like?" For example: Is the problem to create a new future or is it to fix operational problems today? Is the problem to produce a breakthrough result or just some small improvements in an ongoing way? Does the problem involve stretching your resources and knowledge or does it involve using what you already think and know?

After you have framed the problem, the next step is to look at any pet approaches for dealing with such problems to see if they are a match. This often involves reflecting on the group's paradigms or frames of reference. For example, perhaps the problem lies in creating a marketing breakthrough and the organization is operating from a design and manufacturing mentality rather than a marketing and service one. Oftentimes, people in groups are trapped in old paradigms that are socially constructed and reinforced.

The key to engaging people in high-quality dialogue is to make disagreement acceptable so that people focus on what they can learn in the conversation rather than on winning or avoiding losing. Encouraging diverse views and perspectives often leads to shared understanding as well as to discovering something new. Why is dialogue important? It is the primary way by which groups think and interact. Lack of dialogue leads to poor decisions, lack of team learning, and a general deterioration of the group.

SKILL FOUR. Reflecting on Mental Models

Reflecting on Mental Models Is Missing
- *When people keep doing the same thing even though they don't get different results;*
- *When the dialogue in a group is incoherent; and/or*
- *When people are enacting defensive routines without being aware of it.*

Although each person in a company may see the world somewhat differently, most by and large operate from the same managerial frames of reference. The lessons from the past become like a DNA code that is passed from one group of managers to the next. This can prevent people from recognizing changes in reality, seeing the big picture, or seeing alternative ways to solve complex problems.

In most cases, people are not even aware of the frames that define their possibilities and choices. And what makes matters worse is that these frames prevent people from seeing that other possibilities and choices exist for solving the problem. The role of a coach in this process is to continually question what people take for granted. One powerful way to help people to begin reflecting on their mental models is to use stories to make a point. This is a story I often use:

"I heard a story about a group of monkeys. One monkey runs up a pole in a shower to get some bananas. When the monkey gets to the showerhead, the bananas turn out to be plastic decorations and instead of a bite to eat, he gets a cold drenching. He does this four times. The other monkeys watch him and repeat the same procedure. Eventually, they stop climbing the pole. Then, one of the monkeys from the group is removed and a new one replaces him. The monkeys teach the newcomer never to climb up that pole. Eventually all the monkeys from the original group are replaced, yet the new monkeys quickly learn to never go up that pole, even though none of them has had a cold shower. They just accept that pole climbing is discouraged. Here are some powerful questions that foster reflection:

- *What are our pet theories for doing something?*
- *Does the solution require doing something different or doing the same thing better?*
- *What does people's explicit language reveal about their deep beliefs and assumptions?*
- *What are the standard practices that we act on?*
- *What could we do that is fundamentally different?*

SKILL FIVE. Systems Thinking

Systems Thinking Is Missing When
- *You want to provide "great customer experience" and to do so requires business integration;*
- *People are stuck in stove pipe thinking and can't collaborate; and/or*
- *People are protecting their turf rather than thinking of the good of the whole.*

Over the past decade or so, companies have gone to extraordinary lengths to develop integrated business units, create teams, and reengineer processes. Yet despite all this, the real barriers to communication and collaboration remain: the ones in people's heads. People still tend to think in terms of optimizing their individual part as opposed to optimizing how the different parts interact together.

Teaching people the discipline of "systems thinking" often starts with penetrating the illusion of separation by giving people a greater sense of the interconnectedness of everyone and everything. In practical terms, it involves thinking in terms of balancing the big picture and the small picture, the long-term view and the short-term view, and making sure that all the different pieces of the organization fit together to make a whole.

One of the best ways to teach systems thinking is to ask people to take a helicopter ride over their entire business. For example, if you had an airline business you would see that, when the customer purchases a ticket, it is not an isolated event, but part of a whole stream of processes such as scheduling flights, servicing planes, and catering meals. Things like customer satisfaction, growth, and profitability are directly related to how well the different parts of the system interact.

A METHODOLOGY FOR BUILDING NEW SKILLS AND CAPABILITIES

Now we will look at a four-step methodology for teaching people new skills and capabilities (see Diagram 12.1). It is based on the transformational learning process, which calls for reframing people's mindsets, then building new skills (see Diagram 12.2).

DIAGRAM 12.1 *Methodology for teaching new skills and capabilities*

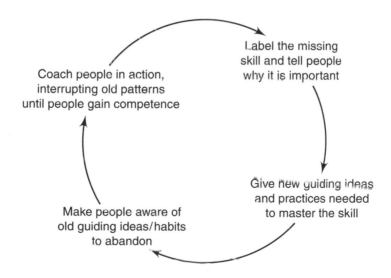

Coach people in action, interrupting old patterns until people gain competence

Label the missing skill and tell people why it is important

Give new guiding ideas and practices needed to master the skill

Make people aware of old guiding ideas/habits to abandon

DIAGRAM 12.2 *Building new skills*

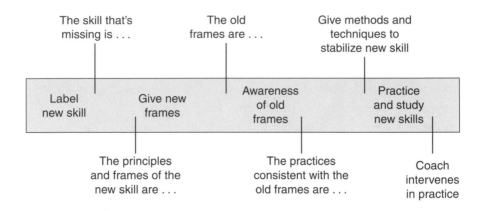

The skill that's missing is . . .

The old frames are . . .

Give methods and techniques to stabilize new skill

| Label new skill | Give new frames | Awareness of old frames | Practice and study new skills |

The principles and frames of the new skill are . . .

The practices consistent with the old frames are . . .

Coach intervenes in practice

1. Label the Missing Skill and Tell People Why It Is Important

One of the most important phases in the process of coaching people to develop new skills is labeling the missing skills. Until people can distinguish these missing skills by putting them into words, they will not be able to act effectively. For example, "We need to develop the skill of coming up with *game changing* ideas to regenerate our company (and industry). This is key to coming up with fundamentally new products and services."

The act of putting an idea into language has real generative power. To begin with, it announces a new domain of practice that is different from everything else that people are doing. Also, if the idea is expressed powerfully and precisely, it helps refocus people's actions. For instance, my friend Bob Fritz makes the distinction between "being creative" and "creativity." Being creative leads to creating something that never existed before, such as a new industry or a new product or service. Creativity is more about creative or artistic expression. Once people know what it means to "be creative," they can begin to learn about the behavior that will allow them to create something new.[1]

Once the new skill is labeled, the next step is to make sure people understand why it is important. "We can cut costs all day long, but if we don't come up with some innovative product ideas in this development process, we may miss the turnoff to the future and our customers will go somewhere else.

2. Distinguish New Guiding Ideas and Key Practices Needed to Master the Skill

Leadership and team collaboration, like golf or skiing, have a set of guiding ideas that shape, limit, and define the actions that a person takes. One guiding idea I want to emphasize here is that *thinking drives behavior.* When people think differently, they act differently. The idea here is not to replace one guiding idea or belief system with another that is superior. It is to distinguish new frames of reference that touch people with new possibilities and choices and that lead to new skills and capabilities.

For example, most managers grow up in a culture in which they get ahead by being smart, always having the right answers, and being right at the expense of making others wrong. It becomes the set of guiding ideas that they bring into every meeting they go to and has an enormous impact on how they think and interact with others. Ask yourself: "What would be the guiding ideas that a coach would introduce in order to empower people to have a real quality of dialogue?"

SWISS AIR LINES: GIVING PEOPLE THE RIGHT GUIDING IDEAS

How do you teach people the skills and capabilities that are needed in a job? "To start, you have to hire people who like people," says Philippe Chéhab, division manager of Swiss Air Lines, "and they have to like them enough to be able to embrace their idiosyncrasies rather than be intolerant and judge them.[2]

"Our commitment is to offering world-class service on our flights. We have special orientation programs for all our flight crews that help people break down the walls that usually separate them from other people and lead to premature judgments and emotional reactions." Chéhab continues, "Besides hiring people who like people, we try to give them the right mind-map. Our mind-maps shape our behavior.

"We tell people that Swiss Air Lines is about being of service and ask them to identify with that and to put themselves in the customer's shoes. If our flight attendants like people, identify with being of service, and have the right mind-map so they can see things from the customer's perspective, the rest takes care of itself. We don't have to tell them how to behave. We no longer have to tell them to put the fork here or there. That's our strategic edge."

Chehab and his group also help people to look at the busines from a systems thinking perspective. Diagram 12.3 shows this perspective. Says Chéhab, "At Swiss Air Lines, people are expected not only to notice breakdowns and make improvements in their areas, but to take responsibility for noticing things and suggesting improvements in other areas that might have consequence on a system level. When we get information about a problem, we try to find the systemic cause."

DIAGRAM 12.3 *A systems thinking perspective*

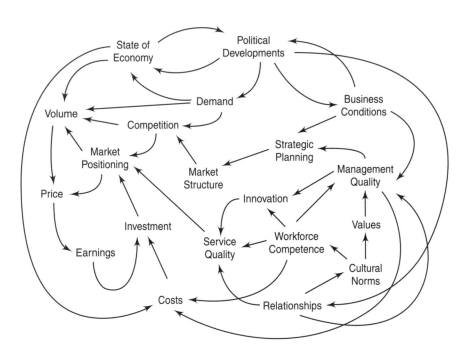

"This starts out as being an interesting idea for people and is something they have to get used to," says Chéhab, "but in time, it becomes part of a whole new identity structure for them. What we are always looking to do is to find ways to accelerate this process." The combination of reframing, plus the reinforcement over time, results in a real spirit of cooperation that probably would never have happened if you had just told people to cooperate." According to Chéhab, "It leads to a feeling of community, of being part of a network that extends to people around the world."

---

3. Make People Aware of Old Guiding Ideas/Habits to Abandon

When you are teaching people new skills, it is not as if you are projecting new guiding ideas and practices onto a blank screen. People already have deeply embedded mindsets and habits, which may fly in the face of what you are trying to teach them. For example, let's say you are coaching a leader who has taken on a stretch goal that will require her to transform her part of the business. Yet she has a lifelong paradigm of looking good, and a slew of skillful behavior around this. I sometimes call this "skilled incompetence"— skilled behavior that leads to unintended results.

Teaching people new skills and capabilities may start with teaching new theory and practices, but quickly becomes a matter of breaking old paradigms and habits people are barely aware of. For example, Joe Mueller, a manager I once coached, had learned some of the juicy vocabulary of leadership such as "taking a stand" and went around talking about it all the time. Yet he got himself into trouble because he was so highly skilled at trying to please others and at altering what he stood for according to the political situation. He was also good at suppressing his awareness of what he was doing. This is what I call "skilled unawareness," any attempt to suppress self-protective behavior inconsistent with the person's value system.

The coach's first role in teaching people new skills and capabilities often involves making them aware of what they are unaware of. I asked Joe, "Do you know that you take one stand on one day, another stand the next day, and a third on the next, depending on which way the political winds are blowing?" This information hit Joe like a wake-up call. He said, "I was completely unaware of what I was doing."

I then said to Joe, with the intent of doing some triple loop learning, "What makes you believe you have to act this way?" Use whatever people say or do as an opportunity to help them reflect more deeply on their history as well as on their deep beliefs and assumptions. If they say, "I don't know" or make light of the issue, make a provocation: "It sounds to me like you are protecting yourself.

Why do you feel like you have to do that?" After I posed some questions like these, Joe asked me to work with him over the course of a one-year period to be resolute in the face of his stand. I remember telling him: "I am going to be like a steel peg in the frozen ground so as to relentlessly support you in being able to speak, listen, and act from your stand."

4. Coach People in Action, Interrupting Old Patterns Until People Gain Competence

Saying is one thing, doing another.
    —Montaigne

We can have a beautiful theory about how to play the piano, but until we raise our finger in the air and press a key, we do not even know what a piano sounds like. Practice is where we learn by doing. The beautiful thing about practice, especially if there is a coach around, is that it gives us an opportunity to get some feedback. We either hit good notes or sour notes. If we take our theory of action and put it into practice and it doesn't produce desired results, we can see that something is off.

Obviously, a key coaching role is to observe what happens as people begin to practice. If people are not getting desired results, we can help them by questioning the assumptions behind their theories or we can coach them on the specific actions they are taking so that they can develop more competence. Practice is what makes observation possible and what allows people to adjust their actions according to the feedback they receive.

Making adjustments as people move from theory to action could involve either transformational coaching (intervening in people's frames of reference) or coaching for incremental improvement (intervening in what people do). As the coach, you have to make observations and assessments of individual and group behavior. Are people taking wrong-headed actions? Do they have the wrong theory of action? Is what they are doing different from what they think they are doing? Do they need to take more time out to study and practice new skills and capabilities that will help them to solve these problems? Are people managing impressions in order to look good, or are they talking about problems and trying to learn from one another?

One powerful method for coaching people to teach people new skills that integrates well with a *learn-by-doing* approach is to help people find a role model who embodies those skills in a similar context. Sometimes the easiest way to learn to play golf or to ski is to play with someone really good at it or to follow along behind him or her mimicking the moves. If a project manager in a big firm wants to learn how to create a real team, he or she might find project managers in the same category are doing it successfully. A key is not just to focus on one role model, but to scan the horizon for many different role models. This is helpful in incorporating the skills or capabilities into one's personal style.

MOVE BETWEEN PERFORMANCE AND THE PRACTICE FIELD

In most groups, getting the job done happens in one box; training and learning happens in another. Because the traditional training situation is often separated from what really needs to be done, there is often no way for people, and especially teams, to learn on the job. There is no place where managers can go to reflect on what they are doing and learn new skills in the context of obtaining the results that they need. I predict that, in the next ten years, there will be many innovations in regard to creating a learning organization infrastructure so that learning happens by design, not by chance.

One of these innovations is coming from Peter Senge and his colleagues at the MIT Organization Learning Center. It has to do with an idea called the "managerial practice field."[3] This idea comes out of distinguishing environments where learning and work are integrated from those environments where they are not. For example, in the field of competitive sports and in the performing arts, players continuously move back and forth between the practice field and the performance field. The idea is to expand people's capacity. It is difficult to imagine a football team learning without practice or a symphony orchestra learning without rehearsal.

Yet this is precisely what is expected of managers and teams. Managers frequently have to act on their strategies when there is no chance to test them, when the fear of personal failure is great, and when there is no way to develop new team skills or replay an important decision. They are also asked in three-day training sessions to develop complex skills, such as building shared vision, enhancing dialogue, or reflecting on mental models, with little opportunity to practice them in real-world situations.

> *The basic idea of performance and practice fields is to make sure that learning occurs in the context of doing the job rather than as a separate activity.*

Examples of Practice Fields

The MIT group has set up a number of different managerial practice fields with prominent companies like Ford, EDS, and GS Technologies. In the Lincoln Continental Division at Ford, in a project that focused on speeding up product development and quality, managers set up regular one- or two-day learning labs to deal with the issues that were coming up. These learning labs helped managers discuss problems that would normally be undiscussable.

EDS decided that it wanted to create a learning organization infrastructure shown in Diagram 12.4. A learning lab was developed by Fred Kofman that focused on developing twenty or thirty coaches who would be proficient in the skills of a learning organization, such as sharing vision, team learning, and systems thinking. These coaches would later be "seeded" into the organization. The infrastructure consisted of (1) special conferences where new skills and practices could be developed; (2) concrete projects where the skills and practices could be applied to key performance criteria; (3) practice and reflection assignments; and (4) personal coaching meetings. Today a high number of EDS employees report directly or indirectly to these program participants.[4]

DIAGRAM 12.4 *EDS infrastructure*

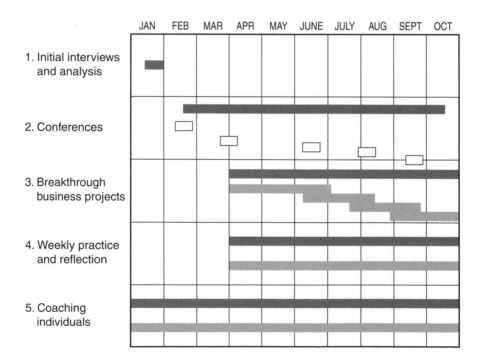

At one company, over a year's time we coached members of a team who were in charge of a big supply chain project that would require significant change. To empower the group, we created a managerial practice field that met on a monthly basis to develop a variety of skills and capabilities that were missing. The members would study skills such as leadership, dialogue, and systems thinking and then look at how they could directly apply these to the task at hand. They also used the breakthrough technique to forward the project through a widening circle of short-term successes. (See Chapter Nine.)

In each case, in order to help the process along, various coaches were used, along with learning methods and tools that were appropriate to the different issues that were arising. "The Learning Lab," according to one participant, "wasn't structured like most training environments we are used to. [The boss] didn't begin with an overview of 'the ten things we are going to tell you.' Instead, he said 'We're going to learn together as we go along.'"[5]

Practice and Reflection Go Together

According to Senge, 90 percent of the learning that occurs in these learning labs is on the personal and interpersonal level. He says, "When people in most companies have a problem, they normally blitz right by it by coming up with ten solutions, picking one, and implementing it. American managers really believe in this 'ready, fire, aim' stuff and are extraordinarily non-reflective. In the practice field, you create an environment where people can slow down. If there is a problem, they can actually start talking about what might be causing it. We can also give people the tools and methods to help them understand it.[6]

"In the practice field, there is also a chance for people to learn to use these tools without fear of making mistakes. As people become used to being reflective and to using the various tools and methods, they start to see that a lot of the problems have to do with their own thinking and reasoning process."

According to Senge, "I like the metaphor of the practice field because both in the practice field and in the rehearsal hall what you do is slow things down. In a real performance, there is a certain pace to things, often a certain frenzy to it, but in the practice field you stop, you try it, you try it a different way. At the same time, you see it from different angles. This creates a much more reflective environment."

Designing Practice Fields

One of the things that the coach can do to give people an experience of dignity is to keep certain ground rules in mind when designing practice fields. These rules go back to our governing values. First, the group members set their own stretch goals that require learning. Second, the learning agenda and practice field are determined by the group members or are based on what they consider important. Third, the practice field experience is something that should not only encourage study and practice, but should be fun. If practice isn't fun, people won't want to practice. The fourth point is that people should have some way to measure their own progress in the practice field.

PRACTICE FIELD ASSIGNMENTS

The following exercises can be used in the practice field. The first section of exercises is on leadership transformation and the second is on group transformation.

Leadership Transformation

EXERCISE 1. Videotape a meeting to show the group leader how his or her way of speaking and listening contributes to the group's problems

I was told a story about a manager who observed that his people agreed in meetings but did not seem to act according to the agreement outside the meetings. As the manager investigated this with the help of a coach, he discovered that people never really agreed in the first place. What happened was the people believed that they had to agree publicly with what the boss said. When the manager found this out, he told the people, in no uncertain terms, that he expected them to challenge him and one another when they disagreed.

The coach then taped some of these meetings, and it turned out that every time people disagreed, the boss would say things like "Damn it! I can't seem to get the point across to you guys" or "Hell, you guys are driving me up the wall." When the manager was shown the videos, he was shocked to see the difference between what he practiced and what he preached.

Once you have made a videotape, use it to observe and make assessments about the behaviors of the leader and group. Illustrate your assessments in a feedback session by playing back selected passages of the videotape. Once you give people these examples, rather than confront them, it's better to ask some questions that allow them to gain insight into what is going on: "What's your take on this?" "What do you think led people to this conclusion?" "What's in your thinking that might cause you to say one thing and do something else?"

EXERCISE 2. Engage in a conversation about a big dilemma

Coaching people to become senior leaders is about coaching them to deal with dilemmas, puzzles, or complex issues. People prefer easy and obvious answers and therefore tend to minimize or suppress dilemmas rather than face them. The result is that they wind up in a quagmire of escalating consequences. It is important to stay centered in the face of a dilemma while you spend time mulling on the problem or dilemma or take experimental action to test for solutions. The following exercise gives people an experience of staying centered.

Three people work together in this exercise. Two people hold onto the arms of a third person and pull down. The person in the middle responds in three different ways. First, the person resists as much as he or she can. Second, the person does not resist at all. And third, the person thinks of an image that represents being centered and gently keeps his or her focus on that image, breathing in an easy and regular way.

Next, the person thinks of a dilemma that he or she is facing and briefly tells the others what it is. Each person then takes one side of the dilemma and, while again pulling down on the person's arm, makes a simple statement that represents the dilemma. The person in the middle again focuses on his or her centering image, staying centered in the face of the dilemma. Centering yourself and holding the tension of the dilemma moves from being a good idea to something that is viscerally felt. This may be very confronting to people or very liberating.[7]

EXERCISE 3. Study and practice one skill for one week in the context of getting the job done

Practice is a form of inquiry in making distinctions that leads to deep learning and allows people to embody new skills and capabilities. As with a ski, golf, or tennis lesson, one way to help people learn new skills is to focus on one skill at a time for a week or so. This is distinctly different from bombarding people with information that they cannot use. For example, in teaching people leadership, one key skill is "taking a stand." This starts with saying what you really want to say, consistent with your commitments, rather than altering what you want to say to protect yourself or others. Have people notice where they need to take a stand and focus on doing so for a period of time. Have periodic conversations to help them be successful in their actions and have them continue practicing until they gain some mastery. Then move on to another leadership attribute.

EXERCISE 4. Recommend articles and books to further people's learning

Some of our recommendations are the following:

Books

- Theory in Practice *by Chris Argyris & D.A. Schön*
- Overcoming Organizational Defenses *by Chris Argyris*
- Knowledge for Action *by Chris Argyris*
- The Skilled Facilitator *by Roger Schwarz*
- The Fifth Discipline *by Peter M. Senge*
- E Leader *by Robert Hargrove*
- The Breakthrough Strategy *by Robert Schaffer*
- Art of the Possible *by Benjamin Zander*

Articles

- *"Good Communication That Blocks Learning,"* by C. Argyris, Harvard Business Review, *July–August 1994*
- *"The Reinvention Roller Coaster,"* by Tracy Goss, Richard Pascale, & Anthony Athos, Harvard Business Review, *November–December 1993*
- *"Strategy as Stretch and Leverage,"* by Gary Hamel & C. K. Prahalad, Harvard Business Review, *March–April 1993*

Group Organization Transformation

EXERCISE 1. Have people write a case study and discuss it with colleagues

An approach to helping people in groups become more aware of any discrepancy between their espoused theory and theory-in-use is to have each person in the group write an honest, one-page case study of what he or she sees as the issues. Then call people together to discuss the case studies. Writing the case study allows people to look at what is going on and, at the same time, disengage from the situation emotionally. It also allows people to have a frank and open discussion about the situation and the feelings people have about it.

Case Study Format
- *What results do you or your group intend to produce?*
- *How do you and your team think you act?*
- *What is the feedback gathered about your actual behavior?*
- *What unintended results are occurring?*
- *What are the thinking patterns or actions that produce your behavior?*

EXERCISE 2. Take a controversial issue, then use conversational protocols that help with team reflection and learning

The protocols in Diagram 12.5 were developed by some colleagues and friends at Innovation Associates. They are useful in helping groups move from an unproductive discussion to a real quality of dialogue and for encouraging teams to self-intervene in their own conversations. When talking about a business topic, such as strategic operation issues, quality and service issues, or team learning issues, post the questions from the diagram to serve as guides. Appoint a facilitator to balance inquiry and advocacy by bringing the group back to the questions from time to time. After a while, the group members will get the hang of it and do it themselves.

DIAGRAM 12.5 *Questions to ask*

---

1. *Am I willing to be influenced? Am I open to learning?*
2. *When advocating a position:*
   - *Do I reveal my thinking/my mental models?*
   - *Do I explain my assumptions?*
   - *Do I share the observable data from which I drew my conclusions?*
   - *Do I encourage others to explore my model/my assumptions/the data?*
   - *Do I listen to really hear?*
   - *Do I stay open?*

3. When faced with another's view with which I disagree:

- *Do I ask "What leads you to that view?"*
- *Do I seek to truly understand the view?*
- *Do I explore, listen, and offer my own views in an open way?*
- *Do I listen for the larger meaning that may emerge out of honest, open sharing of alternative models?*

EXERCISE 3. Completing relationships

Often relationship problems are at the source of many of the problems people face in implementing a strategy or, for that matter, in doing anything. As people tend to be sensitive and to take things personally, it is quite common for relationships to break down. Providing some structure to completing relationships has proven successful. This exercise starts with two people who need to do what I call "get complete" with one another sitting down together. One person has a pen, which we call the "talking stick." The person with the talking stick starts and says everything he or she needs to say to feel complete. When someone has the talking stick, the other person cannot speak, only listen. When the first person is finished, he or she gives the pen to the other person. Then that person speaks until he or she is complete. This goes on until no one needs to pick up the talking stick and speak any more. It is important at this point for each person to acknowledge that he or she is complete. We have noticed that, after doing this exercise with an intact group, the efficiency of the group improves dramatically.

EXERCISE 4. The hot seat exercise

This group feedback exercise is a very powerful, yet delicate exercise that, if managed well, can have a big impact on both the individual and the group. Seat the members of the group theater-style; then place one chair in the front and center—the "Hot Seat." Provide some general guidelines about giving and receiving feedback, such as the following.

When Giving Feedback

- *Talk straight; don't sugar coat.*
- *Speak with the intent to make a difference.*

- *Focus on changeable behavior, not personality.*
- *Use intellect and intuition.*

When Receiving Feedback

- *Sit with arms and legs uncrossed.*
- *Listen whether you agree or disagree.*
- *Listen with the intent to learn something new.*
- *When everyone is done, take a minute to acknowledge that you received and understood the feedback.*

When people understand the guidelines, one person goes to the hot seat and each person in the group gives him or her feedback using exactly the following three sentence stems:

1. "One thing I appreciate about you is. . . ."
2. "One thing I have difficulty with is . . ." or "A next step for you might be. . . ."
3. "One thing I want to create with you is. . . ."

It's vital for people to have generosity of spirit, both in giving feedback on strengths as well as on areas that need improvement.

The person in the hot seat is asked not to speak so that he or she can receive the feedback rather than have a knee-jerk reaction to it. As more and more people in the group speak, there starts to be a common thread to all the feedback the person receives. This feedback is enriched by different people's personal experiences of the person—their wisdom, insights, and intuition, as well as their unique forms of self-expression. When everyone is finished, the person is asked to say something about what he or she learned in acknowledgment of the feedback. One of the first things people often do is wipe their brow and say "Wow! It really is hot up here." In a group of six to eight people, allow fifteen to twenty minutes per person.

As a result of giving authentic feedback to one another, people have an experience of stronger relationships with each other and the efficiency and the effectiveness of the group go way up.

CHAPTER THIRTEEN

TO GET PEOPLE TO BRING THEIR WHOLE SELVES TO WORK

Give Them an Opportunity to Make a Difference

Coaching is about challenging and supporting people, giving them the gift of your presence.

One of the most powerful observations I made with Masterful Coaching is that most organizations give people a big title and pay people big, big bucks with a view toward motivating them to do excellent work. And yet in my experience, (1) the most motivated people are those who are doing something to make a difference in their world and (2) the best work is often done by volunteers. The key inquiry for organizations today lies in being able to elicit people's voluntary commitment.

What do big profit-making corporations need to learn that many small philanthropic organizations already know? Simple! The answer is to design organizations that are consistent with human nature. Though many things have changed in the last five thousand years or so of human cultural history, there is one thing that hasn't—human nature. Human beings want the experience of being lovable (appreciated), being capable, and knowing that their existence makes a difference in the world.

Creating an organization that is consistent with human nature starts with an inspiring vision that people passionately care about, asking leaders to set significant leadership and business challenges that will make a difference rather than just fulfilling a functional role. It also involves acknowledging people for what they actually contribute to the company's being a market leader with a powerful bottom line.

Yet what about the side of human nature that has nothing to do with being a market leader, getting those productivities and efficiencies, or the bottom line? If you ask people what they passionately care about, they will usually tell you their families, schools, communities, war and peace, the earth, and so forth. They have a deep desire to make a difference in these areas of life. Yet given the hectic pace of daily life at the dawn of the 21st Century, they just don't often have the opportunity.

A NONTRADITIONAL PERSPECTIVE

What a growing number of companies are finding is that, if you give people the opportunity to make a difference in these other areas, they will bring their whole selves to work. Some companies have labeled this with a specific term: "strategic philanthropy." This idea involves setting up programs that encourage employees to make a meaningful contribution to their local schools, their community, and the world they live in.

People's Bank in Massachusetts, for example, has a program whereby employees are encouraged to take three months off with pay every three years, to do some kind of philanthropic work in schools, hospitals, or social programs. The result is not only one of reaping the community's good will but also employees who return full of inspiration and motivation with a desire to be of greater service to their colleagues and customers.

At Masterful Coaching we have a "Youth at Risk" mentoring program. Some of our coaches spend a minimum of two to three hours a month "mentoring" youth who have a great deal of potential, but who are in some way at risk. For example, the first person I mentored was a very talented black person in Roxbury, Massachusetts (the ghetto). Despite the fact that she was the class valedictorian of a special school and the winner of a national poetry award, she was not enrolled in college and was in danger of being married off to a fifty-year-old man in Haiti. I found offering this person a powerful assist at a time when she needed it really satisfying. For me, working with her was a breath of fresh air and resulted in a renewed sense of purpose to the work I was doing with clients.

One day, I visited the financial district of New York City to meet with people at the Chase Manhattan Bank. The Chase building sits in a large plaza and its architecture is very tall, formal, and imposing —not the kind of place you would want to apply for a loan if you missed your last car payment. As you walk into the lobby, you see a statement emblazoned on the wall. It says, "Our purpose is to provide financial services to those companies that support the well-being of our customers, whether they be individuals, companies, communities, or countries."

What caught my eye, and made the rest of the message stand out in that imposing lobby in the heart of New York's financial district, was the word "well-being." It told me business was not just about making money or making and selling products and services—that it could be about contributing to the well-being of people, communities, and the planet that we share. The people whom I talked to in the bank said that when Chairman Tom Labrecque first saw the message, it was only a small banner. He insisted that it be put in huge letters. Labrecque believes firmly that, if the company contributes to the well-being of people, communities, and customers, it will have a very profitable relationship with them.

Every coach should ask the question: "Does our work contribute to people's well-being?" As we've seen, it is important to create a work environment that allows people to delight customers and to improve operations. But it is hard for a company to add value if it is not supporting the ecosystems, educational institutions, and other institutions that it touches. The following stories illustrate how companies like Reebok and Bally encourage their people to make a difference in the world, as shown in Diagram 13.1.

DIAGRAM 13.1 *The cycle of stewardship*

If people feel good about themselves, they are more creative and productive.

Reebok: Bringing Your Whole Self to Work

Over the last one hundred years or so, a macho management culture has evolved, based on the belief that the only thing that matters is work and that the business of business is business, that is, to make money. The personal parts of people's lives were supposed to be checked at the door when people showed up for work. Yet, a growing number of powerful executives, many from the Baby Boom generation, have found that, while making money matters, the other things that people care about matter too. One of these executives is Sharon Cohen of Reebok. Cohen joined the company in the early days when there were only twenty employees and later wound up working for CEO Paul Fireman as Reebok's vice president of advertising, a powerful job in the competitive, frenetic world of athletic footwear and apparel.[1]

Says Cohen, "I came to work for Paul Fireman because I liked his values. He talked about honesty, about taking a stand for the things you believed in, about keeping your word, and about family." At forty-five, Cohen's life changed: "I had a baby girl." She left her job in Reebok's marketing area and became vice president of public affairs and executive director of the Reebok Foundation. One of her roles is to help Paul Fireman create an environment in which people can bring their whole selves to work.

"You have to look at the person as a whole," says Cohen. "People spend a lot of time at work. You can't compartmentalize personal life and work life, individual and family concerns, personal concerns and social concerns. People are not just workers by day and good parents by night. In the same sense, you can't pretend that people just bring their minds to work and sit at a desk all day. They also have a body, a spirit, a soul."

CEO Paul Fireman is a believer in corporate responsibility. Says Cohen, "I doubt if there are very many CEOs, if there are any at all, who would admit to social irresponsibility. But there's a long way between the rejection of irresponsibility and the acceptance of responsibility. If you think of a bell curve, what you will find under the bell of the curve, where most companies gather, is what we might call social indifference. That's all those companies and managers who don't regard the matter of responsibility as part of their corporate mission."

According to Cohen, "The things that we do in the area of social responsibility—like the Reebok Human Rights Award and Human Rights Program—make people feel proud of the company and good about themselves. When people feel good about themselves, they are naturally more creative and productive. They add a lot of value to their jobs. You can't measure it, but you can feel it when you take a walk through the halls. It's not coaching in the traditional sense, but it's a kind of indirect coaching." What does the company do in the human rights area? In the fall of 1994, Reebok found out that a factory in China was housing its employees in an unsafe building. Reebok called the factory and said that the employees would have to be moved. The factory manager said, "We will have them out by the end of the month." The Reebok representative said, "That's not good enough." The factory workers were in better housing by the end of the week.

Then there is the Reebok Human Rights Award. Each year, the program recognizes four young people on the front line of human rights work who, early in their lives and against great odds, have had significant impact in their communities. Another Reebok human rights program, "Witness," is designed to arm the human rights movement worldwide with the weapons of mass communication, such as hand-held video cameras and fax machines.

"A video camera in the hands of the right person is more powerful in stopping the violation of human rights than a tank or a gun," said musician Peter Gabriel. Former President Jimmy Carter has hailed the company as doing more for human rights than any other company in the world.

Reebok also has a volunteer program that provides opportunities for people to be of service in the community. According to Cohen, "We do a big effort with the City Year Serve-a-Thon—a youth development program that has become the new urban Peace Corps. Our employees get together on the day of the Serve-a-Thon and paint a school or do whatever the project happens to be."

"We also do other things," says Cohen, "like serving Thanksgiving dinner to the homeless in our cafeteria. We know that this is creating a real benefit for our employees, not just the guests. It is great for employees to see themselves not just as people doing a job to support themselves, but as people who are doing something to make a difference in the world.

"We don't do these projects for economic reasons, but we know that whatever good it does for people to be able to make a real contribution, we get it back tenfold. It's part of what makes the Reebok environment one of commitment, caring, and possibility. It becomes part of the way managers interact with the people who report to them and this becomes part of the value that people create and bring to customers. Can you see it in profitability? Yes! How do you know? We can't measure it . . . but you just know it."

How might it all add up in dollars and cents? Reebok's performance over the last ten years has been 30 percent compounded in sales and almost the same in profits. According to Cohen, who has a marketing person's ability to zero in on a single phrase that says a lot about a company, "Someone referred to our brand about a year ago as 'pure performance plus humanity.' When I heard that, it clicked."

Bally: An Organization Consistent with Human Nature

It is one thing to be able to create a context that inspires and empowers people to add value if you are the CEO of a large company, but how do you do it if you are a middle manager or a team leader? John Egan, marketing and sales manager for Bally retail shops in the United Kingdom, found a way. Egan not only has a philosophy and a system, but knows how to inject it with fun and excitement.[2]

Bally's U.K. management has nurtured a particular business culture where employees pay attention to personal needs, ask customers what they think, and send thank you notes. According to Egan, "I've learned that for people doing front-line jobs, it's not the salary and it's not the benefits package that make a difference, it's the small things—a bit of recognition or a bit of praise or a bit of sharing in success."

The key to creating a value-added culture is to have a philosophy about people. One thing that Egan has realized is that most so-called ordinary people are capable of extraordinary things.

One of the biggest mistakes that managers make is seeing people as ordinary just because they are doing ordinary jobs, and therefore they expect ordinary things from them.

Egan strongly believes that if you look after the staff first, they will look after your customers. A lot of companies introduce a customer-focused approach but don't take into account that employees are angry and resentful because they haven't had a day off in three weeks. "We teach our managers," says Egan, "to look after the needs of the staff in every single way.

"For example, we tell them to put themselves in the other person's shoes if someone has to pick up a child, or has a doctor appointment, or is taking a class and wants to leave the store early. We teach them to say 'yes' instead of saying 'no, it's a busy afternoon and you are going to have to wait until the normal time.' If you do look after the small things, like letting people go ten or fifteen minutes early, they'll come back and work late or forgo their lunch break, not because they have to, but because they want to. Furthermore, their happiness will come through in their smiles or in their eyes when they are actually talking to a customer and trying to sell them a pair of shoes."

Egan continues, "It helps to just talk to people on an individual basis. The first thing that we would do when we go into a Bally store is to greet everyone in a very enthusiastic way to make sure people know that we think they are important. Then we find the opportunity to ask them how the job is going, what they've done previously, what they like, what they don't like, and if they found the training useful.

"Once you've had a chat with a person, make it clear how much you think he or she can contribute. 'Have there been any problems and how can we improve that?' or 'If you owned your own shop, what would you do?' We all share the philosophy of recognizing people and making them feel part of an organization, no matter what part they play, how big or how small. Even if the cleaner walks by while I am there, I will ask him what he thinks."

One of Bally's reasons for success is training, which is headed up by Susan Wellman. "We know that people aren't going to want to work in a shoe shop for the rest of their lives," says Wellman. "We recognize that people do want to progress and to develop as people, so we've got to give them the mechanics to do that." Bally makes sure that the courses it runs are not just for the company's benefit, but for the employees' development as well. This includes courses in creative writing, leadership, and interdisciplinary management.[3]

Along with asking people for their ideas and providing training, recognizing performance is very important. "We also do things," says Egan, "to recognize the good performers, not just the superstars. Sometimes, it's finding out snippets of things—someone might have had to work on her day off just to solve a problem in the store. Usually what we do is send her flowers, a bottle of champagne, or a note." Personally, Egan believes that as long as recognition is sincere and honest, it's impossible to overdo it.

"I was at work one day and we were looking at the absence and sickness record. We noticed that we had quite a few people who had 100 percent attendance records. These were people who instead of turning over and staying in bed when they woke up with a headache decided that they were going to work. We felt we should recognize this achievement, so we sent beautiful boxes of hand-made chocolates to over seventy people.

"We sent the chocolates straight to their homes, right out of the blue. When they arrived home, there was a mysterious box and a letter from me saying: 'Thank you very much for your perfect attendance record over the last twelve months.' And the next day they went to work and said 'Bloody hell, look what happened!'" They were as inspired, empowered, and motivated as they could possibly be. They showed up like people who were really up to something—putting a man on the moon—not just finding a size 9 shoe for someone in a shoe store.

A FINAL REFLECTION

Stewardship is taking a stand for the future of the people, communities, complex social systems, and the world we care about.

This book is about coaching leaders at all levels to create inspired, high performance organizations that work in both human and business terms. Today every business leader I know would like to leave such a legacy to their corporation and its stakeholders and their own families. Yet it often doesn't occur to them that our legacy to our families should not just be a few material possessions but the raising of our collective vision from a foundation of socially constructive values deeply embedded in our society, communities, and schools.

The primary reason is that the leaders of our institutions rarely see themselves as stewards of the planet, communities, and employees, but as voyagers on the road to personal and corporate success. We design organizations based on the idea of becoming more productive without taking into account the far-reaching consequences of a production culture. It seldom occurs to us that our way of living is not sustainable and we are existing off the capital of future generations.

This is because we live in a culture that stresses not stewardship/service, but rather an abundance of self-interest. We lead, manage, and coach people out of this context, setting goals that often camouflage personal ambition as organizational ambition. We do not take into account what people passionately care about or the purposes they hold as sacred. Then we cannibalize people's time and energy, turning them into what the Japanese call a "salary man." As a result, people bury their deep feelings of caring for their organizations, their employees, and their work.

Masterful Coaching doesn't start with setting goals, motivating people, and appraising their performances, so as to get more out of them. It starts with looking in the mirror ourselves and asking about what really matters to us so as to unearth the fact that we do care. This naturally leads to stewardship, choosing service over self-interest, taking the longer and deeper view rather than just being concerned with next door or next week. It means seeing who we are in the context of taking a stand for the future of people, institutions, and the world. It means creating business enterprises that are not only outstandingly productive, but that also nurture the human spirit and allow people to learn and grow.

There are many opportunities in every organization to make stewardship real. For example, being an executive who makes strategic decisions that regenerate the company's future and the community and environment at the same time; helping a client make his or her customer successful; serving as a mentor for an up-and-coming player; or making sure the team gets the support, direction, skills, and capabilities it needs to succeed, regardless of the consequences to the coach. "What are your vision, values, and real goals?" "How do you see your next steps?" "How can I help?" People who truly embrace the quality of stewardship stand out.

In writing this book, I met many men and women whose definition of leadership, coaching, and teaching went beyond the usual parameters and included the notion of social responsibility. These were often men and women whose personal (corporate) commitment to good stewardship involved investing in a common cause. They made this an integral part of their lives, investing their time and energy and resources in it, rather than making a mere gesture. As one executive put it, "I invest in the recognition of the unity of the world, my connectedness with all people, and my own highest human aspirations.

NOTES

INTRODUCTION

1. The idea of unfreeze, change, and refreeze was first introduced by Kurt Lewin, *Resolving Social Conflict: Field Theory in Social Science* (American Psychological Association, February 1997) and also put out by Edgar H. Schein, *Process Consultation: Its Role in Organization Development* (Vol. 1) (Reading, MA: Addison-Wesley, 1988).
2. I am grateful to Fred Kofman for permission to use the idea of the learning enzyme from his paper entitled "Leading Learning Communities."

CHAPTER ONE

1. Dan Goodgame, "The Game of Risk," *Time* magazine, August 14, 2000.
2. I am grateful to Veronica Pemberton, friend and colleague at Masterful Coaching, for conversations that have enriched my view of Masterful Coaching. She is truly a masterful coach and has contributed greatly to the work that we are doing.
3. I am appreciative of the opportunity to work with Richard Severance, executive vice president of Conoco, and I am honored to work with him on creating an Impossible Future for the Conoco Downstream organization. In that coaching engagement, I learned as much as I taught.
4. I am also grateful for the opportunity to work with Jim Nokes of Conoco. I will write more about that coaching relationship in later chapters.
5. "Teachable point of view" was a phrase coined first by Noel Tichy and Ram Charan in *Every Business Is a Growth Business* (New York: Times Books, 1998).
6. Tracy Goss first wrote about executive reinvention in *The Last Word on Power: Executive Re-Invention for Leaders Who Must Make the Impossible Happen* (New York: Currency/Doubleday, 1995).
7. The Ladder of Inference is a tool introduced by Chris Argyris, a pioneer in the area of understanding and overcoming the human defensive behavior at work in organizations. He is the author of numerous publications and has developed many tools for management learning; see C. Argyris, *Overcoming Organizational Defenses* (Needham Heights, MA: Allyn and Bacon, 1990), C. Argyris, *Strategy, Change, and Defensive Routines* (Boston: Pitman, 1985), and C. Argyris, *Knowledge for Action* (San Francisco: Jossey-Bass, 1993).

CHAPTER TWO

1. Jacob Bronowski, *The Ascent of Man* (London: British Broadcasting Corporation, 1973).
2. Fernando Flores has done extensive work in the area of linguistics. See also Terry Winograd & Fernando Flores, *Understanding Computers and Cognition* (Norwood, NJ: Ablex Publishing, 1986).
3. I am especially appreciative of conversations with my friend and colleague at Masterful Coaching Michel Renaud. Michel has contributed enormously to the body of knowledge that makes up Masterful Coaching and to the ideas put forth in this book.

CHAPTER THREE

1. Again, my sincere appreciation to friend Michel Renaud.
2. This chart on social grease versus coaching communication has been developed from the work of Chris Argyris.
3. I am appreciative of this example from David Korkosz, a very old friend and Masterful Coach at Masterful Coaching Inc.

CHAPTER FOUR

1. Tracy Goss, *The Last Word on Power, Re-Invention for Leaders and Anyone Who Must Make the Impossible Happen* (New York, Currency/Doubleday, 1995).
2. Jerome S. Bruner, *Making Stories* (New York: Farrar Straus & Giroux, 2002).
3. My appreciation for this example from my friend and colleague at Masterful Coaching Hans Peter Hartmann, whose uplifting spirit shines through in all of his coaching.
4. The notion of Master Programs comes from the work of Chris Argyris.
5. Dawna Markova, Ph.D., coined the terms "river story" and "rut story." See D. Markova, *No Enemies Within* (Berkeley, CA: Conari Press, 1994).

CHAPTER FIVE

1. Martin Heidigger, *Basic Writings: From Being and Time (1927 to the Task of Thinking)* (San Francisco: Harper San Francisco, 1993).
2. I am appreciative of the opportunity to sit in on a class led by Benjamin Zander, director of the Boston Philharmonic Orchestra and author of (with Rosamond Stone Zander) *The Art of Possibility, Transforming Professional and Personal Life* (Boston, MA: Harvard Business School Press, 2000).
3. I was introduced to the reinvention paradigm by colleague Andres Gomez.
4. Peter Drucker, *The Effective Executive* (New York: HarperBusiness, 1993).

CHAPTER SIX

1. Malcolm Gladwell, *The Tipping Point: How Little Things Can Make a Big Difference* (Boston, MA: Little and Brown, 2000).

2. A special thanks to Jim Nokes of Conoco, whom I have enormously enjoyed coaching.
3. Malcolm Gladwell, *The Tipping Point: How Little Things Can Make a Big Difference* (Boston, MA: Little and Brown, 2000).
4. Ibid.
5. Again thanks to Jim Nokes.
6. Also thanks to Richard Severance.

CHAPTER SEVEN

1. David Bohm, *On Dialogue* (Ojai, CA: David Bohm Seminars, 1990).
2. Harrison Owen, *Open Space Technology: A User's Guide* (San Francisco: Berrett-Koehler, 1997).
3. I am appreciative of conversations with Joan Holms, director of the Hunger Project, an organization dedicated to the ending of hunger.
4. You can read about the work of Gail and Matt Taylor of MG Taylor Corporation in a book by Chris Peterson and Gayle Pergamit, *Leaping the Abyss: Putting Group Genius to Work* (Palo Alto, CA: knOwhere Press, 1997).
5. These governing values are based on the work of Chris Argyris. See C. Argyris, *Knowledge for Action* (San Francisco: Jossey-Bass, 1993).
6. The ground rules are written here with the permission of Roger M. Schwarz, *The Skilled Facilitator* (San Francisco: Jossey-Bass, 2002).
7. The Diagnosis/Intervention Cycle is used with permission of Roger M. Schwarz, *The Skilled Facilitator* (San Francisco: Jossey-Bass, 2002).

CHAPTER EIGHT

1. Many of the ideas in this chapter are based on the work of Chris Argyris, whose work in the areas of getting people to discuss the undiscussable is documented in many publications. See C. Argyris, *Overcoming Organizational Defenses* (Needham Heights, MA: Allyn and Bacon, 1990) and C. Argyris, *Strategy, Change, and Defensive Routines* (Boston, MA: Pitman, 1985).
2. I am appreciative of conversations with Peter Senge on his work creating learning organizations. See Peter M. Senge, *The Fifth Discipline* (New York: Doubleday, 1990) and P. Senge, C. Roberts, R. Ross, B. Smith, & A. Kleiner, *The Fifth Discipline Fieldbook* (New York: Doubleday, 1994).
3. Again a special thanks to Peter Senge.
4. I am appreciative of conversations with Wright Elliot of Chase Manhattan Bank about the change process the bank has been going through the past few years. Also see "A Chastened Chase," *Business Week*, September 26, 1994, p. 106; "Chase's New Vision: Putting Teamwork First," *American Banker*, Wednesday, June 16, 1993; and "Still Waters Run Deep," *Forbes*, October 25, 1993.
5. Bob Putnam of Action Design Associates in Newton, Massachusetts, graciously shared about his work of facilitating groups to move beyond defensive routines and design effective actions.

6. The first three steps to sustaining a learning process are from Bob Putnam. The fourth step comes from Roger Schwarz, professor at the Institute of Government at the University of North Carolina at Chapel Hill. See also Roger Schwarz, *The Skilled Facilitator* (San Francisco: Jossey-Bass, 1994).

7. I am grateful for the time Roger Schwarz made for conversations about his experience of working with people to disperse defensive routines.

CHAPTER NINE

1. Charles R. Day, "Go Find Yourself a Crisis," *Industry Week,* July 4, 1994, p. 23.

2. Shawn Tully, "Why to Go for Stretch Goals," *Fortune,* November 14, 1994, p. 148.

3. Commentary from the *Boston Business Journal,* August 5–11, 1994, p. 15.

4. These questions for designing breakthrough goals were designed by Greg Goff, a Conoco executive I worked with to create the Impossible Future for ConLim.

5. I am grateful for the conversations with Stephen Pook, senior vice president in charge of information technology, who led a task force that spearheaded a breakthrough at Engelhard Corporation. I am also appreciative of colleague Fernando Assens for his initial interview with Stephen Pook.

6. I am grateful for conversations with Robert Schaffer, in which he shared his ideas and expertise on developing high-performance teams using the "breakthrough strategy." Many of the ideas in this chapter are based on his work in this area. See Robert Schaffer, *The Breakthrough Strategy* (New York: Ballinger, 1988).

7. Charlie Baum graciously shared his insights about high-performance teams and how to introduce these teams into an organization where there is no ready-made slot for them.

8. I am appreciative of the time Mike Berkin, performance quality manager of Dun & Bradstreet Information Services, and Sharon Shelton spent with me sharing about the breakthrough projects they have successfully initiated at D&B.

CHAPTER TEN

1. Peter Scott-Morgan of Arthur D. Little, Inc., graciously shared his work about the "unwritten rules" that is the basis for this chapter. See Peter Scott-Morgan, *The Unwritten Rules of the Game* (New York: McGraw-Hill, 1994).

2. Brian Dumaine, "Mr. Learning Organization," *Fortune,* October 17, 1994.

3. Again, appreciation to Peter Scott-Morgan.

CHAPTER ELEVEN

1. See Kurt Lewin, *Resolving Social Conflict: Field Theory in Social Science* (American Psychological Association (APA) June 1999). See Edgar H.

Schein, *Process Consultation: Its Role in Organization Development,* Volume I (Reading, MA: Addison-Wesley, 1988).
2. I appreciate having had the opportunity to work with Rick Hamm of Conoco and for being able to share this example of using metaphors in coaching.
3. Pat Riley, *The Winner Within* (New York: G.P. Putnam's Sons, 1993).

CHAPTER TWELVE

1. Robert Fritz, *Creating* (New York: Ballantine, 1993).
2. I am appreciative of conversations with Philippe Chéhab, division manager of Swissair, on the truly inspirational work he is doing at Swissair with systems thinking and shifting people's mindsets and identity from separate to related.
3. Again, special appreciation to Peter Senge for conversations about his work in the MIT Organization Learning Lab. A number of his ideas are expressed in this chapter.
4. My appreciation to Fred Kofman of the MIT Organization Learning Center.
5. Again, a special thank you to Fred Kofman.
6. Again, a special thanks to Peter Senge for his fine work.
7. This dilemma exercise is from Bill Isaacs and Dia Logos in Cambridge, Massachusetts.

CHAPTER THIRTEEN

1. I am grateful to Sharon Cohen for conversations about Reebok and its inspiring work in the area of social responsibility.
2. I am appreciative of conversations with John Egan about what Bally is doing to nurture a culture wherein people can add value.
3. Thanks to Susan Wellman from Bally for her comments on the educational programs for employees.

ABOUT THE AUTHOR

Robert Hargrove is the founder of Masterful Coaching Inc., a leading executive coaching firm. He is the author of Masterful Coaching, Revised Edition *and* Masterful Coaching Fieldbook; Mastering the Art of Creative Collaboration; *and* E-Leader, Reinventing Leadership in a Connected Economy. *He is a renowned speaker on the subject of becoming an extraordinary leader, the collaborative corporation, and masterful coaching for managers.*

Hargrove was a co-director of the Harvard Leadership Research Project, and was a founder of Innovation Associates, with Charles Kiefer and Peter Senge (author of The Fifth Discipline—The Art and Practice of the Learning Organization). *He has designed and lead paradigm-altering leadership development programs based on a coaching context for Global 1000 firms like Adidas, Motorola, Fidelity Investments, Novartis, Zurich Financial, and Conoco that produced fundamental shifts in mindset and behavior.*

Robert Hargrove lives with his wife and children in Brookline, Massachusetts, and can be reached through Robert.Hargrove@masterfulcoaching.com or by phone at 617–739–3300.

MASTERFUL COACHING PRODUCTS AND SERVICES

At Masterful Coaching we call ourselves the world leader in executive coaching, not because of the size or geographic spread of our handpicked Masterful Coaching World Network, but because we are changing the conversation about executive coaching in the world. We believe that masterful coaching can only take place in the context of inspiring our clients to be the source of a powerful new future, not be merely reacting to events; to create what's possible rather than what's predictable; to accomplish what they really need to accomplish by bringing power and velocity and to the whole process. We offer the following products and services.

THE MASTERFUL COACHING WORKSHOP

- *Inspires leaders and managers to become coaches and mentors, and provides them with the guiding ideas, tools and methods to do so.*
- *Makes it clear that coaching takes place in the context of accomplishment, not therapy.*
- *Recognizes and disperses the five myths of coaching so as to create a positive conversation about coaching in the company.*
- *Introduces people to Masterful Coaching, the Method.*
- *Builds coaching conversation skills through the 6 Cap Coaching System.*

ONE-YEAR EXECUTIVE COACHING PROGRAM

"Masterful Coaching impacts leadership capability and bottom-line business results."
    —Rene Jaeggi, CEO, Adidas
Create a powerful partnership with a Masterful Coach over the next 12 months that enables you to . . .
- *Inspire an Impossible Future*
- *While becoming an extraordinary leader*
- *And producing extraordinary business results*

People meet with their Executive Coach monthly and have weekly tele-coaching conversations.

ACTION COACHING FOR TEAMS

"Achieve mastery as a coach while impacting the leadership development and business performance of your team in less that twelve months."
    —Tom Kaiser, Zurich Financial
- *Create a team of "A" players vs. "B's" and chronic "C's"*
- *Achieve business breakthroughs with measurable results that make or save the company money*
- *Build a high performance team that delivers on hot projects*

The team meets with the team leader and an Action Coach monthly as a group. Each player also gets one 90-minute individual coaching phone call per month.

THE COLLABLAB—A STRATEGIC FORUM

After an executive takes a stand for an Impossible Future, we lead a CollabLab to foster the company "buy in" and *creative collaboration* necessary to make it happen.
- *Get your organization aligned behind a game changing strategy or major change.*
- *Develop a shared approach to implementation; not just the what, but the how.*
- *Generate action that leads to a rallying momentum.*

The *CollabLab* is an accelerated solutions environment that compresses time and dramatically improves how people think and interact.
Visit us at MasterfulCoaching.com for more info or call 617–739–3301.

INDEX

A

ABCD performance management system, 29–30, 147

Abernathy, R., 142

Acknowledgment, 59–60, 63

Action language, 170d

Action learning, 212

Action maps, 240–244, 243d

Actions: changing assumptions and
redesigning, 192–193; creating
goals and case for, 199, 201;
expanding people's ability to take
successful, 41; forwarding powerful
and effective, 75–76, 140d; from
stand that individual matters,
149–150; to gain competence in
new skills, 258–259; initiatives to
ground new context in, 145–147;
leaders fostering effective, 132;
SPIA (Strategic Planning in
Action), 120–123; strategic planning with leaders/group, 120–123;
unintended consequences of,
191–192. See also Goals

Activism, 58–59

Adidas, 199

Advanced beginner stage, 17

Advocacy/inquiry balance, 169–170,
188–189d

"Alignment of wholes," 147–148

Allied Signal, 130

Antigen, 35–36

Argyris, C., 70, 173, 177, 181

The Art of Possibility (Zander), 234

"Artful Victim" story, 99

The Ascent of Man (Bronowski), 45

Assessments, based on observable
behavior, 237–238

Assumptions: learning to change,
192–193; testing, 190–191

Auerbach, R., 240

Automatic self distinction, 93–94

B

"Bad humeurs," 47

Bally, 274–276

Barzun, J., 32

Baum, C., 208, 213–215

Becoming Masterful Coaches: it's who
you are being/not just technique,
44–48; as matter of distinction,
49–59. *See also* Masterful Coaches

Beginner stage, 1

Behavioral approach, 47

Being: an activist, 58–59; "body of
declarations" commitments about,
48–49; Masterful Coaches as state
of, 44–48; through power of language, 47–49; power to actually
choose who we are, 46; psychological and behavioral approaches
to, 47

Bennett, B., 80

Berkin, M., 213–215

BHAGS (Big Hairy Audacious Goals), 27

"Body of declarations": commitments
to future using, 48; examples of
three powerful declarations, 49;
power in becoming Masterful
Coaches, 63–64; for taking

Changing the Game" theme of, 155; Estee Lauder, 158–159, 161–162; used to explore more innovative environment, 89; role of Masterful Coach in, 157–158; seven accelerators of, 156–157; three phases of, 159–163. *See also* Creative collaboration

CollabLab phases: designing WOW! solutions, 161–162; do a deep dive, 162–163; generate possibilities, 160

Collaborative conversation facilitation: creating framework for, 166; using diagnosis/intervention cycle for, 168*d*–169; encouraging balancing inquiry with advocacy, 169–170, 188–189*d*; establishing governing values, 166–167, 182–183; establishing ground rules, 167, 182–183; starting with high level of intention, 165–166

Commitment: to being a Masterful Coach, 61–62; "body of declarations," 48–49; declared at the onset, 236–237; declaring at beginning of conversation, 80–81; to giving acknowledgement, 59–60, 63; to giving up old patterns, 62; to honesty and integrity, 54–55; to Impossible Future person is creating, 55–56; to making a difference, 51–52, 83–84; to person you are coaching, 52–53; recall when you were given, 53; to transformation, 56–57

Committed listening: described, 66–67; elements of, 69*d*; as foundation for all-powerful coaching, 67–68

Committed speaking, 68–70

Compass Points: I: coaching is a powerful partnership, 19–24; II: stand in the future people want to create, 24–31; III: leaders must reinvent themselves first, 31–35; IV: coach as thinking partner, 35–40; V: expanding people's ability to take successful action, 41

Competent stage, 17

Completing relationships, 266

Conflict resolution skills, 250–251

Conoco Cevolution, 110, 137

Conoco CollabLab, 160–161, 163

Conoco Downstream North America, 24, 26, 106, 109–110, 127, 143, 150

Conoco Refining and Marketing Europe, 238

Content/context bowl, 142*d*

Context: building shared, 249–250; distinction of, 91–92

Conti, C., 36, 37, 39

"Controlled burns," 185

Conversations: on big dilemma, 263; coaching, 66–84, 143; dialogue vs. discussion in, 153–154; facilitating collaborative, 165–171; joy of authentic, 175; stages of evolution toward collaborative, 155; on the undiscussable, 175–177, 183*d*. *See also* Dialogue

Cook alone/cook together conversation model, 154

"Crazy wisdom," 19

Creative collaboration: coaching groups to transform them for, 153–154; dialogue and, 153–154; facilitating conversations for, 165–171; need for building, 151–153. *See also* CollabLab model; Partnership

CSC Index, 197

CTB (Creating the Business), 26, 105

"The Customer, Changing the Game" (CollabLab theme), 155

Cycle of stewardship, 271*d*

Cycle to Success team (Motorola), 208

D

"Dancing with what is occurring," 72

Dead Poets Society (film), 61

context of, 132; requirements for realizing, 119; taking a stand for the, 133–137; unwritten rules and impact on, 225–226
"Impossible goal," 198
Inquiry/advocacy balance, 169–170, 188–189d
Inspirational leadership, 52
Inspired organizations, 136–137
Integrity commitment/role models, 54–55
Intervention levels, 183–185
"It starts with me" stand, 137–141

J

James, W., 244
Jarvi, J., 31–32, 33
Johnson, L., 142
Jones, G., 87–88, 89
Jordan, M., 20
The journey: creating the Impossible Future, 24–31, 28d; importance of having goals to, 87–88; mapping the five compost points, 17–41; as not just destination, 16–17; workplace setting of, 17
Just-in-time training, 208

K

Kennedy, R. F., 142
King, M. L., Jr., 142
Knickel, C., 136–137
Kofman, F., 8, 260
"Kokoro" (perfecting inner nature), 44–45
Korkosz, D., 80, 234, 235

L

Labrecque, T., 175, 178
Ladder of interference, 39d, 187d–188
Language: action, 170d; power of, 47–49
Language paradigm, 47–48
Lauder, A., 161–162

"Law of the few," 145
Leaders: choosing breakthrough, 210; declaring "impossible goal" for, 198; developing teachable point of view, 144–145d; enrolling in extraordinary coaching relationship, 111–113; example of 360-degree feedback for, 106–110; extraordinary distinguished from ordinary, 129–130, 248–249; generative vs. predictable, 114; guiding principles for reinventing organizations and, 130–132; using the Method for, 110–126; monthly follow-up for, 123–126; performance opportunity defined by, 209–210; providing feedback to, 242; Pyramid of Accomplishment diagram for, 115d; reinvention plan for, 116–119; strategic planning with, 120–123
Leadership Reinvention Plan, 116–119
Leadership transformation exercise, 262–263
Learn-by-doing approach, 258–259
Learning: action, 212; developing capacity of, 186; Double and Single Loop, 90; recommended articles/books for furthering, 264; steps to sustaining process of, 181–183; stretching, 196d–197. *See also* Transformational learning; Triple Loop Learning
Learning by doing, 63
"Learning enzyme" metaphor, 8
Left-hand column exercise, 70, 72d, 186–187d
Life narratives, 86–89
Listening: balancing inquiry with advocacy and, 169–170; committed, 66–68, 69d; to create greatness environment, 23–24
Little, A. D., 223

M

McNealy, S., 130

Mueller, J., 257–258
Myth of Icarus, 103–104

N

Nahill, B., 53, 56, 57
Nay, D., 214
Nelson, J., 150
New skills: abandoning old ideas/habits for, 257–258; building, 254d; distinguishing guidelines/practices to master, 255; gaining competence in, 258–259; labeling missing, 254; methodology for teaching capabilities and, 253d–259; moving between performance/practice field and, 259–267; studying/practicing for one week, 263–264; Swiss Air Lines case study on, 255–257
Nicklaus, J., 20
Nike, 199
Nokes, J., 25, 106–108, 110, 136, 143, 146, 150
Nontraditional perspective: Bally use of, 274–276; cycle of stewardship and, 271d; Reebok use of, 272–274; value of, 270–271
Norton Company, 150

O

Observation/intervention cycle, 237d
"One Strategy Wonder," 92
Ontological system, 137
Organizations: guiding principles for reinventing, 130–132; promoting stewardship by, 271d, 277–278; shifting context of, 142; taking stand for inspired, 136–137; transformation process for, 94–95; value of nontraditional perspective to, 270–276. *See also* Unwritten rules
Outrageous goal setting, 201, 202–203
Owen, H., 159

P

Parks, R., 142
Partnership: qualities of a great, 22–24; Tiger Woods/Butch Harmon, 19–22. *See also* Creative collaboration
Paul, St., 87
Pemberton, V., 24, 56, 77
People's Bank in Massachusetts, 270
Personal transformation: Compass Point III on, 31–35; process of, 94–95
Phillips, T., 214
Pook, S., 200–203
Power of language, 47–49
Practice field assignments: on completing relationships, 266; using conversational protocols for team learning, 265–266; engaging in conversation about dilemma, 263; hot sea exercise, 266–267; leadership transformation, 262–263; recommended articles/books for furthering learning, 264; studying/practicing one skill for one week, 263–264; writing case study, 264–265
Practice fields: designing, 262; examples of, 260–261; moving between performance and, 259; using practice/reflection in, 261
Principle of calling forth: as Masterful Coach, 61d; steps in, 60–64
Provocative statements, 239
Psychological approach, 47
Psychological system, 137
Putnam, B., 181, 183–189
Pyramid of Accomplishment diagram, 115d

Q

Questions. *See* Coaching questions

R

Rapid prototyping, 162–163

Reebok, 199, 272–274

Reebok Human Rights Award, 273

Reframing thinking/attitudes, 74–75

Reinventing organizations: guiding principles of, 130–132; using The Method for, 133–150; Step 1: taking stand for the Impossible Future, 133–137; Step 2: "it starts with me" stand, 137–141; Step 3: creating powerful context, 141–147; Step 4: generating alignment of wholes, 147–148; Step 5: act from stand that the individual matters, 149–150

Reinventing organizations guiding principles: breaking the grip and excelling as, 131–132; leaders fostering effective action, 132; leaders must communicate/act from Impossible Future, 132; leaders must reinvent themselves, 131; person at top must support process, 131

Reinventing yourself, 32–35

Reinvention paradigm, 117–118d

Relationship assignment, 266

Renaud, M., 54, 67

Riley, P., 240

River stories: creating, 101–103; described, 95–96; recognizing, 96–97; transforming rut stories into, 97d

Road to Damascus, 87

Role models: looking for, 62; looking for honesty/integrity, 54–55

Rosen, J., 197

RTB (Running the Business), 26, 28, 105

Rules. See Unwritten rules

Russell, B., 36

Rut stories: consequences of, 98d; described, 95–96; recognizing, 96–97; recognizing/interrupting, 98–100; transforming into river stories, 97d; understanding nature of, 100–101

S

Schaffer, R., 128, 205, 206, 207, 208

Schwarz, R., 167, 181, 182, 189–193

Scott-Morgan, P., 223, 226

Self-awareness, 48

Self-deception patterns, 239

Senge, P., 174, 175, 259, 261

Seven Coaching Conversation System: CAP 1: declaring possibilities, 73; CAP 2: being a thinking partner, 73–74; CAP 3: drawing others out, 74; CAP 4: reframing thinking and attitudes, 74–75; CAP 5: teaching and advising, 75; CAP 6: forwarding action, 75–76; CAP 7: giving honest feedback, 76; described, 72–73d; putting to use the, 81–82

Severance, R. W., 24–31, 127, 136, 147

Shearing Inc., 35

Shelton, S., 213–215

Shifting organizational context, 142

Simon, F., 224–225

Single Loop Learning, 90, 104

Six Sigma, 32, 150

The Skilled Facilitator (Schwarz), 167, 181

Skills: five essential (and often missing), 248–253; labeling missing, 254; methodology for teaching new, 253d–259; sources of, 247–248

"Small game" playing, 114

"The smartest man in the room" syndrome, 152

Solution specification criteria, 158

"Sounding board" function, 38–40

"Sourcing document," 143

SPIA (Strategic Planning in Action), 120–123

Sponsors: breakthrough, 209–210; finding, 229–230

Steel, S., 35, 36, 37, 38, 39

Stewardship: cycle of, 271d; promoting, 277–278

Stories (rut and river), 95–103

Strategic philanthropy, 270–271

Strategic planning, 120–123

Stretch goals, 196d–197, 198d

Structure for fulfillment, 27–29, 122

Subway crime, 145–146

Sun Microsystems, 130

Swiss Air Lines, 255–257

Systems thinking perspective, 252–253, 256d

T

Teaching/advising cap, 75

Team dialogue skills, 250–251

Teamwork, 207–208

Testing assumptions, 190–191

Thinking partner concept, 35–40, 73–74

3M, 197

360-degree feedback, 4, 56, 95; example of, 106–110; Leadership Reinvention Plan from, 116–119; *unfreeze, transform, refreeze* model on, 232, 233–235. *See also* Feedback

The Tipping Point (Gladwell), 142

TROV (Teachable Point of View), 26–27, 28, 29, 144–145d

"Tranquilizing" story, 99

Transformation distinctions: be an activist, 58–59; be a cheerleader, 59–60; be commitment to honesty/integrity, 54–55; be commitment to Impossible Future person is creating, 55–56; be a commitment to making a difference, 51–52; be commitment to transformation, 56–57; be total commitment to person you are coaching, 52–53; masterful coaching as matter of, 49–50;

seven powerful, 50d; Triple Loop Learning, 91–94

Transformational learning: good example as best gift for, 87–89; life as narrative and, 86–89; three guidelines for, 86; Triple Loop, 89–90d, 91–104, 117–119

Triggers category, 227, 228d

Triple Loop Learning: described, 89–90d; mastering definitions/distinctions of, 91–95; post-feedback conversation using, 117–119; rut and river stories and, 95–103; when to use, 104

U

Undiscussables: contrasting models for dealing with, 183d; conversations on the, 175–177

Unfreeze, Transform, and Refreeze model: on giving feedback, 117; phases of, 232–233

Unintended consequences, 191–192

Unwritten rules: to achieve Impossible Future, 223–224; awareness of gap between Impossible Future and, 228–229; coaching for uncovering/realigning, 225–230; deciding to alter or keep, 229–230; defining, 219; Ford Motor Company and, 224–225; making them work, 228d; recognizing changes in, 222–223; things which prevent understanding of, 220–222; understanding power of rules and, 220. *See also* Organizations

V

van Leeuwenhoek, A., 47

Virtuoso stage, 17

Vision: action based on Impossible Future, 132; building shared, 249–250